Counterinsurgency Wars and the Anglo-American Alliance

Counterinsurgency Wars and the Anglo-American Alliance

The Special Relationship on the Rocks

Andrew Mumford

Georgetown University Press / Washington, DC

Library of Congress Cataloging-in-Publication Data
Names: Mumford, Andrew, 1983– author.
Title: Counterinsurgency wars and the Anglo-American alliance : the special relationship on the rocks / Andrew Mumford.
Description: Washington, DC : Georgetown University Press, 2017. | Includes bibliographical references and index.
Identifiers: LCCN 2017002310 (print) | LCCN 2017008405 (ebook) | ISBN 9781626164918 (hc : alk. paper) | ISBN 9781626164925 (pb : alk. paper) | ISBN 9781626164932 (eb)
Subjects: LCSH: Counterinsurgency—United States. | Counterinsurgency—Great Britain. | United States—Military relations—Great Britain. | Great Britain—Military relations—United States.
Classification: LCC E183.8.G7 M86 2017 (print) | LCC E183.8.G7 (ebook) | DDC 355.0310973041—dc23
LC record available at https://lccn.loc.gov/2017002310

♾ This book is printed on acid-free paper meeting the requirements of the American National Standard for Permanence in Paper for Printed Library Materials.

18 17 9 8 7 6 5 4 3 2 First printing

Printed in the United States of America

Cover design by Martyn Schmoll. Cover image by llhedgehogll/iStock/Getty Images..

For Elodie

Contents

Acknowledgments

The book you are reading is the product of much-appreciated help and support from many people and organizations.

Colleagues and friends were kind enough to read parts of the manuscript. I am therefore indebted to Rory Cormac, David Fitzgerald, Adrian Guelke, Karl Hack, Clive Jones, and John Young. The book is better for their valuable insights, but of course any errors or omissions remain my responsibility.

I have enjoyed the chance to discuss elements of the US-UK "special relationship" and the nature of Anglo-American military and diplomatic history with numerous others whose arguments helped clarify my own. In particular I would like to thank Richard Aldrich, Huw Bennett, Louise Kettle, Wyn Rees, and my colleagues in the Centre for Conflict, Security and Terrorism at the University of Nottingham for being willing sounding boards.

A special mention must be made of the late Alex Danchev. I was fortunate to be a colleague of Alex's for four years. He was gracious enough to give me input when this book was in its infancy. Alex gave me characteristically sound advice, encouraged sharper thinking, and, in a way only he could convey, urged the need for a reduction in "excess verbiage." Alex was arguably one of the most incisive observers of the special relationship on this side of the Atlantic. Our scholarly community is poorer for his loss.

I am extremely grateful to those institutions that awarded funding in order for me to undertake the research contained in this book. The University of Nottingham granted me an Early Career Research and Knowledge Transfer Award, which facilitated transatlantic research visits. I am thankful also to the British Association for American Studies for the award of a Visiting Fellowship at the Eccles Centre for American Studies at the British Library in London where I was able to take advantage of their superb resources. My appreciation extends to the staff at the UK and US National Archives for their help in tracking down numerous files.

My editor at Georgetown, Don Jacobs, took an interest in this project from a very early stage, and I am hugely appreciative of the faith he showed in guiding the book from sketchy idea to final publication. Thanks also to the anonymous referees who reviewed the first draft of the manuscript for their constructive critique, as well to as my scrupulous copy editor, Don McKeon.

Finally I turn to my wife, Hannah, who is a constant source of support and inspiration. The book is dedicated to our daughter, Elodie. She was born two weeks after I finished writing the first draft of the manuscript. She has taught me the real meaning of a special relationship.

Introduction

The "Special Relationship": Origins, Meaning, and Dynamics

> Neither the sure prevention of war, nor the continuous rise of world organization will be gained without what I have called the fraternal association of the English-speaking peoples. This means a special relationship between the British Commonwealth and Empire and the United States.
>
> —Winston Churchill, March 5, 1946

The "special relationship" is surely one of the most overindulged yet vacuous phrases in the modern diplomatic lexicon. It is a Churchillian construct initially designed to tie the flag of a fading imperial power to the mast of the new rising global hegemon. The very phrase is seldom used in Washington. On occasion it may be muttered by a president welcoming a visiting British prime minister at a Rose Garden press conference, but it rarely features in policy discussion.[1] The continued use of the term in common transatlantic parlance owes more to paying lip service to past glories than reflecting any meaningful mutual political need.[2] Indeed, the special relationship is a chimera seen only by the British. Such patterns show no sign of fading. Soon after becoming prime minister in 2010, David Cameron used his first trip to Washington to state that he and President Barack Obama were in "violent agreement" on key security issues and the sanctity of the US-UK special relationship.[3] Prime ministerial hyperbole aside, this book is dedicated to exploring whether British and American leaders have indeed been in "violent agreement" but more specifically to analyzing levels of agreement in times of violence—namely, "irregular" wars against insurgent opponents.

Counterinsurgency has been one of the most frequent types of war that American and particularly British forces have been deployed to since the end of the Second World War, spanning nearly every continent. Therefore an analysis of US-UK interaction during these campaigns speaks profoundly to the very existence of a special relationship at all. This is an increasingly important intellectual undertaking—and an exposé of the special relationship at large—given the way in which a sustained assessment of counterinsurgency wars since 1945 intersects so many fundamental geostrategic components that underpinned the postwar transatlantic alliance, including the molding of a postcolonial balance of power, the fight against communism in the Cold War, and the twenty-first-century "War on Terror."

An assessment of each nation's respective private political perceptions and public diplomacy toward the other's counterinsurgency wars reveals a thin layer of "specialness" at work. As Patrick Porter has convincingly argued, in order for US-UK relations to be considered "special," they "must not only entail beneficial transatlantic relations but also must pass a higher test of 'exceptional influence.' "[4] The most recent wars in Iraq and Afghanistan have largely failed to demonstrate the existence of the important latter characteristic, given the prevalence of mutual recrimination over tactical approaches and operational performance. Indeed, we cannot fully understand the fallout from the two-front War on Terror unless we fully contextualize Anglo-American interaction in previous counterinsurgency wars. This book posits that we should be less surprised about US-UK tensions over interference or underperformance in Basra and Helmand if we are more aware of the high politics of friction between London and Washington during the numerous preceding counterinsurgency wars. Operational frustrations may be temporary, but strategic self-interest has proven perpetual. In asymmetrical wars, the special relationship has proved to be thoroughly asymmetrical too.

Counterinsurgency and the Challenge to Specialness

Subverting the traditional focus of the special relationship on conventional war alliance, nuclear weapons, and other defense issues, this book will tap into the most prevalent and hotly debated form of modern conflict—namely, counterinsurgency warfare—and seek to place US-UK relations in this context, one that is overlooked and underanalyzed. By doing so, this book takes on three key research themes that challenge assumptions in the fields of Anglo-American diplomatic and military history. First is to assert that the "small wars" of British decolonization, far from aggravating anticolonial sentiment in Washington, made acquiescent imperialists out of the Americans as Cold War anticommunism trumped all other concerns. The second is to highlight the role that domestic political concerns in Washington had on White House interference with British military action—a sign of the utter imbalance in the relationship. The third is to assess the overall levels of specialness at work in counterinsurgency wars as a litmus test of the overall working relationship of these two allies. The objective of the book, therefore, is to frame irregular warfare against insurgent enemies as a key dynamic through which the late twentieth- and early twenty-first-century special relationship fluctuated and allowed the two nations to pursue strikingly dissonant policies during frequent counterinsurgency wars.

The book also intends to challenge writing prevalent during and after the Cold War that perceived the special relationship as an inherent "force for good" in international affairs. By honing in on the frequency of counterinsurgency wars, this book seeks to explore how the mutual use of force was projected globally and the consequences this had. Given the origins of the modern special relationship in antifascist solidarity and the "just war" to liberate Europe from Adolf Hitler's yoke, it is an inevitable consequence that the Anglo-American alliance has been traditionally interpreted as a persistent force for good in the world. Lauding the common ideological investment in freedom and liberty (politically and economically), analysts such as Walter Russell Mead have perceived the post-1945 continuation of a strong US-UK friendship as "less a result of policy choices made by either the British or Americans than it is the cause of the similar choices the two countries so frequently make."[5] But there have been some forceful challenges to the liberal consensus. Never backward at coming forward, the late polemicist Christopher Hitchens (himself an Englishman at home in America) labeled the special relationship a "transmission belt by which British conservative ideas have infected America, the better to be retransmitted to England." What Britain found returning to its shores, repackaged by the Americans, was a predilection for class-bound conformities and, as shall be discussed in the next chapter, "the temptations of empire."[6]

In attempting to evaluate the political interplay between each other's counterinsurgency campaigns, the book will focus on three identifiable themes that underpin the relationship: first, political attitudes toward specific conflicts, tracing levels of diplomatic support or disquiet in regard to counterinsurgency in official dispatches and private correspondence, in order to assess just how important and consistent the political dynamic was to the special relationship when put under the unique strains of this form of warfare; second, the reciprocity of military assistance, taken as the ultimate demonstration of alliance solidarity in war; and third, the level of intelligence cooperation as a means of ensuring military success and securing strategic goals.

The book will utilize historical and contemporary cases from the post–World War II era of US and UK irregular war campaigns to contribute empirical evidence to this thematic analysis. These wars were conducted by an array of characters, from belligerent generals to coercive diplomats, from transatlantic gun smugglers to jungle-bound insurgents, drawing the attention of presidents and prime ministers. The influence of politicians from Churchill to Obama and soldiers from Gerald Templer to David Petraeus will be traced throughout this book, which will bring a new angle to the story of one of the most defining, albeit shallow, diplomatic and military relationships of the modern era. The largest campaigns have been selected as a means of analyzing respective levels of influence on the political management and strategic direction of each other's counterinsurgency wars. The American campaigns in Vietnam, Afghanistan, and Iraq will be considered in relation to how the British interpreted US actions, and the inspiration that Britain's colonial small wars has given the contemporary American "COINdinistas" will be questioned. Conversely, the British campaigns in Palestine, Malaya, Cyprus, South Arabia, Northern Ireland, Afghanistan, and Iraq will be assessed in the context of American perceptions and levels of assistance.

Given the extensive British exposure to counterinsurgency wars during the mid-twentieth century, the case selection in this book has omitted the campaigns against the Mau Mau in Kenya (1952–60) and against the People's Front for the Liberation of the Occupied Arabia Gulf in Dhofar (1964–75). Kenya and Dhofar have not been overlooked for reasons of space but because of the peripheral nature of those campaigns to either the future of the British Empire, the general course of the Cold War, or Anglo-American relations in general. Even Gen. Sir Frank Kitson, who had made his name as an assiduous exponent of counterinsurgency tactics against the Mau Mau, came to label the Kenya campaign "a sideshow amongst sideshows" amid the broader tumult of 1950s international relations.[7] The absence of any discernable support from Moscow for the isolated and quasi-mystical Mau Mau meant that Washington paid little attention to Britain's efforts to brutally reimpose security over Kenya.[8] The Dhofar campaign is not covered here, because the troops involved were not under British command. The British officers served under the sultan of Oman, meaning this was not an outright counterinsurgency campaign but one of counterinsurgency assistance to an ally.[9] Similarly, the American "low-intensity operations" in Central America and the Caribbean of the 1980s will not be addressed here, given how they were conducted largely by special operations forces and were not undertaken under what would commonly be perceived as a counterinsurgency rubric. Grenada in 1983 and Panama in 1989, for example, were invasions designed to bring about outright regime change.

The core issue this book seeks to address is the nature of the Anglo-American alliance in warfare, specifically diplomacy in counterinsurgency conflicts. This will be tackled from a very precise angle: by exploring how one of the most enduring alliances in contemporary international relations has been affected by one of the most perpetual forms of conflict in the modern era. It will assess the role of transatlantic diplomacy in irregular warfare and the important impact counterinsurgency has played in wider diplomatic relations between the United States and the United Kingdom in wars against Zionist, communist, nationalist, and Islamist insurgents. This is a crucial topic, given how the book will trace the increasing politicization of such campaigns, in particular the political management of British decolonization (of which counterinsurgency played a large part) and the fallout within America from the Vietnam War on the conduct of the "long war" on terrorism after the attacks of September 11, 2001 (9/11). It is precisely because counterinsurgency is such an inescapably political form of warfare (given the inherent strategic desire to reestablish political control over a region or country via the winning of local "hearts and minds") that this book offers extra weighting to the analysis of the civilian management of the conflicts in respective capital cities above that of the military conduct of the campaigns on the ground. It also places each campaign in the wider context of other key geopolitical events that were affecting both the conduct of the war specifically and US-UK relations in general at the time. This becomes crucial when assessing, for example, how the Korean War and debates about the recognition of communist China impinged on the fight against communist insurgents in Malaya or how the Suez Crisis in 1956 affected Washington's attitude toward Britain's efforts to hold on to Cyprus in the face of insurgent opposition at the same time. No counterinsurgency war takes place in a vacuum, and the subsequent chapters duly frame such conflicts within the broader sweep of regional and global developments in order to offer a fresh perspective on Anglo-American relations in an international context.

The Origins of the Special Relationship

Since the end of the Second World War, it has been patently clear that Britain has needed America more than America has needed Britain. The attritional conflict against Germany and her allies pushed the two countries closer together than at any point since American independence, yet the exhausting impact it had on the British economy contrasted starkly with the effervescence of postwar American wealth. Postwar loans from Washington to London came to symbolize a lasting economic reliance that soon spread to other areas of policymaking. A report by the Foreign Office's Permanent Under-Secretary's Committee (PUSC) in November 1949 wryly observed that "the Anglo-American partnership will for some time inevitably be an unequal one."[10] Although accepting the asymmetry of the relationship, postwar British foreign policy clearly posited close ties with the Americans as a prerequisite for preserving British power and interests globally. Fast-forward to a few months after 9/11, and the British foreign policy establishment was still trying to couch its entire raison d'être through proximity to America: "The United States is the United Kingdom's foremost political and military ally, its single greatest trading partner, its largest source of investment, its largest recipient of investment, and the world's sole remaining superpower."[11]

Undoubtedly, the oft-vaunted "personal chemistry" between presidents and prime ministers plays a part in setting the tone for broader Anglo-American relations. Attempts by Harold Wilson to inject some personal warmth into the special relationship were quickly quashed by Richard Nixon. Henry Kissinger delightfully recalls a dinner at Chequers in February 1969 when the prime minister "suggested to Nixon that they call each other by their first names. A fish-eyed stare from Nixon squelched this idea." The adoption of an avuncular attitude toward Nixon left Kissinger with the impression that Wilson was acting "like a small-town bank manager who had decided that the best way to deal with his most improvident customer was to give him a reputation of parsimony to uphold."[12] Contrast this with Nixon's relationship with the next occupant at Downing Street, Edward Heath, which Kissinger described as "the most complex of Nixon's Presidency." The two notoriously insular men "never managed to establish the personal rapport for which Nixon, at least, longed in the beginning."[13] This in part may have come down to Heath's overriding emotional investment in forging much closer British links with Europe, to which proximity to the United States may have proved a hindrance.

It was clear that some presidential and prime ministerial relationships have been close enough on a personal (and political) level to warrant the revival of the special relationship label. Margaret Thatcher clearly saw Ronald Reagan as "one of us," spawning an anticommunist, pro–free market transatlantic partnership. But even Thatcher and Reagan had moments when the purportedly special nature of US-UK relations was fundamentally challenged, most notably American hesitance to provide significant support to Britain during the Falklands War in 1982 and Reagan's decision to forcibly remove the leader of the Commonwealth island of Grenada in 1983.[14] More recently Tony Blair and George W. Bush forged a close personal friendship based on shared faith, similar views on the imperative of spreading democratic values globally, and, as one mutually appreciative press conference revealed, the use of the same toothpaste. But close personal chemistry between leaders is not proof of a special relationship, first because British leaders do not have a monopoly on friendship with American presidents and second because an emphasis on agential proximity belies the deeper structural elements that even Churchill alluded to when talking about a "fraternity of English-speaking peoples."

Debating the Meaning and Purpose of the Special Relationship

It was amid the grandeur of a black-tie White House dinner that Harold Wilson, guest of honor during a Washington trip in December 1964, delivered arguably the most realistic assessment of the meaning and purpose of the special relationship ever by a British prime minister. Standing to give a toast to his host, Lyndon Johnson, Wilson detached from the accustomed sentimentality with which British and American leaders usually wax lyrical on such occasions:

> I have heard this often enough about whether there is a special relationship between the United States and Great Britain. Some of those who talk of the special relationship, I think, are looking backwards and not looking forward. They talk about the nostalgia of our imperial age. We regard our relation with you not as a special relationship but as a close relationship, governed by the only things that matter and that is a unity of purpose and that is the unity of objective.[15]

Eschewing the traditional rhetoric pertaining to common language and fraternal bonds forged in war, Wilson implicitly acknowledged how such sentimentality counts for little when the defense demands of the Cold War alliance and the diminution in political stature as decolonization took hold, not to mention domestic economic constraints, meant that Britain brought less to the table than the Americans may have wished. Quoting the essayist Charles Lamb, Wilson summoned all his Yorkshire bluntness to self-effacingly acknowledge to his Texan host that "there is nothing so irrelevant as a poor relation."[16] The prime minister's desire to emphasize a shared mission, if not a shared burden, represents the most clear-eyed interpretation of the inescapable power imbalance at the heart of post-1945 Anglo-American relations.

But Wilson's demure recognition of Britain's inherent junior-partner status in the alliance has not prevented consistent reference to a special relationship by subsequent leaders who have become inured to the rhetoric of decline and irrelevance. Former British ambassador to Washington Sir Robin Renwick once remarked that despite being "the subject of obituary notices," the special relationship has since the Second World War "shown a Lazarus-like tendency to survive."[17] Yet the alliance has not so much shown good survival skills as a flair for reinvention. In the post-1945 era we have seen the bonds shift in the nature of its specialness from wartime solidarity to ideological symmetry. Reinventing reasons why US-UK relations remain exactly special has been a perpetual political and academic task for the past seventy years, with emphasis being placed alternately on common heritage, language, identity, ideology, and personal chemistry between the leaders. This reinvention has been the offspring of necessity, namely an imperative on behalf of the British to demonstrate ongoing worth to their American cousins in the face of ever-increasing disparities in political, economic, and military power.

The cheerleaders and naysayers of US-UK relations have provided a substantive corpus of literature on aspects of transatlantic ties from its Churchillian heyday to its 1970s nadir, through to its personality-driven reignition under Thatcher and then Blair. As one of the most scrutinized of modern international diplomatic relations, the Anglo-American alliance has created analytical lines in the sand, dividing observers into several identifiable camps. Alan Dobson and Steve Marsh have identified three predominant issues that have emerged from academic debates about the special relationship. First, there is a divergence of understanding, which is essentially a dichotomy of "sentiment versus interests." Second, there are more existential questions surrounding the mythologizing of the relationship. Third, there are fundamental divergences in explaining its rise and fall.[18] Despite these divergences, there is a large pool of literature that has built up over the past few decades, offering grand chronological sweeps of the high politics of Anglo-American relations in which the big themes of defense, economics, and leaders' personalities prevail.[19] Alex Danchev delineated between the "evangelists," who pursue close transatlantic relations with missionary zeal (personified by Churchill), and the "functionalists," whose more pragmatic assessment emphasizes commonalities but omits sentiment (epitomized by Wilson and arguably Dean Acheson too). Danchev went further by identifying a new strain of special relationship observers: the "terminalists." To this camp the special relationship is pure fiction, a convenient Cold War construct that was rendered obsolete after 1989.[20]

Riffing off Danchev's typologies, this book would offer itself up as being between the functionalist and terminalist camps—"termo-functionalist," if you will. Admittedly there was, and still is, much political hot air about Anglo-American specialness that is purely rhetorical and reliant on heavily romanticized interpretations of past glories that gloss over present difficulties (or irrelevancies). This book has empathy with Ronald Hyam's description of the special relationship as "ambivalent and intermittent," most notably during the mid-twentieth century when it was based precariously on "a vague sense of affinity."[21] More often than not, successive American administrations have seemed slightly embarrassed by persistent British references to a special relationship. Even Kissinger, a known Anglophile inside the Nixon White House, felt the need to dampen grandiloquent allusions to specialness when devising transatlantic security policy. In a briefing note to Nixon before his departure on his inaugural foreign tour as president, Kissinger came across as almost uncomfortable with the term and sought to dispel conceptions of exclusivity: "I would think that the answer to the special relationship of Britain would be to raise other countries to the same status, rather than to discourage Britain into a less warm relationship with the United States."[22] If this was Kissinger's "answer to the special relationship," then we can certainly intimate that Nixon had a "problem" with Britain in the first place.

Indeed, there is perhaps very little that is special about ties between London and Washington since the end of the Second World War. A search of the public papers of the presidents (via the online American Presidency Project) reveals how, from Harry Truman to Barack Obama, American presidents have used the phrase "special relationship" in statements and press conferences to describe

American bonds with twenty-two countries other than the United Kingdom.[23] If there is a special relationship between the United States and the United Kingdom, the specialness is certainly not marked by exclusivity. The word "special" has been an excessively used semantic device in American diplomacy in the Cold War and post-1989 era. In turn, British politicians have been naive in assuming that a special relationship with the US was seen as a monogamous one by Washington. As Richard Neustadt reminded us back in 1970, "relations of alliance are not altogether different from relations of indifference."[24] A truly "special" relationship must surely be defined as one that can ably demonstrate a *mutual level* of exceptional influence on each other's policy outlook, and, crucially, this relationship should be discernibly monogamous, with no other country coming close to levels of influence, patronage, and good will. Britain and America have never truly maintained this level of specialness after the end of the Second World War.

Over the past seventy years there have been occasional instances when the two nations have interacted over counterinsurgency wars in a truly cooperative way, in a manner above and beyond the mere functionality of a standard alliance. The case-study chapters that follow sketch out instances of intelligence-sharing, political codependency, and the cross-pollination of counterinsurgency theory and practice. But more often than not, such examples of close assistance were undertaken to meet some domestic political need (as discussed in the next chapter) or to opportunistically fulfill some broader foreign policy goal. As a result of post-1945 power imbalances and increasing economic dependence, the rationale of successive British governments that all must be done to preserve close transatlantic relations simply became the same as acceding to American demands or policy whims in an effort not to rock the boat. The price of specialness for the British was perpetual acquiescence.

Yet there are some signs that the British political establishment has at last acknowledged the fallacious nature of the special relationship discourse. In 2010, the House of Commons Foreign Affairs Committee went as far as to recommend the use of the phrase "special relationship" be avoided altogether by British diplomats and politicians. Pushing for a more pragmatic understanding of ties between London and Washington (that they enjoy *a*, but not *the*, special relationship), the committee concluded that the label was "misleading" and created "unrealistic expectations about the benefits the relationship can deliver to the UK."[25] Its successor committee in the next parliament applauded this recommendation and in April 2014 asserted that "the Coalition government seem to have . . . adopt[ed] a more hard-headed, less deferential attitude to the US . . . without jeopardising the warmth of the tie or the utility of the relationship for the UK."[26] But this conclusion grasped the wrong end of the stick. The ability of the British government to adopt a "less deferential" approach to the United States was more of a reflection of how the United Kingdom was on the periphery of the foreign policy radar of the Obama administration, to the extent that the British government could afford to make noises about asserting itself, knowing full well that no one in Washington was really listening. The election of Donald Trump in November 2016 set off a similar bout of hand-wringing about the ongoing relevance of the special relationship, with the British press obsessing over the fact that Prime Minister Theresa May was only the tenth world leader Trump phoned after becoming president-elect.[27]

The Traditional Realms of the Special Relationship

There are three predominant realms in which the special relationship has been traditionally defined: intelligence relations, nuclear relations, and conventional wars. Arguably, these spheres of close Anglo-American cooperation in the wake of the Second World War came to shape our understanding of the intertwined nature of transatlantic security relations. Yet the perceptible intimacy between London and Washington in the shady world of intelligence, the high-risk domain of nuclear secrets, and the mythologized unity of large-scale war-fighting belied tensions on a much wider and deeper range of defense and security issues, including the management of counterinsurgency wars.

Several Anglo-American intelligence-sharing agreements during the Second World War were topped off in 1948 with what has come to be commonly known as the UKUSA intelligence treaty (which was not a singular agreement and also included the Commonwealth partners of Canada, Australia, and New Zealand).[28] This provided the basis primarily for cooperation in the realm of signals intelligence (SIGINT), although this has never meant that each party received unfettered access to the others' material. Intra-alliance politics and friction ensured that UKUSA never created a system of joint intelligence collection, analysis, and dissemination. Transatlantic intelligence fiefdoms maintain a fierce independence. As Richard Aldrich has pointed out, the foundation of cooperation was starkly realist and operated on a quid pro quo basis in which the British traded the placement of American SIGINT sites in far-flung corners of the empire for access to the latest technology operated by the US National Security Agency.[29]

Any significant joint sense of purpose was driven by a mutual suspicion of their erstwhile Soviet ally as world war gave way to cold war. But as a result of several high-profile defections to the USSR, including the exposure of the infamous "Cambridge Five" spy ring, the intelligence dimension of the special relationship in the 1950s was at a very low ebb. The American intelligence agencies began to develop a wary distrust of their British counterparts, and this resulted in the search for alternative intelligence alliances.[30] Indeed, the Cold War extended Washington's intelligence horizons to such a large extent that the transatlantic exclusivity of the 1940s was transcended and the intimacy of US-UK intelligence efforts against Nazi Germany faded into memory.[31]

Another key area in which Anglo-American relations have purportedly demonstrated a high degree of specialness is that of nuclear weapons. This was symbolized in July 1958 with the signing of the Atomic Energy Defence Agreement, which facilitated the biggest piece of bilateral nuclear cooperation to date.[32] This reversed the nuclear secrecy enshrined in the 1946 McMahon Act, which aimed to build American nuclear supremacy by blocking allies' access to expertise and technology.[33]

Yet far from being a cornerstone of a special relationship, nuclear and intelligence cooperation were arguably components of manipulation by Washington in order to garner greater influence over other areas of British defense commitments, including spending. They were used as carrots to encourage London to take particular paths regarding defense policy, most notably during the turbulent economic crisis of the 1970s, which spawned defense reviews that recommended slashing the budget of the Ministry of Defence. This caused alarm in Washington, most acutely with Kissinger, who was concerned at the detrimental effect on American intelligence that the closure of British bases in the Mediterranean would have.[34]

Even cooperation in the realm of conventional warfare, so soon after the triumphant alliance against the Axis powers, proved to be a troubled ghost of its former self. Take as a prime example that of the Korean War. Already faced with demanding troop deployments overseas (including, as we shall see later, in Malaya), the British chiefs of staff were at first reluctant to accede to the American request to contribute to their UN-badged force. The Foreign Office was wary of what such a refusal could do to Anglo-American relations. Some Whitehall mandarins felt that the British needed to deploy alongside the Americans if only to act as a brake on any rash decisions by President Harry Truman to utilize nuclear weapons.[35] Eventually the Foreign Office position won out, and two infantry battalions were sent to the Korean Peninsula.[36]

Despite this deployment, fundamental differences remained between London's and Washington's perceptions of how the Korean War should be handled politically, most significantly over how to interact with China. The government of Clement Attlee felt that Beijing needed to be brought into negotiations to end the war, while the Truman administration remained loath to make Mao Zedong a legitimate regional actor.[37]

Foreign Office hopes that British participation in the UN mission would restrain the Americans were dashed almost single-handedly by the forceful belligerence of Gen. Douglas MacArthur, the US commander. Aiming to capitalize on the successful landings at Inchon in September 1950, MacArthur planned an offensive beyond the Yalu River two months later. This aggressive strategy provoked a massive Chinese response in support of their North Korean allies, pushing UN forces back. Rosemary Foot has argued that MacArthur's Yalu offensive represented a pivotal moment in US-UK relations during the Korean War. The Attlee government had been compliant in supporting Washington's war effort from the outset of hostilities in June 1950. But by the time of the Yalu offensive in November of that year, British divergence from American policy became more pronounced in an effort to avoid the war spilling over into an outright conflict with China.[38] Consistent American refusal to take on board any British advice over Korea led Sir William Strang, the permanent undersecretary to the Foreign Office, to gloomily conclude in January 1951 that the US "behaves insufferably to its allies."[39] London had clearly deluded itself into thinking that it could mold American actions at a time when US grand strategy had become so ideologically entrenched. This fallacy of influence, as seen during this conventional war, would be repeated in unconventional wars as America's Cold War increasingly intersected with Britain's small wars of decolonization.

Structure of the Book and a Note on Case Selection

At its heart, this is a book of Anglo-American intrigue, fallout, and rivalry. It poses fundamental questions about the nature of transatlantic relations over the last seventy years that arise due to the consistency of counterinsurgency war-fighting since 1945. The three themes identified earlier that drive the research and analysis of the book can be translated into question form: Why did America compromise its anticolonial tradition by helping Britain maintain its empire in the face of rebel insurgents? How did successive American administrations pander to domestic electoral blocs in a way that undermined British conduct of counterinsurgency wars against certain ethnic groups? What level of specialness was at work in counterinsurgency wars?

Answers to these questions will be sought by ordering the book in a particular manner. The first two chapters deal with the two broad thematic issues of politics and military culture that underpin this book. Chapter 1 addresses the political dimension that shaped over half a century of US-UK cooperation (or, more commonly, friction) in counterinsurgency wars. This was initially driven by the awkward policy position Washington found itself in at the beginning of the Cold War, having to wrestle with the often mutually exclusive policies of anticommunism and anticolonialism in the face of Britain's small wars of decolonization in Southeast Asia and the Middle East. The shifting political base of post-1945 geopolitics, heralded by a crumbling British Empire and a newly minted American superpower, has given rise to contentious debates regarding notions of an "American Empire." It has often been during American counterinsurgency wars (particularly Vietnam and Iraq) that such accusations have reached a crescendo. The chapter finishes by accounting for the role of

American domestic political pressures in the decisions made by successive White House administrations in regard to positions taken about British counterinsurgency wars. Collectively this allows us to account for the multiple layers of pressure (at the global, regional, and national level) that impinged on US and UK political management of their respective (and frequent) counterinsurgency wars, therefore making an exploration of such types of conflict a useful vehicle to explore the broader special relationship at work in the political and military spheres.

Chapter 2 shifts focus from the political dimension of the relationship to the military one by assessing the origins and evolution of American and British approaches to counterinsurgency warfare. "Doctrine" is a word seldom used to describe the body of British military thinking on this form of warfare. Indeed, there is a traditional British aversion to codifying strategic thought that stands in stark contrast to the reams of official doctrine produced by their American counterparts. This chapter evaluates the collective body of experience built up by the British during the so-called classical era of counterinsurgency in the mid-twentieth century and identifies what the American military has distilled (erroneously perhaps) from them. Following from the traumatic experiences of the Vietnam War, counterinsurgency was firmly shut out from the collective consciousness of the American military. However, the imperatives of the war in Afghanistan and then the shifting security landscape in Iraq made for a fierce intellectual battle within the US military. This chapter will show just how influential the British historical experience was in shaping the debate in the United States—but for mostly the wrong reasons.

Having established the key thematic premises of the book, the subsequent chapters are each dedicated to particular case studies that showcase in chronological order exactly how the contending political pressures (foreign and domestic) and respective military approaches affected the special relationship at work in counterinsurgency wars since 1945. They demonstrate that far from being something that cemented ties between London and Washington (which might reasonably be expected when violent substate actors threaten the national interest of a supposedly special ally), counterinsurgency wars created multiple schisms between the two nations. We begin in Palestine (1946–48) in chapter 3. The first British counterinsurgency war of the postwar era triggered massive American interest, given President Truman's desire to recompense the Jewish people in the wake of the horrors of the Holocaust and Britain's inability to disentangle itself from a mess of its own making. In Palestine we see the first example of unilateral American decision making that was fundamentally designed to alter the outcome of a British counterinsurgency war, as well as the first American diplomatic missions designed to place Washington's interests at the center of any postconflict settlement, regardless of the British position. Palestine also set a precedent for generating significant American domestic political lobbying based on ethnic diaspora sympathy for an insurgent group fighting the British. This pattern would be repeated many times in subsequent wars.

Chapter 4 turns to the much-covered story of the Malayan Emergency (1948–60) but offers a new take on the conflict by highlighting the American dilemma of wanting to prevent the spread of a communist insurgency at the same time as being reluctant to condone ongoing British colonial rule in the early Cold War period. From the Malayan case we can see how London deliberately attempted to portray its counterinsurgency war as one of crucial importance to Western anticommunist objectives. Importantly, Washington bought this line, allowing the Cold War in Asia to be a Trojan horse for the reassertion of colonial control.

Whitehall also played the communist card, but to less effect, during the concomitant counterinsurgency war in Cyprus (1955–59), which is the focus of chapter 5. American concern over the regional dynamic of the outcome of the war led to some covert American diplomacy that went behind British backs to prep Greek negotiators. But the shadow of the Suez Crisis cast itself darkly over the Cyprus campaign. Washington did not take kindly to this rash act of imperial muscle-flexing amid broader signs that Britain was a fading colonial power. Another counterinsurgency campaign was yet again influenced by the broader rubric of Cold War regional dynamics and delicate politics of decolonization.

Regional concerns, this time in the Middle East, propelled the administrations of John F. Kennedy and Lyndon Johnson to maintain a wary position in regard to the British campaign in South Arabia from 1963 to 1967. Chapter 6 shows how initial US-UK friction of the issue of recognizing the newly declared Yemen Arab Republic soon spilled over into American incredulity at covert action inside the borders of the new state as London sought to enhance the counterinsurgency war.

The Johnson and Nixon presidencies are indelibly associated with the Vietnam War. This particular counterinsurgency conflict became the albatross around the neck of the American military, and US foreign policy in general, for a generation. Chapter 7 shows how the massive expansion of the American war effort in Vietnam created a policy quandary for London, which tried to tread a fine line between offering direct counterinsurgency military assistance and noninterference in an increasingly controversial war. The result was a haphazard combination of ad hoc indirect assistance, through the creation of the British Advisory Mission to Vietnam under its revered boss Sir Robert Thompson, and occasional peacemaking initiatives conjured up by the government of Harold Wilson. Neither was ultimately satisfactory, allowing us to see how the ineffectualness of British opinion and action regarding one of Washington's counterinsurgency wars reveals the true vacuity of the label "special relationship."

Another prime showcase of American political efforts (this time from Congress, not the White House) to undermine the British management of a counterinsurgency campaign is that of the first decade of the modern Northern Irish

"Troubles" (1969–79). A sizeable Irish American diaspora, and the attendant lobby groups it created, placed significant political pressure on the British government to halt its campaign against the Irish Republican Army (IRA) in order to pave the way for a "united" Ireland. But the United States was not only a welcoming political platform for Irish republicans. It also provided a mass market for weapon purchasing and fund-raising within sympathetic communities. The American connection to Irish republican activity was arguably the greatest external challenge faced by the British military in its attempts to reduce the potency of the IRA. Chapter 8 chronicles this struggle.

The events of 9/11 and the subsequent waging of a global War on Terror by the administration of George W. Bush was blown off course by the formation or recalibration of potent insurgent forces. First, the overthrow of the regime of Saddam Hussein in Iraq paved the way for the unleashing of a multivariate and bloody insurgency that coalition forces spent from 2003 to 2010 trying to tackle. Chapter 9 shows how involvement of the British in the Iraq War—predominantly through their civil-military control over the Shia-dominated south of the country—led many American political and military leaders to reappraise their opinion as to the effectiveness of the British Army as a counterinsurgent force. The Iraq War sparked fundamental tensions in US and UK approaches to this particular type of war. The result was a loss of American faith in British abilities and British exasperation at American attitudes.

Such outcomes were mirrored in the parallel war in Afghanistan (2001–14). Chapter 10 details how American frustration at perceived British timidity in their conduct of operations was matched by British annoyance at American overreliance on kinetic solutions. The British deployment to Helmand Province ended without reducing insurgent control over key areas and required US Marine Corps assistance in accomplishing basic objectives. This all reinforced negative opinions within the American military and political hierarchy pertaining to the competence of British forces in a form of conflict with which it had become synonymous in previous decades.

The book is rounded off with a conclusion that ties the common strands of the campaign case studies together—namely, the imbalance of Anglo-American relations, the role played by domestic politics in shaping policy toward counterinsurgency campaigns, and the fluctuating fortunes and perceptions of specialness between the United States and the United Kingdom in this type of war. Counterinsurgency wars, given their frequency in the tableau of conflict since 1945, are a revealing lens through which to look at a supposedly special relationship in the diplomatic and military sphere. They demonstrate the absence of specialness between London and Washington in the conduct of the most frequent form of noncovert military operation the two leading Western powers used in the latter half of the twentieth century. What is striking, in fact, is the utter ordinariness of the relationship inasmuch as it is marked with self-interest and mutual irritation—and the conduct of counterinsurgency operations by the US and the UK from 1946 to 2014 provided ample opportunity for both.

Notes

Epigraph: Winston Churchill, "Sinews of Peace" speech, Fulton, Missouri, March 5, 1946, https://www.nationalchurchillmuseum.org/sinews-of-peace-iron-curtain-speech.html.

1. House of Commons Foreign Affairs Committee, *Global Security: UK-US Relations.*
2. Dickie, *"Special" No More*, xi–xii.
3. "PM and President in 'Violent Agreement,' *Times* (London), July 21, 2010, http://www.thetimes.co.uk/tto/news/politics/article2652542.ece.
4. Porter, "Last Charge of the Knights?," 357.
5. Mead, *God and Gold*, xii.
6. Hitchens, *Blood, Class and Empire*, 5.
7. Kitson, *Bunch of Five*, 3.
8. For a thorough analysis of the British counterinsurgency campaign against the Mau Mau, see Bennett, *Fighting the Mau Mau*; Branch, *Defeating Mau Mau*; Anderson, *Histories of the Hanged*; and Elkins, *Britain's Gulag.*
9. For a thorough analysis of the Dhofar campaign, see Ladwig, "Supporting Allies in Counter-Insurgency," 62–88, and DeVore, "Complex and Conventional Victory," 144–73.
10. PUSC report #51: "Anglo-American Relations—Present and Future," November 9, 1949, The National Archives, UK (hereafter TNA), FO 371/76386.
11. House of Commons Foreign Affairs Committee, "British-US Relations."
12. Kissinger, *White House Years*, 92, 416.
13. Ibid., 932–33.
14. For an assessment of the turbulence beneath the surface of the Thatcher-Reagan relationship, see Aldous, *Thatcher and Reagan.*
15. "Toasts of the President and Prime Minister Harold Wilson," December 7, 1964, Papers of the Presidents, Lyndon Johnson papers, document #796, http://www.presidency.ucsb.edu/ws/?pid=26749.
16. Ibid.
17. Renwick, *Fighting with Allies*, xi.
18. Dobson and Marsh, "Introduction" in Dobson and Marsh, *Anglo-American Relations*, 8.
19. For example, see Burk, *Old World, New World*; Dumbrell, *Special Relationship*; Louis and Bull, *Special Relationship*; and Watt, *Succeeding John Bull.*
20. Danchev, *On Specialness*, 2–3.
21. Hyam, *Britain's Declining Empire*, 27.
22. Kissinger, *White House Years*, 91.
23. These countries are, in chronological order of their reference, the Philippines, Puerto Rico, France, Panama, Mexico, Japan, India, Liberia, prerevolutionary Iran,

Israel, Thailand, Yugoslavia, Canada, Italy, Australia, Egypt, Jordan, Portugal, Greece, Poland, Pakistan, and Romania. See www.presidency.ucsb.edu.

24. Neustadt, *Alliance Politics*, 2.
25. House of Commons Foreign Affairs Committee, *Global Security: UK-US Relations*, 22.
26. House of Commons Foreign Affairs Committee, *Government Foreign Policy towards the United States.*
27. "Donald Trump Finally Calls Theresa May—After Egypt, Turkey and Ireland," *Metro*, November 10, 2016, http://metro.co.uk/2016/11/10/donald-trump-finally-calls-theresa-may-after-egypt-turkey-and-ireland-6249448/.
28. Aldrich, *GCHQ*, 89.
29. Ibid., 7.
30. Walton, *Empire of Secrets*, 122, 142.
31. Jeffreys-Jones, "End of an Exclusive Special Intelligence Relationship," 721.
32. Baylis, "Exchanging Nuclear Secrets," 33–61.
33. Ball, "Military Nuclear Relations," 439–54.
34. Robb, "'Limit of What Is Tolerable,'" 322.
35. Dockrill, "Foreign Office, Anglo-American Relations," 460.
36. For broad overviews of the British military and political stance during the Korean War, see Stueck, "Limits of Influence," 65–95, and Greenwood, "'A War We Don't Want,'" 1–24.
37. Dockrill, "Foreign Office, Anglo-American Relations," 460–61.
38. Foot, "Anglo-American Relations," 43–58.
39. "Minute by Strang," January 3, 1951, TNA, FO 371/92067.

1

Empires, Old and New

The Politics of Counterinsurgency

> As the United Kingdom maintains her position as a world power and increases her economic strength and stability the United States may be expected to continue to welcome her as an intimate, but not exclusive, partner.
>
> —Sir William Strang, permanent undersecretary, Foreign Office, April 1950

Counterinsurgency is intrinsically political in its conduct. Its fundamental strategic premise is the (re)assertion of authority for the civil powers, which has traditionally required a mix of coercive and conciliatory measures to convince local populations to abstain from supporting insurgent violence. Lip service to phrases such as "winning hearts and minds" or repetitions of French warrior-scholar David Galula's maxim that counterinsurgency warfare "is 20 per cent military action and 80 per cent political" have underlined the importance of the nonkinetic component to this form of warfare.[1] It is therefore imperative to ascertain the political context in which British and American counterinsurgency wars since 1945 have been operating if we are to comprehend the machinations behind the causes, conduct, and consequences of these frequent conflicts and the implications they have had on the "special relationship."

Such machinations were calculatedly constructed in Washington and London in the postwar era. The United States sought to solidify its position as the preeminent global power and prevent the expansion of Soviet influence. The United Kingdom, conversely, sought to carefully manage the unraveling of its empire and readjust to its diminished standing in the world order. Dean Acheson famously stated that after the Second World War, Britain had "lost an empire and has not yet found a role" in world affairs. Yet seen through the lens of counterinsurgency (from which so many moments of decolonization occurred), Britain's role during the Cold War becomes readily apparent: to hold the line against the spread of communism in parts of the world where British influence, be it coercive or consensual, provided better intelligence cover or a residual military bulwark against Soviet or Chinese expansion.

But this is only part of the story. Imperial counterinsurgency conflicts by the British involved formal colonial structures that gave rise to metropole-periphery frames of analysis. Yet as the recalibration of the postwar world order saw the United States accrue significant global political and economic power, questions regarding the ambitions of the US to eclipse Britain as an "imperial" power will be addressed in respect to the conduct of American counterinsurgency wars.

The final piece of the puzzle is what might be labeled capital *P* politics. The inescapable desire to win elections encouraged domestic-party political agendas in the United States to encroach on foreign policy debates that were raging during the early Cold War period. This had the specific effect of creating a permissive environment for lobby groups representing ethnic diasporas to pressure the White House, Congress, and State Department to take particular stances on British counterinsurgency conflicts where the insurgent opponent had a shared kinship with their members. The maintenance of (or at least the semblance of) a special relationship was thus at the mercy of the domestic political scene in Washington and goes to reinforce the utter imbalance of US-UK relations, given how the reverse situation would not be manifest as British domestic influence over American policymaking diminished hugely after the Second World War.

This chapter will unravel these intertwined themes in order to reveal the motives Washington had for formulating its policies toward many of Britain's colonial-era counterinsurgency wars.

The Early Cold War, Counterinsurgency, and Decolonization

By the early 1950s, Britain's foreign policy makers had come to accept that the country's best interests on the global stage were best served by closely aligning themselves with the United States. America had been identified by Foreign Secretary Ernest Bevin in a note to the cabinet in May 1950 as one of the "three main pillars" that would shape the direction of British policy in the years to come, alongside the Commonwealth and Western Europe.[2] But recalibrating Britain's foreign policy outlook for the nascent Cold War was not an automatic prelude to decolonization. London decided that the perceived economic and strategic value of empire would increase British prestige in the eyes of Washington. This was a rather astute decision for Whitehall to come to, given American acquiescence toward some of Britain's counterinsurgency wars against procommunist guerrillas and other beneficial side effects of the British Empire, especially access to a wider intelligence network in the Far East. The increasing importance of anticommunism to British, not just American, foreign policy in the 1950s ensured that the maintenance of imperial control, and the careful management of its eventual dismantling, was undertaken with a firm eye on the Cold War objective of preventing Soviet or Chinese expansion in parts of Asia and the Middle East where the Union Jack flew. The process of decolonization was the eventual result of the interaction between local conditions on the ground within the colony and the broader international political environment.[3] As this book aims to show, many of the local dynamics were shaped by vicious insurgencies, while the changing nature of international relations in large part was affected by superpower grand strategy. Britain's "small wars" of decolonization were thus subject to a two-way set of pressures from above and below that impinged on the British diplomatic handling of the conflicts, the political management of the withdrawal from empire, and the British military's actions in these counterinsurgency wars. The stories of the early Cold War and British decolonization are thus intricately linked.

In the early Cold War the United States had tacitly acknowledged that the maintenance of the British colonial presence in some parts of the world was a cheaper alternative to its own military deployments. So pervasive was suspicion of communism within American political circles that successive administrations developed a benign acceptance of the British Empire.[4] It possessed a certain strategic utility for Washington that permitted the West a greater reach into regions susceptible to Soviet or Chinese influence.[5]

The bipolar nature of Cold War power struggles, however, did not play out quite so simply on the ground in colonial wars or within the corridors of Whitehall, where a contentious set of local, national, and regional actors impinged on the process of arresting imperial decline. This was particularly true within Britain's intelligence machinery, where there was a great reluctance to credit the significance of the agency of colonial actors, given their obsession with Cold War threats. This led, as we shall see later, to an inability within Britain's intelligence agencies to rationally frame their understanding of the causes and consequences of colonial counterinsurgency.[6]

It would be all too easy to depict decolonization as the end of British usefulness to the Americans. Britain did not cut political ties or curtail the presence of important military or intelligence networks within the newly independent nations. The necessity of maintaining such vestiges of the security state across what some corners of Whitehall still called "the British Southern World" meant that in reality decolonization did not end the British presence—it merely redefined the power relationship.[7] Far from representing a panicked and incoherent response to colonial insurgencies, the exit strategies implemented in Britain's small wars of decolonization symbolized a carefully managed withdrawal from empire that attempted, not always successfully, to secure the best possible terms for London. The former colonies were still to be held in orbit within a British, and therefore by default an American, sphere of influence.[8] For its part, Washington would appear to be quite comfortable with such implicit power-sharing arrangements.

Embodying this pragmatic American approach to empire in the early Cold War years was Dean Acheson. As secretary of state in Harry Truman's second administration, he was, according to one biographer, a "romantic imperialist" who saw "American and British interests as the same."[9] Seeing an inherent value in the maintenance of the British Empire, Acheson placed Anglo-American solidarity at the heart of his foreign policy outlook and lobbied London to not cut and run from problematic colonies. The inevitable result of this was the Foreign Office being lulled into a false sense of security about the attitude toward imperialism within the rest of the Truman administration. Underlying hostility in some quarters of Washington regarding Britain's role in the third world of Cold War geopolitics boiled to the surface once Dwight Eisenhower took office, and Anthony Eden's hubristic military adventure with France and Israel over the Suez Canal in 1956 caused a breakdown in relations.

A year before the tripartite covert effort to undermine the regime of Col. Gamal Abdel Nasser in Egypt by forcefully taking the "renationalized" Suez Canal, Eden had told his cabinet that "we should not allow ourselves to be restricted overmuch by reluctance to act without full American support. We should frame our own policy in the light of our own interests and get the Americans to support it to the extent we can induce them to do so."[10]

Such a mind-set, based on a misconceived understanding of British independence from American will, set the United Kingdom on a path to what Keith Kyle has described as an "ice age" in the special relationship, characterized by distinctly chilly diplomatic relations and London being temporarily frozen out of Washington's inner circle of trusted friends as a result of the Suez Crisis.[11] In the run-up to the invasion, Eden remained perplexed by American opposition to using force against Nasser. The Egyptian ruler had links to Moscow and was making a power play to become the regional strongman. Eden's confusion at the inflexibility of the Eisenhower administration was fueled by both his self-perception as an enlightened advocate of steadily managed decolonization and Secretary of State John Foster Dulles's interpretation of anti-Nasser bellicosity as a new British colonial ruse.[12] The effect of this cocktail of misunderstanding and miscalculation was, as Dulles himself put it at the height of the crisis, "the destruction of our trust in each other."[13] By the time Harold Macmillan had replaced the ailing and alienated Eden in 1957 after Eisenhower had effectively issued an ultimatum calling for the British to withdraw from Suez or face bankruptcy, it was now starkly apparent that the United States held the reins of British power on the global stage. Macmillan's core task was to go about repairing the damage done to Anglo-American relations and mitigating the effects of the "winds of change" that he perceived to be blowing through the remnants of the empire. The Suez Crisis bluntly demonstrated, if it was not clear before, that a changing of the international guard had occurred. Britain was no longer capable of imposing its will on the global stage without American permission. The bigger issue remained whether the concomitant British retreat from empire and the American rise to global superpower status during the early Cold War essentially necessitated the construction of a new "American Empire." The complex relationship Washington had with the lingering British presence in strategically sensitive parts of the third world, and indeed with the way in which successive presidents went about implementing foreign policy goals during the Cold War, has resulted in the inevitable claims that a Pax Americana was created. American perceptions of, and influence over, the management of Britain's colonial counterinsurgency wars certainly exacerbated such an assertion.

Counterinsurgency and the "American Empire" Debate

The story of British decolonization is inextricably tied to that of counterinsurgency. The stage-managed withdrawal from empire was occasionally threatened, even hastened, by the sparking of a violent insurgency. Britain's retreat from parts of Asia, Africa, and the Middle East was controlled not just by a political desire to herald independence and the economic need to reduce imperial expenditure, but also by the military's ability to stem the tide of communists in Malaya and ethnonationalists in Cyprus and South Arabia. Yet the centrality of counterinsurgency to discussions of the British Empire (particularly its demise) should not be seen as an exclusively British phenomenon. Debate surrounding the existence and nature of an American Empire has raised its head, especially at times when the exercise of American power on the global stage is proving robust or controversial. Over the past seventy years, the recurrent debate about American Empire peaked during American undertakings in protracted and bloody counterinsurgency wars, namely those in Vietnam and Iraq. The twin tales of empire and counterinsurgency are shared Anglo-American stories.

American political culture has since the days of the Boston Tea Party had a distrust of colonialism engrained within it. The population developed a politically socialized repellence toward empire in its traditional sense. This attitude was not substantially shaken as world war gave way to cold war. A May 1950 State Department assessment of "Certain Current Problems with the UK" cited "Policies Towards Colonial and Dependent Territories" as a key area of concern. This briefing document, circulated in advance of the London Tripartite Meeting (along with France) played up the main differences in approach toward the maintenance of empire by contrasting Washington's "traditional dislike of colonialism and belief that independence is desirable for all peoples" with London's emphasis on "the need for gradualism in colonial development."[14] This discomfort toward British colonialism within the wider American population at the beginning of the Cold War was, however, trumped by perceptions of a greater threat. As British ambassador to Washington at the time, Oliver Franks, wrote to Foreign Secretary Ernest Bevin in May 1950, "the broad masses of the American people, including the liberals, are convinced that the supreme danger confronting their civilisation is not old-fashioned colonialism but modern communism." A fear of "reds under the bed" was recalibrating the American political consciousness. Ambassador Franks acknowledged that the Americans perceived the issue of colonial independence with a "woolly sentimentality" and that American public opinion needed "educating" on the "realities of present-day colonial administration." More important, Franks argued, American policymakers needed to be encouraged to "recognise that anything which weakens the colonial powers also weakens the United States."[15] The British foreign policy establishment had realized during the early Cold War that the best way to ensure American acquiescence toward the maintenance of the empire was to tie it to the emergent priorities of stemming communist expansion in Asia, Africa, and the Middle East. Anticommunism eclipsed anticolonialism in policymaking circles, which paradoxically increased the American need for a British colonial presence in certain parts of the world at a time when Britain was beginning to scale back its imperial responsibilities.[16] Anticommunism made acquiescent imperialists out of the Americans in the early Cold War.

But not all in Washington were willing to swallow this line. In June 1953, Secretary of State Dulles used a national radio address to berate his own administration's policy for becoming "unnecessarily ambiguous" in respect of its attitude toward "the old colonial interests of our allies."[17] This was a view clearly shared by what the Colonial Office euphemistically labeled "unattributed United States intelligence elements," most likely the Central Intelligence Agency, run by John Foster's brother Allen. The Colonial Office cataloged in 1957 how unrest across British colonial territories was being fomented by foreign sources, leading officials to surprisingly conclude that American anticolonialism ranked alongside Soviet propaganda and indigenous nationalism as one of the three "main sources of subversion" across the empire, arguing that the American intelligence agencies' "policy of interference is taking the shape of *control without responsibility*."[18]

American attitudes toward British colonialism, particularly those of the Dulles brothers, did not always extend to a reflection on the nature of American power itself. Expansionism across the frontier in pursuit of a "manifest destiny" has been a marked feature of the American republic since independence in the late eighteenth century. As the nation grew from its original thirteen colonies, the push westward triggered wars with Native Americans, Spaniards, and Mexicans in the nineteenth century as Thomas Jefferson's self-proclaimed "empire of liberty" annexed land to fulfill a nascent set of ideological, economic, and strategic national interests. Yet the territorial expansion of the nation halted with the connection of two oceans.[19] The United States dominated the continent as the nation consolidated its expanse. Through participation in two world wars and the creation of a dominant economy via a huge workforce and massive resources, American isolationism in world affairs gradually eroded. The bigger questions, though, remain whether this made America an empire in some form and whether the exercise of its power abroad constitutes acts of American imperialism.

How best to label the role and character of American power in the world? Raymond Aron was in no doubt that America constituted an "imperial republic" in its actions during the early Cold War because of the way he perceived the United States expanded the concept of containment to become an imperially imposed doctrine for a new international order.[20] Numerous sobriquets have been used by other scholars, each of which, Michael Cox has argued, seems inadequate: "Superpower" is a little blatant; "hegemon" too vague; "unipolar" too restrictive.[21] "Empire," however, is a tag imbued with both ideological and military functions that allows for the normative character and the resource capabilities of the country to be taken into consideration—an important facet when assessing the exercise of power in expeditionary counterinsurgency wars.

Michael Doyle's seminal definition of empire constructs it as "a system of interaction between two political entities, one of which, the dominant metropole, exerts political control over the internal and external policy—the effective sovereignty—of the other, the subordinate periphery."[22] Notions of America as an empire have more often than not been used alongside some adjective to characterize a particular aspect of American power projection. We therefore have America as an "incoherent empire" (Michael Mann), as an "empire in denial" (Andrew Bacevich), and as "empire lite" (Michael Ignatieff). The decades-long debate about the existence of an American Empire has broadly created four schools of thought, which I will label the Advocates (those who embrace the label and benefits of modern imperialism), the Cautious Optimists (those who believe that, if used properly, modern American imperialism can be a liberal force for good), the Critics (those who decry American imperial pretension), and the Deniers (those who argue that no such thing as an American Empire exists). Each school of thought brings with it a whole host of implications about how to interpret American power, and each speaks directly to its application in conflicts where the asymmetry of power against an insurgent opponent magnifies the conduct of the "dominant metropole."

Leading the Advocates school of thought are modern neoconservatives such as Niall Ferguson and Max Boot. Their forceful advocacy of a proimperial interpretation of modern American history leads Advocates to not see "empire" as a dirty word. Ferguson has gone as far as to claim that Americans should shrug off any timidity around using the label "empire" to describe their country's global influence because American power projection is not only expansionist and self-righteous—it is, Ferguson posits, also an unquestionable force for good.[23] As with the self-styled liberal empire built by Britain in the nineteenth century, the rhetoric and actions that have come to define the modern American imperium has led to a perceptible historical irony whereby, as Ferguson has mischievously put it, the anticolonial foundations of the United States are so compromised by similarities to its British imperial predecessor that the rebellious child has now grown up to resemble the once despised parent.[24] One of the main catalysts to such a transformation has arguably been America's engagement in a series of counterinsurgency wars to fend off substate threats to gradual expansionism of the frontier in North America and abroad as a "sphere of influence" spread. Boot made this connection when writing a history of American small wars in the early twentieth century, observing that he was simultaneously "chronicling the political course of American empire."[25] American success in counterinsurgency wars before the Second World War benignly created, to Boot's mind at least, a "family of democratic capitalist nations that eagerly seek shelter under Uncle Sam's umbrella."[26] The American Empire, for the Advocates, is benevolent and held together consensually.

This assumption is challenged to some extent by the Cautious Optimists, such as Michael Ignatieff. This position shifts the basic ideological interpretation of American Empire from a neoconservative one to a liberal one. From such a standpoint, Ignatieff has argued that although not seeking to build an empire in a traditional sense, the United States has built a version of "empire lite" whose touchstones are the advocacy of human rights, the spread of democracy, and free markets—all of which are aggressively protected by unrivaled military prowess.[27] Liberal notions of American Empire being used as a force for good in international politics by occasionally using military intervention to uphold fundamental rights informs Geir Lundestad's description of America establishing an "empire by invitation" in the early Cold War. This was a consensual process where the US supported allies in rebuilding their economies after the Second World War and provided a military bulwark against Soviet encroachment. Invitations from European nations to America to provide economic, political, and military assistance, Lundestad argues, were extended by countries on other continents in subsequent decades. These governments saw American protection as an important mechanism to uphold democratic rights that would have been curtailed by communist rivals.[28] For the Cautious Optimists, this makes the foundation of the American Empire one of accident, not design, in reluctant fulfillment of its own liberal, perhaps utopian, worldview.[29]

But the use of the very word "empire" really only received a positive tone in recent decades. Its origin in the American debate was as a label of denigration used by the third identifiable school of thought, the Critics, in regard to American foreign policy actions in the Cold War. The Critics perceive American foreign policy since 1945 as being so imbued with perceptions of benevolence and righteousness (something the Cautious Optimists applaud) that

William Appleman Williams coined the phrase "the imperialism of idealism" to describe the ideological zeal that accompanied American expansionism and interventions abroad.[30] More contemporary Critics, such as Chalmers Johnson, perceive that the nature of American imperialism lies in its mass network of foreign military bases in countries all over the world. This provides the United States, Johnson argues, with the capacity to "garrison the globe" via the permanent deployment of over half a million service personnel to over seven hundred military bases on every continent bar Antarctica.[31] In short, America's empire is militaristic and predicated on the sheer physical presence of its armed forces. This is a theme recurrent in Michael Mann's characterization of America as an "incoherent empire" that practices what he critically labels "new imperialism"—a blend of coercive and occupationist tendencies with more informal modes of hegemonic influence in political and economic realms.[32] The Critics coalesce on the left of the political spectrum and decry the course and conduct of American foreign relations most audibly when used in the counterinsurgency contexts of Vietnam and Iraq.

The final discernable set of scholars to have staked a claim in the American Empire debate are the Deniers. They argue, as Desmond King and David Lake have done, that although the United States may act in an imperial fashion, this is not the same as being an empire.[33] The Deniers counter the notion that American actions even fit within the rubric of a debate about imperialism. Benjamin Barber has argued that far from being an interventionist or expansionist imperial power, the majority of American foreign policy actions abroad have been undertaken to ensure future reductions in expeditionary warfare. As such, any Pax Americana is based "not to secure the world for US purposes, but only to secure the USA from the world."[34] Yet the implications of the contemporary "security dilemma" have arguably nullified such a distinction. America's search for absolute security at home, especially in a post-9/11 context, has necessitated controlling the internal and external policies of other states, through both hard- and soft-power mechanisms.

Although not an empire builder in the traditional sense in which nearly every vestige of the occupied territory is controlled by the metropole, America has got itself, in Andrew Bacevich's words, "an imperial problem" that successive presidents have refused to acknowledge.[35] This has been a particularly acute issue during expeditionary counterinsurgency wars when forcible regime change has been followed by extensive military operations involving punitive measures against elements of the population. Whether American leaders decide to use the label "empire" or not is largely irrelevant; if world opinion decides that if it looks, sounds, and acts like an empire, the label will stick. America's decision after 1945 to rigorously defend and help expand the boundaries of global democracy left it in a self-created position of being the guardian of a global liberal order. As Britain demonstrated in the nineteenth century, some nations go in search of an empire.

What American has shown in the twentieth century is that some nations have empires thrust on them. The domestic political ramifications of such foreign policy prescriptions are considerable and, indeed, are mutually constitutive, as the next section investigates.

Wars at Home and Abroad: The Impact of Domestic Politics on Counterinsurgency

The inability of London to reconcile the maintenance of empire with the rise of America as a global power was a key driver behind mid-twentieth-century decolonization.[36] Another major factor was the impact of American domestic politics on US policy toward British military efforts to maintain their imperial reach. As Richard Neustadt reminds us, "foreign relations begin at home."[37] This was certainly the case when analyzing how successive White House administrations shaped their policy toward Britain's counterinsurgency conflicts across the empire after the Second World War. Domestic political concerns remained paramount in the minds of foreign policymakers. This was certainly not restricted to the implications of Britain's small wars of decolonization. On a visit to Washington at the height of the Suez Crisis in November 1956, Air Chief Marshal Sir William Elliot met with Eisenhower. The president informed Elliot that "he had known that we [the British] did intend at some point to strike against Egypt. But he did not think it would be so soon. He thought it would be after the [US presidential] elections."[38]

Worries over the effect of British colonial military action on American electoral mathematics are a recurrent theme in American political attitudes toward the British case studies analyzed in this book. Since 1945, the British military has found itself fighting counterinsurgency wars against groups whose ethnic demographic or national allegiance had a large American-based diaspora: Jews in Palestine, Greeks in Cyprus, Irish in Northern Ireland. As the later chapters go on to demonstrate, an astute political wariness of the importance of such large ethnic blocs to the outcome of mayoral, gubernatorial, congressional, and presidential elections impacted on the ways in which American policymakers acted in regard to Britain's wars against their ethnic kin. As Robert Dallek, the eminent biographer of Kennedy, Johnson, Nixon, and Kissinger, astutely observed, "trolling for ethnic votes was standard election year politics" in the United States.[39] The special relationship in counterinsurgency wars was thus at the whim of American domestic politics.

International relations and domestic politics are, in Robert Putnam's words, a "puzzling tangle."[40] The relationship between the two, in particular the balance of interactive cause and effect, is complex. Putnam urged in the late 1980s that analysis should aim for an integrated understanding of both spheres. His theoretical modeling of what he called "two-level games" (nominally instances where negotiations are conducted by actors at the national and international levels) creates a platform on which to base an assessment of the US-UK special relationship in general and during counterinsurgency wars in particular. Consider for a moment Putnam's explanation of how two-level games work: "At the national level, domestic groups pursue their interests by pressuring the government to adopt favourable policies. . . . At the international level, national governments seek to maximise their own ability to satisfy domestic pressures, while minimising the adverse consequences of foreign developments."[41]

Bearing this in mind, we can see how American leaders had to placate domestic concerns about British imperialism while at the same time ensure that British counterinsurgency campaigns simultaneously aided US Cold War strategic aims in the third world. Given the complexities of this particular two-level game, where the central dilemma for successive American presidents was either gain domestic votes (mainly Jewish or Irish American) but risk ostracizing a close ally or lose the votes in order to maintain a special relationship with Britain. The chapters that follow reveal that national-level concerns trumped international-level most times. Winning elections mattered more than supporting a British small war. The importance of key demographics to swing elections was higher in the minds of US politicians than the upkeep of Anglo-American relations.

The reflection of domestic political concerns in consecutive American administrations' foreign policy decisions relating to colonial-era British counterinsurgency campaigns is recognizable in Kenneth Waltz's "second image" of international relations. In his seminal text *Man, the State and War*, Waltz posited that actions relating to war are driven by an interconnection between three main causes, or "images," as he labels them: human behavior (individual agency), the internal structure of states (essentially domestic politics), and international anarchy (the nature of world order). The second image is important to Waltz's overall construct because "the internal organization of states is the key to understanding war and peace" and that "war most often promotes the internal unity of each state involved."[42] A contemporary, and perhaps more cynical, reworking of that last dictum based on American political maneuverings in relation to Britain's colonial-era counterinsurgency wars would instead read: "War, or interference in a war, often promotes internal electoral dividends for each leader involved." Thus we can better understand Truman's intervention in the Jewish migration issue that was a catalyst to insurgent violence in the British Mandate of Palestine immediately after the Second World War as predominantly an electoral stunt to shore up the sizeable Jewish American vote for Democratic candidates. Similarly, we see domestic political concerns effect congressional plays for the Irish American vote through vehement critiques of British security policy in the early phases of the "Troubles." Such "internal defects," as Waltz calls them, help explain "external acts of the state."[43] When analyzing declassified documents relating to the special relationship at work during counterinsurgency wars since 1945, one sees that the "internal defects" of the US Electoral College and the demands they place on party machines to win over blocs of voters impinged significantly on the "external acts" of those in power to adopt particular stances on British counterinsurgency campaigns. This frequently nefarious American political influence on the British management of certain conflicts stands in contrast to the percolation of military doctrine regarding counterinsurgency warfare between the two nations. The British tradition has provided fertile material for reinterpretation by a new generation of American warrior-scholars, but, as we shall see in the next chapter, this has still provided ample scope for transatlantic tension.

Notes

Epigraph: "Extract from a Memorandum for the Permanent Under Secretary's Committee—Anglo-American Relations: Present and Future," document #27, in Documents on British Policy Overseas (hereafter DBPO), series II, vol. 2, *The London Conferences: Anglo-American Relations and Cold War Strategy, January–June 1950*, 82.

1. Galula, *Counterinsurgency Warfare*, 63.
2. "Extract from Conclusions of a Meeting of the Cabinet held at 10 Downing Street on Monday, 8 May 1950, at 11am," document #74, in DBPO, series II, vol. 2, 261. Interestingly, Bevin's triptych predates Sir Winston Churchill's identical, but more famous, enunciation of "three concentric circles."
3. Heinlein, *British Government Policy*, 5–6.
4. Burleigh, *Small Wars*, 2–3.
5. Anne Deighton, "Britain and the Cold War, 1945–55," in Leffler and Westad, *Cambridge History of the Cold War*, 127.
6. Cormac, *Confronting the Colonies*, 209–10.
7. Hale, *Massacre in Malaya*, 400.
8. Grob-Fitzgibbon, *Imperial Endgame*, 2.
9. McNay, *Acheson and Empire*, 6, 62.
10. "Cabinet Meeting," Cm (55)34, October 4, 1955, The National Archives, UK (hereafter TNA), CAB 128/29 (34).
11. Kyle, *Suez*, 2.
12. Ibid., 274.
13. "Top Secret: from Washington to Foreign Office," October 31, 1956, TNA, PREM 11/1105.
14. "UK—Current Problems," US National Archive and Records Administration (hereafter NARA), Record Group (RG) 43 250/10/16/4 (Box 45).
15. "Confidential: From British Embassy, Washington DC to Ernest Bevin, 14 January 1950," TNA, CO 537/7136.

16. Hyam, *Britain's Declining Empire*, 28.
17. "Radio Address by the Honorable John Foster Dulles, 1 June 1953," TNA, FO 371/103515.
18. "Survey of Subversive Activities in the Colonies, 1957," TNA, CO 1035/139 (emphasis added).
19. For an assessment of the expansion of the American nation, see Reynolds, *America, Empire of Liberty*.
20. Aron, *Imperial Republic*, 304.
21. Cox, "Empire's Back in Town," 5.
22. Doyle, *Empires*, 12.
23. Ferguson, *Colossus*, 2, 8.
24. Ibid., 15.
25. Boot, *Savage Wars of Peace*, xvi.
26. Ibid., xx.
27. Michael Ignatieff, "American Empire: The Burden," *New York Times Magazine*, January 5, 2003, http://www.nytimes.com/2003/01/05/magazine/05EMPIRE.html?pagewanted=all.
28. Lundestad, "'Empire by Invitation,'" 189–217.
29. Simes, "America's Imperial Dilemma," 91–102.
30. See chapter 2 of Williams, *Tragedy of American Diplomacy*.
31. Johnson, *Sorrows of Empire*, 1.
32. Mann, *Incoherent Empire*, 13.
33. King, "When an Empire Is Not an Empire," 163–96; Lake, "New American Empire?," 281–89.
34. Barber, "Imperialism or Interdependence?," 240.
35. Bacevich, *American Empire*, 243.
36. Hyam, *Britain's Declining Empire*, 12–13.
37. Neustadt, *Alliance Politics*, 61.
38. "Record of Conversation between the Secretary of State and Air Chief Marshal Sir William Elliot at Her Majesty's Embassy, Washington on 18 November 1956," TNA, PREM 11/1176. I am grateful to Louise Kettle for bringing this document to my attention.
39. Dallek, *Nixon and Kissinger*, 413.
40. Putnam, "Diplomacy and Domestic Politics," 427.
41. Ibid., 434.
42. Waltz, *Man, the State and War*, 81.
43. Ibid.

2

Anglo-American Military Culture

What Role for Counterinsurgency?

> My overriding impression was of an Army imbued with an unparalleled sense of patriotism, duty, passion, commitment, and determination. . . . Yet it seemed weighed down by bureaucracy, a stiflingly hierarchical outlook, a pre-disposition to offensive operations, and a sense that duty required all issues to be confronted head-on.
>
> —Nigel Aylwin-Foster, British Army brigadier embedded with US forces in Iraq, 2005

As an astute observer of the dynamics of the "special relationship," Alex Danchev once noted how it has "waxed fat on war."[1] Yet this waxing has only occurred, in the academic literature at least, on the fat of particular types of war—namely, large-scale conventional ones. The mythical bonds of fraternity forged during the fight against Nazism in the Second World War lingered long in the historical memory and ensured the overshadowing of the more fraught relationship in more unconventional forms of war. If in general terms the special relationship has waxed fat on war, then it has waned precipitously on counterinsurgency.

Orthodox perceptions of the special relationship rely heavily on assumptions about shared language, history, and, importantly, culture. If we hone in on this particular pillar of the relationship, we can observe numerous types of culture at play, including that of military culture. The origins of the American military, rooted in rebellion against the redcoats of the British colonial forces, serve as a reminder of some fundamental differences in Anglo-American military culture that have ingrained themselves over the past two centuries. As military historian

John Keegan once observed, the officer corps of the two nations exhibit noticeably different behaviors and display dissimilar attitudes toward each other: "There is a marked cultural difference between American and British army officers. . . . The British notoriously exhibit an unhurried and amateur manner, while Americans are formal and conscious of rank. The British officer's tendency to wear odd clothes and use Christian names to other officers strikes Americans as unserious."[2] Taking these observations on board, we see that the old epithet about Americans and Britons being separated by a common language actually runs much deeper.

The history of post-1945 Anglo-American war-fighting is in large part dictated by the narrative of counterinsurgency conflict. Britain's extensive irregular warfare experience stemmed from numerous insurgent challenges whose casus belli ranged from communism (Malaya) to socialist-inspired nationalism (Yemen) and the nationalist fight for an alternative union (Cyprus and Northern Ireland). It was generally accepted that as the War on Terror morphed into a protracted counterinsurgency campaign, the volume of British experience in such operations would allow them to hit the ground running against new insurgent enemies. Brig. Nigel Aylwin-Foster's (in)famous *Military Review* article in 2005 that admonished American thinking and performance in Iraq came to encapsulate the entrenched British mind-set of superiority when it came to counterinsurgency.[3] "Brits know best" seemed to be the message in the early phases of the wars in Iraq and Afghanistan.

The perception that familiarity had actually bred competency and not complacency inside the British Army was forged in part from an understanding of hostile American attitudes toward counterinsurgency dating back to the Vietnam War. The bitter legacy of America's Southeast Asian quagmire had inured generations of US commanders since the departure from Saigon to calls for greater understanding of, or preparedness for, war against irregular enemies. The result was a hardening of American military culture against the waging of counterinsurgency, a rejection of messy fights against enemies hiding within the broader population, and a safer embrace of high-tech conventional war-fighting against state-based opponents.

However, the British response to the complexities of twenty-first-century insurgencies, in their decentralized and globally networked form, has threatened to expose their competency as a colonial-era myth. Quantity of counterinsurgency combat experience has not equated into outright quality. In parallel to this, American military adaptation to the exigencies of the War on Terror in the wake of the 9/11 attacks, led by an intramilitary intellectual insurgency, brought about one of the biggest challenges to orthodox US military culture in decades. Such recent developments make an exploration of comparative Anglo-American military cultures vis-à-vis counterinsurgency war relevant for three key reasons. First, it reveals the high-profile role that counterinsurgency has played in shaping the entire dynamic of US and UK military cultures in both positive and negative ways. Second, it helps us understand the process of cultural adaptation on both sides of the Atlantic in the face of the changing threats posed by insurgent groups to national security. Third, it helps us trace the process of intermilitary learning as a way of gleaning whether any "specialness" was or is present when it comes to US-UK cooperation during these sorts of war. Overall we can see how both the British and American militaries are hostages to their own history in counterinsurgency terms. For the British, it has imbued in them a false sense of competence, given the erroneous equation of quantity of campaigns with quality of execution. For the Americans, the albatross of the Vietnam War has hung heavily around their necks, resulting in the automatic discounting of enhanced counterinsurgency preparedness and the shunning of irregular war as a widely accepted component of US military culture. Both militaries have paid the price for such historical and cultural miscalculations.

The British Military and the "Counterinsurgency Myth"

The British approach to counterinsurgency after the Second World War rested on a track record of extensive colonial policing duties and military aid to the civil powers across large swaths of territory that constituted the extensive empire. When combined with the exigencies, and perhaps the eccentricities of British military culture, such historical exposure to insurgencies created a discernable approach to counterinsurgency warfare that over time came to be heavily mythologized as revolving around concepts of "minimum force," the adoption of "hearts and minds" operations, and discernable strategic results. A revisionist turn has occurred in assessments of British counterinsurgency warfare as a result of the return to some of the lessons from key colonial campaigns as a means of improving the potency of the stalled campaigns in Iraq and Afghanistan. More analysts of the British experience noted how a myth had been perpetuated about British competency in irregular war-fighting.[4] This mythologizing process has, in part, occurred because of the relative absence of other counterinsurgency success stories. Benevolent observers have noted that during the "classical" counterinsurgency period of the mid-twentieth century, "the British approach had yielded more success than that of any other nation faced with internal conflict. . . . Nothing like an Algeria or Vietnam tarnishes the British record."[5] The absence of a catastrophic counterinsurgency failure, however, should not detract from the drawn-out strategic inertia that came to characterize consecutive campaigns and is perhaps an outcome more indicative of the preparedness and efficiency of the insurgent opponents that the British have faced. It is not that the British were or are better at counterinsurgency than any other nation. It is just that they were able to wring more from their failures.

David Ucko and Robert Egnell note that another reason why the British track record has been so mythologized is that there has been a scholarly predilection to conflate the theory and practice of counterinsurgency.[6] The impact of works by Charles Calwell, T. E. Lawrence, Robert Thompson, and Frank Kitson has inevitably conjured the illusion that the sheer quantity of theoretical material has been the product, or indeed cause, of a superior qualitative experience in theater. Since the launching of the War on Terror and the difficult adaptation to counterinsurgency in Iraq and Afghanistan, the American military commentariat have been the most profound peddlers of this myth as US commanders sought ways out of their modern imbroglios.[7]

More often than not, insurgent rebellions and the counterinsurgency wars that follow produce a plague on both houses, resulting in mutual loss of blood and treasure. In campaign after campaign, as the following chapters show, the British military was hampered in its efforts to win counterinsurgency wars by inadequate political and security resources within the colonies, by a misreading of insurgent enemy aims and objectives, by frequent resort to the coercive stick instead of the conciliatory carrot, by the absence of an effective collective lesson-learning mechanism across civil-military channels, and by question marks over the entire sustainability of the British imperial project.[8] The accumulative effect of these misperceptions was a thoroughly artificial interpretation of British military performance in counterinsurgency within transatlantic security circles.

According to John Nagl, the British succeeded in Malaya, specifically in contrast to the American failure in Vietnam, because the British Army had an organizational culture akin to a "learning institution," whereby the army quickly adapted to counterinsurgency conditions and changed tactics accordingly.[9] The array of operational experiences the British Army has undergone, from limited to total war, has arguably led to a greater degree of pragmatism in its military outlook. A dogmatic adherence to rigid military doctrine has been absent, which, when compared to the generation-long postmortem on the failure of US strategy in Vietnam, perhaps explains more than most other factors why this mythological aura has been built around the British. However, this does not explain, nor should it detract from, the languid application of appropriate irregular warfare tactics and the absence of swift strategic design. The early phases of nearly every campaign in the classical era (as we shall see in the later chapters) were marred by stagnancy, mismanagement, and confusion. For example, it was two years into the Malayan Emergency before the army conceived of a cohesive civil-military strategy in the form of the Briggs Plan. Despite building a military culture around proficiency at counterinsurgency, the British have been consistently slow to instigate an effective strategy and achieve operational success. The vast body of campaign experience has not translated into a cogent counterinsurgency lesson-learning process within the British Army. The very need to "relearn" counterinsurgency in the post-9/11 conflict environment has undermined assertions as to the British military's existence as an effective learning institution. That exact process of relearning counterinsurgency in Iraq and Afghanistan has occurred in direct correlation to that of their American partners in the War on Terror. But as Col. Alex Alderson, a key figure in shaping the British Army's modern outlook on counterinsurgency, has argued, "the UK was not just the junior coalition partner to the US, but the junior intellectual partner as well."[10]

As Theo Farrell has observed, the process of British military transformation to meet the demands of the modern strategic environment is shaped by resource constraints, domestic politics, and military culture.[11] However, none of these three elements are conducive to quick adaptation in the British case. The military culture of the British Army is essential to the process of counterinsurgency lesson-learning, given the inherent aversion to formalized doctrine. Pragmatic flexibility on a campaign-by-campaign basis has been evident, given the absence of codified strategic manuals (the recent exception to this was the publication in October 2009 of *British Army Field Manual: Volume 1 Part 10; Countering Insurgency*).[12] Counterinsurgency lesson-learning for the British has essentially been a creative and not an imitative process.

Analysis of the conduct of British counterinsurgency, from Palestine to Afghanistan, has frequently rested on assumptions that the adoption of a "small wars culture" was drawn from a static body of knowledge, like the tomes written by the warrior-scholars named above. But this culture, although subject to unwarranted plaudits, has been shaped and molded by the individual leaders residing within the military. Culture and leadership in the military are mutually reinforcing and mutually reinventing concepts. The story of British counterinsurgency since 1945 is in large part a very human tale about the personalities whose charisma and intellect moved doctrinal debates forward but whose hubris and bluster occasionally jeopardized strategic success.[13] Frequently the finger of failure has pointed at the civilian leaders whose beady eye on a timetable for withdrawal has been seen by many in the military as an act of politically motivated cowardice. But the deeply troubling outcomes of campaigns such as Palestine, Yemen, and Iraq also reveal the role played by military commanders unable or unwilling to meet the task set them.[14] This has deep implications because of the way in which mythologized perceptions of British effectiveness at counterinsurgency became commonplace within the American military at the dawn of the "new counterinsurgency era."

American Military Culture and Counterinsurgency

In his address to the 1962 graduating class of the US Military Academy at West Point, President John F. Kennedy extolled the need for the American military to adopt "a versatility and an adaptability" in the face of what he stressed was a contemporary form of conflict that the newly minted officers he addressed that day would find themselves predominantly fighting. This, the president asserted, "is another type of war, new in its intensity, ancient in its origin—war by guerrillas, subversives, insurgents, assassins." Kennedy concluded by urging a thorough overhaul of the American approach to these asymmetrical threats. In cheerleading counterinsurgency, Kennedy rallied, "It requires in those situations where we must counter it . . . a whole new kind of force, and therefore a new and wholly different kind of military training."[15] Half a decade later Kennedy's mantra would be echoed by a new generation of counterinsurgency enthusiasts, mainly drawn from the military establishment that the president had so urgently pressed to embrace irregular war in the early stages of the Vietnam War.

Six months before he delivered that speech, Kennedy had established the Special Group (Counterinsurgency) under the command of Gen. Maxwell Taylor, to stifle insurgencies in countries friendly or important to the United States. Taylor himself referred to the group as "a sort of Joint Chiefs of Staff for the control for all agencies involved in counterinsurgency."[16] But the Kennedy administration's newfound obsession with counterinsurgency, and his exclusive references to the need to quash Soviet-sponsored "wars of national liberation" in the third world, reveal an understanding of irregular war as a specifically Cold War imperative. Counterinsurgency as a mode of imperial war-fighting, in the British or even the French mode, was an anathema as far as Washington was concerned, with few public references made to the comparative experiences of colonial powers' counterinsurgency lessons. Indeed, up until the Kennedy recalibration, the US approach to counterinsurgency had mainly involved the US Army Special Forces training insurgents to overthrow enemy regimes rather than fight them directly.[17]

But the enthusiasm with which resources were thrown into counterinsurgency training in the early 1960s waned drastically as the Vietnam War became more intense and larger in scale under President Lyndon Johnson. The backlash within the military began long before the Paris Peace Accords, and the protracted postmortem of American military performance continued long after the last helicopter left Saigon. As David Fitzgerald argues in his book of the same name, the US military has been "learning to forget" counterinsurgency war-fighting since Vietnam as a result of processes deeply embedded in American strategic culture. After the war, the army derived a set of lessons from Vietnam that relied on a constructed institutional memory of counterinsurgency's challenges. This, in turn, percolated through the army's doctrine, training, and education systems and resulted in the formation of an "American way of war" whose identity closely associated with conventional war. The military convinced itself that Vietnam, and therefore counterinsurgency, had been a temporary distraction from the bigger and more urgent task of preparing for large-scale war-fighting.[18] A brief revival in interest in counterinsurgency during the so-called low-intensity conflicts of the 1980s in Central America under Ronald Reagan did not represent a renewed embrace of counterinsurgency, merely a convenient and half-hearted foray. It would not be until the War on Terror that the expediencies of counterinsurgency were again unwillingly grasped by the broader US military (notably within the US Marine Corps)—but not without a tumultuous intellectual power struggle for the mind-set of the army.

No better symbol of the contemporary institutional wrestle over the significance and role of counterinsurgency in the corridors of the US military is needed than the 2006 *Quadrennial Defense Review* (*QDR*). Included within its writing team were some of the boldest advocates of counterinsurgency working with the military at the time, including David Kilcullen. Emboldened by perceived strategic and tactical failings in what they began to label "the long war," the *QDR* team pressed for the Pentagon to overtly embrace counterinsurgency as a means of energizing the stagnant war efforts in Iraq and Afghanistan. Skeptical of the broader implications on US military culture and applications of American power, senior Pentagon figures including Defense Secretary Donald Rumsfeld sought to row back on some of the more strident pieces of counterinsurgency advocacy in the document. Sitting next to each other at the beginning of the review is a Rumsfeld-influenced preface followed by an introduction sculpted by, among others, Kilcullen. Within these few pages we find the epitome of the tussle to grant or deny counterinsurgency a central role in medium-term US military planning. In the notably cautious preface, the Rumsfeldian desire to pour cold water on calls to adapt to a seemingly new set of priorities built around addressing asymmetrical threats leads to a trenchant opening statement: "Manifestly, this document is not a 'new beginning.' . . . [It] represents a snapshot in time of the Department's strategy for defense of the Nation and the capabilities needed to effectively execute that defense."[19] Pentagon top brass were clearly intent on blunting the obsession with counterinsurgency in some quarters by depicting it as unwarranted due to the temporary nature of the wars in Iraq and Afghanistan. Turn the page to the *QDR*'s introduction, however, and you find a different message. By establishing the premise of America amid a long war against "dispersed, global terrorist networks," the *QDR* writing team asserts that such threats "require the US military to adopt unconventional and indirect approaches." The lines in the sand of this intellectual battle over counterinsurgency were starkly drawn by the *QDR* author's desire to push "two fundamental imperatives" on the Pentagon. First, they argued, was the need to "reorient the department's capabilities and forces" in order to "prepare for wider asymmetric challenges." The second was the associated need to "ensure that organizational structures, processes and procedures" within the bureaucracy were pushed behind a new counterinsurgency-based strategy.[20] The resistance that this plea had even from their own nominal boss at the Pentagon serves as a stark indicator of how irreconcilable the two camps would be on the centrality of counterinsurgency to the modern American "way of war."

The two sides in the "Great Debate" on counterinsurgency have been labeled by Andrew Bacevich as the "Crusaders" and the "Conservatives."[21] The former group, embodied by *QDR* writer David Kilcullen and other counterinsurgency warrior-scholars such as David Petraeus and John Nagl, were determined to overhaul the approaches of the US Army and US Marine Corps to thinking about and doing counterinsurgency based on a population-focused doctrine. The latter group, whose most vocal members include Gian Gentile and Doug Porch, conversely perceived the demands of counterinsurgency as a momentary fad that is a distraction from the bigger strategic priority of conventional war-fighting. The Crusaders certainly achieved the upper hand in the debate by 2007 with the adoption of the new, Petraeus-inspired *FM 3-24: Army and Marine Corps Counter-Insurgency Field Manual* and the subsequent promotion of its lead author to command US forces in Iraq and Afghanistan. A new ethos of astute cultural awareness was radiated by the Crusaders—or "COINdinistas," as their opponents laconically called them. Yet the intractability of the wars in Iraq and Afghanistan, coupled with the eventual downfall of Petraeus, the king of the Crusaders, from his position as director of the Central Intelligence Agency in 2012 saw the pendulum swing back the way of the Conservatives, who have arguably been on a crusade of their own to dismantle the counterinsurgency infrastructure within the US military.

Counterinsurgency is arguably antithetical to the nature of American military culture, in particular its intrinsic aversion to laborious and complex operations. But as the invasion of Iraq in 2003 quickly gave way to a nationwide insurgency, the Crusaders set themselves the task of bringing counterinsurgency away from the fringes of US military specialism and setting it at the heart of its thinking. Counterinsurgency needed to go mainstream. This required a fundamental upheaval in the way the army trained for and conducted irregular warfare, all bound within the confines of an enlightened new doctrine.[22] But, as with all revolutions, it did not take long for counterrevolutionary forces to gather. The new field manual added fuel to the fire. Arch-Conservative Gentile argued that parts of *FM 3-24* were "a jumble of dreamy statements that bordered on some mixture of philosophy, theory and military operational history."[23] Porch went as far as to claim that it was "naïve, impracticable, unworkable and perhaps institutionally fraudulent."[24] Both critics honed in on the notion that the overarching narrative of population-based counterinsurgency that the field manual attempted to portray was a fallacy and took issue with the seeming self-righteousness and strong sense for self-publicity that the COINdinistas possessed. As Gentile despairs at the end of his book, "the belief that counterinsurgency works persists like a vampire among the living."[25]

To complete the critical circle, a backlash against the Conservatives' counter-crusade has begun. This has been led by David Ucko, who accuses Gentile and Porch of "advancing screed-like diatribes based on poor sourcing and contradiction."[26] This refrain is a similar one heard during the post-Vietnam era from some quarters that the hard lessons drawn from difficult wars should not be ignored in order to heal the institutional scars that counterinsurgency has wrought. Similarly, T. X. Hammes has provided a useful corollary to the anti-COINdinista stance by positing the need for a long-term counterinsurgency capability within the US military. Irregular war, Hammes argues, has an "enduring relevance" to patterns of conflict, an ignorance of which could have deleterious consequences on US national security. This capability requires a focus on both enemy and population-centric approaches and, crucially, ploughs resources into an indirect approach through training local security personnel to counter insurgencies on their own turf.[27] In short, the United States needs to distance itself from expeditionary counterinsurgency, but not from counterinsurgency overall.

In a lecture to the Royal United Services Institute in London in 2013, Petraeus weighed into the argument against his Conservative critics by stating, "We cannot lose our proficiency [in counterinsurgency] . . . without degrading the relevance of our militaries to address future threats and achieve foreign policy objectives."[28] But this, in essence, is the same argument put forward by the anticounterinsurgency lobby. The Petraeus-versus-Gentile debates are not about counterinsurgency per se. They are more about the nature of future conflict and emergent threats. This has echoes of the debate about counterinsurgency after Vietnam. In the preface to his important book *Deadly Paradigms*, written the decade following the Vietnam withdrawal, D. Michael Shafer warned that "Vietnam-induced public skepticism" had rendered counterinsurgency "a footnote to a rapidly fading and best forgotten moment in American foreign policy." Despite the waning of interest in counterinsurgency, its relevance to future American deployments, albeit in difference guises (as 1980s low-intensity conflict), had not. Yet a willing collective amnesia about counterinsurgency ensued, opening the United States up to a dangerous level of unpreparedness should the military be required to fight another irregular war in the future.[29] As the War on Terror's foray back into counterinsurgency fades and the foreign policy wounds heal, Shafer's observation still holds true, given the Conservative countercrusade against engraining counterinsurgency in US military culture (and memory) takes place. Trying to understand counterinsurgency better does not have to equate to wanting to do it more. It merely means trying to avoid egregious errors if asked to perform it again.

One of the main strands of learning from past experiences that the Crusaders picked up on was rediscovering the large pool of British doctrinal texts to have emerged out of the small wars of decolonization. The attainment of "must-read" status in COINdinista circles of T. E Lawrence's *Six Pillars of Wisdom*, Charles Calwell's *Small Wars*, Robert Thompson's *Defeating Communist Insurgency*, and Frank Kitson's *Low Intensity Conflict* ensured that modern American counterinsurgency doctrine has a hint of a British accent. Such tomes helped shaped thinking at a time when there was a paucity of American-produced literature and offered mantras that were recast for a twenty-first-century asymmetrical conflict environment. Indeed, the desire to learn from the British experience and tap into the British institutional memory regarding counterinsurgency led the *FM 3-24* writing team to initially propose that the manual be jointly written with the British Army, only to have potential UK collaborators withdraw because of the ambitious timetable for completion.[30] So pervasive has been the influence of such "classical" British counterinsurgency theorists on the COINdinistas who surrounded Petraeus that Frank Hoffman has argued that the percolation of such ideas into *FM 3-24* represents the manifestation of "neo-classical" counterinsurgency that is still stuck in Maoist perceptions of insurgent organization and motivation.[31] Even writers of modern British counterinsurgency doctrine, such as Alex Alderson, have acknowledged that American doctrine "is based on sound classic theory . . . with the British model in mind."[32] Conservative critics leapt at this transatlantic source of inspiration. Doug Porch lambasted the "compendium of predictable platitudes" that have been "lifted from British theory . . . a Lawrence / Liddell Hart victory without battle formulas." The result, Porch declares, was the adoption in Iraq of a quasi-colonialist approach of "divide and rule" that the British had applied during so many imperial counterinsurgency campaigns.[33]

The British legacy is clearly a divisive one in modern American debates about the theory and practice of counterinsurgency. The most significant and sizeable of these campaigns, from Palestine to Northern Ireland, are worth exploring in detail as a means of understanding the historical experience of British counterinsurgency war-fighting and prizing out exactly how American political influence during these campaigns affected not just the dynamic of the conflict but also the broader solidity of the special relationship—a bond severely tested during the War on Terror when the two militaries deployed to a counterinsurgency war together for the first time. It is to exploring these interwoven pasts that the rest of this book is dedicated.

Notes

Epigraph: Aylwin-Foster, "Changing the Army," 3.

1. Danchev, "Cold War 'Special Relationship' Revisited," 582.
2. John Keegan, "Let the Infighting Begin: British and US Rivalry Resumes," *Daily Telegraph*, April 17, 2003, http://www.telegraph.co.uk/news/worldnews/northamerica/usa/1427766/Let-the-infighting-begin-British-and-US-rivalry-resumes.html.
3. Aylwin-Foster, "Changing the Army," 2–15.
4. Mumford, *Counter-Insurgency Myth*.
5. Mockaitis, "Phoenix of Counterinsurgency," 8, 11.
6. Ucko and Egnell, *Counterinsurgency in Crisis*, 24.
7. The most high-profile example of this is Nagl's *Learning to Eat Soup with a Knife*.

8. French, *British Way of Counter-Insurgency*, 5.
9. Nagl, *Learning to Eat Soup*, xxii.
10. Alexander Alderson, "Too Busy to Learn: Personal Observations on British Campaigns in Iraq and Afghanistan," in Bailey et al., *British Generals in Blair's Wars*, 292.
11. Farrell, "Dynamics of British Military Transformation," 783.
12. *British Army Field Manual: Volume 1 Part 10; Countering Insurgency.*
13. Nolan, *Military Leadership and Counterinsurgency*, 7, 28.
14. Edwards, *Defending the Realm?*, 17.
15. John F. Kennedy, "Remarks at West Point to the Graduating Class of the US Military Academy," June 6, 1962, Papers of the Presidents, document #226, www.presidency.ucsb.edu/ws/index.php?pid=8695.
16. Quoted in McClintock, *Instruments of Statecraft*, 165.
17. Ibid., xvii.
18. Fitzgerald, *Learning to Forget*, 58–59.
19. "Preface," *Quadrennial Defense Review*, US Department of Defense, February 6, 2006, v, ix.
20. "Introduction," ibid., 1.
21. Bacevich, "Petraeus Doctrine," *Atlantic*, October 2008, http://www.theatlantic.com/magazine/archive/2008/10/the-petraeus-doctrine/306964.
22. This process is chronicled in Kaplan, *Insurgents*.
23. Gentile, *Wrong Turn*, xvi.
24. Porch, *Counterinsurgency*, xi.
25. Gentile, *Wrong Turn*, 135.
26. Ucko, "Critics Gone Wild," 163.
27. Hammes, "Future of Counterinsurgency," 566.
28. Petraeus, "Reflections on the Counter-Insurgency Era," 86.
29. Shafer, *Deadly Paradigms*, ix.
30. Fitzgerald, *Learning to Forget*, 168.
31. Hoffman, "Neo-Classical Counterinsurgency?," 71–87.
32. Alderson, "Learning, Adapting, Applying," 18.
33. Porch, *Counterinsurgency*, 302, 310.

3

The Changing of the Guard in the Postwar World

Counterinsurgency in Palestine and the Creation of Israel

> A major difficulty in the rule of Palestine was of course the effect of outside influences, notably the United States.
>
> —Sir Alan Cunningham, high commissioner of the British Mandate in Palestine, 1948

The Polo Grounds stadium in Manhattan, known to locals as "The Bathtub," might seem like an odd place for American frustration at British conduct of a counterinsurgency campaign to manifest itself. Yet as Foreign Secretary Ernest Bevin, on a diplomatic trip to New York in December 1946, was announced to the crowd while taking his seat as a guest of honor at a New York Giants game, he was roundly greeted by a chorus of boos and jeers.[1] The sympathy for the effort to establish a Jewish homeland against the stubborn resistance of the civil and military rulers of the British Mandate of Palestine was palpable enough to overshadow the ensuing football game that night in Manhattan. Bevin had been given an up-close taste of American public opinion with regard to the British counterinsurgency effort against the loose coalition of Zionist insurgent groups within Palestine.

Having been the mandatory power in Palestine since 1920, the British had faced an Arab revolt in the 1930s and had been refereeing disputes between the small Jewish population and the Arabs ever since. But after the Second World War, international attention turned to Palestine as a violent Zionist insurgency coincided with growing American pressure on the British to permit greater numbers of Jews who had been persecuted during the Nazi pogroms to establish a state in their ancestral homeland. As such, British policy on Palestine had to juggle multiple demands. It needed to quash the insurgent violence while not jeopardizing relations with Washington. At the same time, Britain needed to conceive of a longer-term plan for the Middle East that met the strategic need and demand for oil. The trouble with these simultaneous pressures was that the conduct of the counterinsurgency campaign made the British look decidedly anti-Zionist, which angered the vocal pro-Zionist elements within the United States, while the need for oil and longer-term stability in the region required the toeing of a pro-Arab line from London.[2] The inevitable result, according to the last high commissioner in Palestine, Sir Alan Cunningham, was the construction of no coherent policy at all, as the British became subsumed "amid turbulence, vilification, assassination and kidnapping."[3]

The British response to this complex insurgency was to cause serious ructions in the "special relationship." Shocked at his reception from the football crowd in New York, Bevin would become so embroiled in the management of the conflict that, according to his celebrated biographer Alan Bullock, the Palestine issue "was to cause him more angry frustration and bring down more bitter criticism on his head than any other issue in his whole career."[4] The White House was to bring down its fair share of that bitter criticism on Bevin and the rest of the Clement Attlee administration. Even after he had left office, Harry Truman still felt that over Palestine the British were "highly successful in muddling the situation as completely as it could possibly be muddled."[5] The conflict in Palestine ensured that the first "unhappy tangle" in the "special relationship" after the end of the Second World War was over Britain's conduct of a counterinsurgency campaign and its associated political fallout.[6] It provides an important corollary to much of the special relationship literature that has tended to focus on the dynamic between London and Washington in the nascent Cold War in Eastern Europe during the same period.

From World War to Counterinsurgency War

Even before Allied victory against Adolf Hitler's Germany had been secured, President Truman was being warned by his secretary of state, Edward Stettinius, that "it is very likely that efforts will be made by some of the Zionist leaders to obtain from you at an early date some commitments in favor of the Zionist program," including a lifting of immigration restrictions into Palestine and the creation of the Jewish state.[7] Almost as soon as the war was over in Europe, the American Christian Palestine Committee wrote to all members of Congress requesting that they press Truman into implementing a pro-Zionist stance on Palestine.[8] The ending of the Second World War brought with it a realization of the full extent of Hitler's genocide against the Jews of Europe. Truman himself admitted that sympathy for the victims of the Holocaust played a key role in shaping his own perspectives on how the British should approach the issue of Jewish immigration into Palestine and deal with Zionist violence inside the mandate.[9] In August 1945, he wrote to the new British prime minister, Clement Attlee, enclosing a copy of a report written by American legal expert Earl Harrison on the state of displaced persons (DPs) across Europe. The president urged the prime minister to scrap immigration limits placed on entry to Palestine, as set out in a 1939 white paper. American inclination to play a large role in influencing the future of the British Mandate had already begun.

This did not go unnoticed in London. Attlee stonewalled Truman's copy of the Harrison Report and instead focused on the recommendations of his deputy prime minister and lord president of the council, Herbert Morrison, who in his own report concluded that there was a need to establish a joint Anglo-American Committee of Enquiry into the situation of Jews in postwar Europe. Even Morrison could not resist a sideswipe at the Truman administration for what he perceived to be its arm's-length interference in the Palestine issue. By establishing a joint committee, Morrison argued, "the United States will thus be placed in a position of sharing the responsibility for the policy which she advocates. She will no longer be able to play the part of irresponsible critic."[10] Attlee also wrote a personal letter to Truman that included a robust defense of the British position on Palestine. In an attempt to stave off American pressure to open up immigration restrictions, Attlee warned Truman that efforts by Washington to help increase Jewish immigration quotas "could not fail to do grievous harm to relations between our two countries."[11] Bevin was also urging the cabinet that "a solution of the problem of Palestine" was urgently needed in part because "the agitation in the United States" over the issue of Jewish immigration to the mandate "was poisoning our relations with the United States Government in other fields."[12]

Intense lobbying by pressure groups, religious organizations, and congressional delegations in Washington was duly noted by the British ambassador, Lord Halifax. A month after Bevin's warning to the cabinet, he allowed his frustration at vocal American interference on the Palestine issue to get the better of him. In rather undiplomatic language, Halifax fired an exasperated telegram back to London in which he claimed "rats were at work" in Washington attempting to undermine the British position.[13] Perhaps he had the new secretary of state, James Byrnes, in mind, with memories still fresh of a testy meeting the two men had held a few weeks earlier in which Byrnes had bluntly told Halifax that the United States was "interested in Jews going to Palestine and not to be scattered all over the earth."[14] By the time of this meeting, Byrnes had already seen War Department plans, drawn up at the request of the State Department's Office of Near Eastern and African Affairs (NEA), for the possible deployment of American troops to Palestine to help British forces "maintain order ... in case disturbances should take place as a result of decisions to open Palestine to Jewish immigration." The War Department estimated that around four hundred thousand troops would be necessary, of which the US would probably have to provide around three-quarters. But the War Department concluded its report on a note of caution, arguing that any Palestine deployment would cause "indefinite delay" to the demobilization of the US military, which was currently occurring just a few months after the end of the Second World War.[15] American preparedness for the possibility of military intervention was stoked by its diplomatic representatives on the ground. The American consul in Jerusalem, Malcolm P. Hooper, cabled Washington days before the War Department report crossed Byrnes's desk, describing Palestine as "the center of a world of nerves" and that "the tinder is laid for racial conflict."[16]

In order to avoid this tinder being set alight by an American-provided spark, Prime Minister Attlee wrote to President Truman in May 1946, calling for the "closest of co-operation between our two Governments on this matter."[17] But this plea was heavily compromised by the violent forces of Zionism within Palestine and the political support for it from inside the United States.

Zionism in Palestine and America

In many ways the violent Zionist opposition to British rule in Palestine was the first example of a modern internationalized insurgency, incorporating arms smuggling from America and bombings against British targets on continental Europe and London.[18] Compounding the difficulty in responding to such a complex insurgency was the inability of British intelligence inside Palestine to discern the relationship between the three main groups—the Haganah, the Irgun, and the Stern Gang.[19]

The Haganah had its roots in the agrarian socialist movement in Palestine and drew sizeable support from Zionists favoring a strategy of "active defense." The Haganah (literally the "Defense Force") was created to protect Jewish settlements across Palestine from Arab attacks, in the mode of armed neighborhood-watch groups. Orde Wingate, who would later find fame leading the British Chindits in a guerrilla war against Japanese forces in Burma in the Second World War, acted on his Zionist sympathies while posted to Palestine during the Arab revolt (1936–39) to help train the nascent volunteers. But this primarily defensive approach did not appeal to all Zionists. A revisionist element emerged out of the Haganah in the late 1930s with a determination to undertake offensive operations against Arab guerrilla units. The Irgun Zvai Leumi (National Military Organization), popularly known simply as the Irgun, emerged as the preeminent Zionist force, advocating violence as a means of protecting and extending

Jewish interests in Palestine. But the dawn of the Second World War resulted in a final split within the Zionist movement. Uncomfortable with the implicit cooperation that the Irgun and the Haganah were offering Britain in wartime, and incensed at a British refusal to acknowledge the need for a Jewish state, militant Zionists broke away from the Irgun to form the Lochmei Herut Israel (the Fighters for the Freedom of Israel, or LHI). Dedicated to attacking the British military presence in Palestine during the war, the LHI became known colloquially as the Stern Gang in 1942 after the group's leader, Abraham Stern, was killed by police.[20]

All three groups did have a major feature in common. They all operated a dual-track approach in which a paramilitary campaign fought for the ability to rule and a parallel political campaign projected to the wider world a message about their right to rule. By mid-1946, the three main groups pledged to work together in order to achieve their shared goals. The result was the establishment of the Jewish Resistance Movement and a rise in coordinated attacks against British interests. This unity, however, was short-lived. The movement splinted in July 1946 amid recriminations toward the Irgun, which had undertaken a bomb attack against the British Mandate administrative headquarters at the King David Hotel in Jerusalem that killed ninety-one people.[21]

This atrocity drew the condemnation of President Truman, who cautioned the Zionists in Palestine that such acts of "wanton slaying . . . will not advance, but on the contrary might well retard, the efforts that are being made."[22] Truman's admonishment was well placed, given the political weight carried by Zionist groups in the United States. The goal of creating a Jewish homeland was pressed on all branches of American government in the late 1940s by a sizeable Jewish American lobby. Groups such as the American League for a Free Palestine undertook anti-British propaganda campaigns with rousing effect. Pressure was exerted on the White House to punish Britain for its actions in Palestine by canceling postwar loans, which were propping up the British economy. As Norman Rose has observed, Britain "had to calculate how much humiliation, international criticism and tension with the United States it was willing to endure before it reached the conclusion that holding on to Palestine, thereby alienating the powerful American Jewish lobby, was not worth the cost."[23]

The conflict in Palestine seeped into the broader American political consciousness as several prominent Jewish Americans used their place in the public eye to enhance the Zionist message. In 1946, the playwright Ben Hecht previewed his latest production in New York, a vitriolic, anti-British play called *A Flag Is Born*, which recounted the horrors that European Jews had been subject to in recent years. On the back of a successful tour, Hecht wrote an open "Letter to the Terrorists of Palestine" in which he encouraged them to continue their fight: "Every time you . . . let go with your guns and bombs at British betrayers and invaders of your homeland, the Jews of America make a little holiday in their hearts." The British consulate in New York was worried enough to convey back to London concern that Hecht's attitude was representative of wider Jewish American feelings toward the British war in Palestine.[24]

But American Zionism did not remain exclusively political. Elements within the Jewish American population, particularly those with Mafia links in New York, provided a constant supply of weapons to insurgent groups in Palestine. Using a hotel suite in the same building as New York's famous Copacabana nightclub as their base of operations, affiliates of the Haganah used donations from the diaspora to purchase army-surplus weapons (in plentiful supply after the Second World War) and smuggle them aboard ships in New York Harbor. The ringleader of this operation was Teddy Kollek (who, after the creation of Israel, became mayor of Jerusalem). Kollek built connections with New York's Mafia underworld, which assisted in money laundering and weapon smuggling on the Zionists' behalf. One Zionist sympathizer with Mafia connections who helped Kollek was a part-time singer named Frank Sinatra, who, on one occasion, delivered bags of money to a waiting ship heading for Palestine when the original courier started to be shadowed by the Federal Bureau of Investigation (FBI).[25] Arms smuggling to the Zionist insurgents had become a *cause célèbre.*

In another high-profile incident in August 1947, French police arrested an American rabbi, Baruch Korff, as he was about to board a plane bound for London that was going to drop anti-British leaflets and, it was wrongly feared, bombs. Korff, whose New York–based Political Action Committee for Palestine had proved an influential lobby group for Zionist interests in Congress, previously considered a plan involving Jewish immigrants parachuting out of planes over Palestine in order to undermine stringent British immigration quotas.[26] These are a few of the more outlandish efforts by Americans to influence the course of events in Palestine. Yet they were just the tip of the iceberg in regard to the broader domestic political forces that were aligned behind a pro-Zionist stance aiming to shape President Truman's dealings with the British over Palestine.

American Domestic Politics and Palestine

By the mid-1940s, there were over four million Jews in America. Their importance as an electoral bloc was significant to the outcomes of the 1946 midterms, the 1948 presidential election, and a string of local elections in between.[27] Over 60 percent of the Jewish population in the United States lived in Pennsylvania, Illinois, or New York—states whose large Electoral College votes could make or break a presidential candidate.[28] It is therefore little wonder that President Truman's Palestine policy was molded in large part by the weight of public opinion, especially the views of the Jewish American community. Speaking frankly to a reception of Arab ambassadors to the US after the November 1945 mayoral elections in several large American cities, Truman openly stated, "I'm sorry, gentlemen, but I have to answer to hundreds of thousands who are anxious for the success of Zionism; I do not have hundreds of thousands of Arabs among my constituents."[29] Indeed, those very same elections caused transatlantic friction due to the White House's decision to delay in agreeing to the remit of a new Anglo-American Joint Committee on Palestine until the Democratic candidate for mayor of New York had safely beaten his Republican (and Jewish) rival, lest some of the terms and conditions of the committee anger New York's sizeable Jewish vote.[30] This decision led to some heated exchanges between Foreign Secretary Bevin and his opposite number at the State Department, James Byrnes. Bevin's attempts to make clarifying statements regarding the function of a new committee of inquiry were slapped down by Byrnes, who accused him of "embarrassing us before this election in New York." The secretary of state requested that the British ambassador, Lord Halifax, ask Bevin to postpone any press releases until after the election.[31]

Truman's obsession with his domestic electoral position was reinforced by a small coterie of advisers who helped shape a pro-Zionist policy platform. These included special counsel Clark Clifford, his assistant Max Lowenthal, and the president's adviser on minority affairs, David Niles. Clifford in particular pushed Truman to adopt a more vocal stance in favor of the Zionists for avowedly political reasons.[32] The covetous eye these advisers had on electoral mathematics was noticed by more objective diplomats. Undersecretary of State Dean Acheson confided in August 1946 to the new British ambassador, Lord Inverchapel, that he felt the president was "the unhappy prisoner of the domestic politics of this country and was looking eagerly for a way of escape."[33] Acheson's observation rooted out a fundamental dichotomy at the heart of Truman's position. Keen to win elections and enhance Democratic majorities at every level of government, the president actually harbored a deep resentment toward many prominent Zionists and the Jewish American lobby as a whole. From the early days of the conflict, Truman had personally taken a lead on shaping the American response, in part so he could mitigate any electoral damage that the British war effort against the Zionist insurgents could do to his chances of keeping the Jewish bloc on board. In a letter to influential Zionist leader Rabbi Stephen S. Wise in August 1946, Secretary of State Byrnes revealed just how heavily Truman was involved in policymaking on Palestine: "For the past year President Truman has had personal charge of the Palestine problem. Communications between the British Government and the United States Government have been carried on by the President and Mr. Attlee—not by Mr. Bevin and me."[34] Toward the end of 1947, Truman had received over one hundred thousand pieces of correspondence on the issue of Palestine. Many of those letters, Truman thought, were Zionist "propaganda" that he wished he had "struck a match to."[35] His exasperation with all parties involved in the conflict was barely concealed in a letter he wrote to an old friend back in Missouri in early 1948: "The situation has been a headache to me for two and a half years. The Jews are so emotional and the Arabs are so difficult to talk with. . . . The British, of course, have been exceedingly non-cooperative in arriving at a conclusion."[36]

But for all the headaches Palestine caused him, it did not diminish his desire to win elections. In October 1946, a month before important midterm elections, Truman delivered a speech to coincide with the Jewish Day of Atonement (Yom Kippur), in which he pressed for the establishment of a viable Jewish state. Prime Minister Attlee saw straight through what he perceived to be a thinly veiled piece of electioneering targeted at the Jewish American vote. An angry telegram was sent from Downing Street to the White House in which Attlee admonished the president for not postponing the speech: "I have just received with great regret your letter refusing even a few hours [*sic*] grace to the Prime Minister of the country which has the actual responsibility for the government of Palestine in order that he might acquaint you with the actual situation and the possible results of your action."[37] Attlee's aggressive response to Truman's politicized interference in the Palestine conflict received a plea of innocence and a mild apology from the president ("If my statement . . . was embarrassing to you, I very much regret it"[38]), but Truman still pressed the case for increasing immigration caps.

In December 1946, a month after the midterms, Truman met at the White House with Bevin—a man the president later accused of being "undiplomatic—almost hostile" in the wake of the Yom Kippur speech.[39] In the meeting, Truman admitted that "it would be easier for him to help now that the US elections were over." The Foreign Office record of their conversation goes on to reveal how Truman "went out of his way to explain how difficult it had been with so many Jews in New York."[40] Such an insight reinforces Michael Cohen's depiction of Truman as a "resentful prisoner of the Jewish lobby."[41] Earlier that year, Truman had felt compelled to reject the recommendations of the initial version of the Anglo-American Joint Committee of Inquiry into the issue of Jewish immigration into Palestine (which did not opt for a full lifting of the immigration cap), based on explicit domestic political pressures: "The opposition in this country to the plan has become so intense that it would be impossible to rally in favor of it sufficient public opinion enable [*sic*] this Govt to give it effective support."[42]

Although no major elections were held in the United States in 1947, that year became an incredibly fractious one for the special relationship due to the role played by ongoing American domestic political concerns shaping White House Palestine policy. Diplomatic talks to end the conflict were reaching the United Nations, and multiple solutions, including the possibility of partitioning Palestine into separate Jewish and Arab states, were being touted. In January that year, the State Department had assured the British embassy in Washington that "the American Government, for domestic and other reasons, would find it easier to support in the United Nations and elsewhere the solution of the Palestine problem calling for partition and the setting up of a viable Jewish state than any other solution at present under consideration."[43] The wording used by the State Department here is interesting. Note how domestic reasons are privileged over any other (indeed, any "other" reasons are left deliberately vague). Furthermore, it is interesting how the statement claims that these domestic reasons would make it "easier" for the US to support partition. The language is indicative of political expedience, especially given the missed chance to assert that the policy position was being supported because the US felt it was right or just. In a series of memos exchanged the following month by Dean Acheson and Loy Henderson (the director of the State Department's NEA), Acheson mused that although the US government had backed the policy of partition up to that point, whether "we will conclude that despite its domestic advantages for us that policy carries too great a weight of international difficulty to put across."[44] Henderson replied sympathetically, stating that "before we begin to make any public announcements committing ourselves to any line of action we should decide only after discussions with Congress, with the White House and with American Jews and other interested American groups what our policy is to be."[45] By this stage in the conflict, even the State Department was keen to shore up the domestic political front first before shaping its foreign policy platform on Palestine.

But the biggest fallout from the politicization of the Palestine conflict for political gains in the United States came in February 1947. In the chamber of the House of Commons, Ernest Bevin let fire a withering attack on President Truman's decision to make a unilateral statement calling for the immediate admission of one hundred thousand Jewish immigrants into Palestine. Angered by what he perceived to be Truman's impatience with and disrespect toward the British handling of the Palestine issue, Bevin sniffed at the president's vulnerability to the whims of the Jewish Agency (a group, he claimed, that was "very largely dominated by New York"). Warming to his theme of domestic political influence over American foreign policy, Bevin lambasted Truman for having his eyes solely fixed on his own electioneering: "I begged that the statement not be issued, but I was told that if it were issued by Mr Truman, a competitive statement would be issued by Mr Dewey [Thomas Dewey, Republican governor of New York]." Bevin excoriated the administration for its misplaced priorities: "In international affairs I cannot settle things if my problem is made the subject of local elections."[46] In the wake of this blistering attack, the White House felt compelled to issue a statement of rebuttal. It labeled Bevin's key charge that "America's interest in Palestine and the settlement of Jews there is motivated by partisan and local politics" as "most unfortunate and misleading."[47] But the foreign secretary was uncowed. A few months later he was harrying the new secretary of state, George Marshall, to ensure that the Truman administration clamp down on "illegal immigrant traffic" whose funds "are largely subscribed in the United States."[48] If Bevin could not press the case for stronger American support for British policy in Palestine, he clearly was not afraid to resort to a politicking of his own kind. This relied on exploiting American Cold War paranoia about Soviet intentions.

Playing the Russian Card in Palestine

In February 1946, George Kennan sent his famous "Long Telegram," which urged renewed American leadership around the world. Tensions between the emergent post–Second World War superpowers and the realignment of international order crystallized the early Cold War. It was against this backdrop that the major source of tension between the United States and the United Kingdom was the conduct of the counterinsurgency campaign in Palestine.[49]

Elements within the Attlee administration were not above trying to exploit American Cold War fears over the Palestine issue in order to get Washington more in line with British policy and counteract the powerful domestic political forces at work on Truman. Bevin in particular stoked concerns over possible Soviet infiltration of Palestine. At a meeting in early December 1947 with Secretary Marshall, he suggested that continuing levels of illegal immigration, which he felt was being tacitly supported by the Americans, was bound to lead to bloodshed "since the Arabs would undoubtedly be incited to massacre the Jews and the situation might require the use of force. The United States government might then find themselves required to provide forces, and the Soviet government might press to provide a force. Would the United States government like this?" Marshall replied that he would not.[50]

The British government had been aware for some time of an inclination within some American diplomatic circles to see the situation in Palestine through a Cold War lens. As early as August 1946, the US embassy in Moscow gave its British counterparts sight of a telegram it was sending to Washington that reported on Soviet policy toward Palestine. It was steeped in suspicion of the Kremlin's motives for stoking anti-Zionist violence inside the mandate: "[A] basic Soviet policy is to weaken British and American influence in the Middle East, and to win over as much sympathy as possible in the Arab countries."[51] This fear was reflected in a report by the US Joint Chiefs of Staff two months earlier, in which they warned that the most deleterious consequence of damaged British and American reputations in the region would be that "the USSR might replace the United States and Britain in influence and power through the Middle East."[52] Fast-forward two years, and the British government had come to convince themselves of this anti-Soviet mistrust as the clock ticked down to the end of the mandate. Bevin circulated a memo to the cabinet in which he postulated that "by supporting partition in Palestine [into separate Jewish and Arab states] the Soviets may well hope to encourage disorder in the Middle East."[53]

On occasion the British resorted to intelligence operations to frighten off American public opinion for greater Jewish immigration levels to Palestine. A secret propaganda campaign by MI6 (Military Intelligence, Section 6—the British agency that collects foreign intelligence) was hatched to fool the Americans into assuming that the Soviets were heavily involved in assisting the illegal immigration of Jews from Europe to Palestine. Creating a fake group called the Defenders of Arab Palestine, MI6 agents sent letters under the auspices of this organization to prominent politicians and media outlets claiming that it was a key goal of Moscow to establish a Jewish puppet state once the mandate had ended.[54]

This was not the only time that the shadowy world of intelligence played a part in the transatlantic disputes about the fate of Palestine. In February 1948, the Joint Intelligence Committee (JIC) agreed to restrict the circulation of two reports on Zionist insurgent violence in Palestine to the Central Intelligence Agency (CIA). JIC personnel in Washington had been advised by the chiefs of US Naval and Army Intelligence that the CIA contained "Jewish sympathisers" who kept themselves "well informed through leakages" from the State Department and the White House. The JIC members debated the implication for US-UK intelligence relations that these revelations could have. It was decided that any future JIC reports on Palestine "should be shown in the first place to the Director of the Central Intelligence Agency but that it be explained to him that if he could not guarantee that they would not fall into pro-Zionist hands, then they would not be left with him."[55] Declassified CIA reports from 1947 reveal that not only did the agency stake out a position opposing dual partition ("US commercial and strategic interests in the Near East will be dangerously jeopardized"[56]), but also that it felt that the British were being remarkably restrained in their dealings with insurgents on all sides, noting how the authorities seemed "unwilling to resort to ruthless measures of suppression."[57]

Although the British intelligence machine had reservations about the reliability of the CIA, the FBI proved a more effective partner in abating transatlantic Zionist arms smuggling. In January 1947, FBI director J. Edgar Hoover presented the State Department with a report on the activities of Betar, a Zionist youth movement with links to Irgun. Adding to previously known information about the group's branches in the United States, including a training regime based in Harlem for new recruits, the FBI unearthed intelligence from an informant that Betar had a cell of members within US Army units based at Fort Knox, Kentucky. Further intelligence gathering revealed suspicions about a ship bound for the French port of Marseille that was anchored in New York. FBI agents deduced that this ship was carrying an excessive amount of kosher food and medical supplies, as well as contained hidden storage compartments. The ship was registered with the American Sea and Air Volunteers for Hebrew Repatriation (ASAVHR), an organization dedicated to helping "transport Jews of Europe to Palestine via sea and air and to support the fighting resistance armies of Palestine." ASAVHR membership was open to former members of the US Navy and any active merchant seaman. The ship in question, the MS *Abril*, was owned by the Tyre SS company, whose secretary admitted to an undercover FBI agent when drunk that "although cleared for Marseille [the MS *Abril*] is intending to run the British blockade [of Palestine]."[58] The FBI also had an agent inside the National Jewish Coordination Committee, who reported back on efforts by American Zionist groups in early 1947 to work more closely together.[59]

In addition to this, a series of FBI sting operations in early 1948 resulted in the seizure of fifty-six tons of explosives bound for Palestine, as well as the arrests of two prolific New York arms dealers who were in collusion with Irgun.[60] But it was immigrants, not guns, on ships that caused most concern to MI6. Leaning heavily on a network of informants across Palestine and the DP camps in Europe, MI6 went about trying to stem the flow of illegal immigrant ships across the Mediterranean. Secret agents in Italy undertook sabotage operations against five empty ships in the summer of 1947 by using limpet mines to scuttle them while still in harbor before they had chance to set sail with cargoes of Jews bound for the mandate in breach of immigration caps.[61] Yet intelligence concerns over illegal immigration were only secondary to the main priority of preventing Zionist groups from transferring their campaign from Palestine to the UK mainland—an issue that arguably eclipsed even intelligence collection on the growing threat of the USSR in the late 1940s.[62]

It would be wrong, however, to conclude that the British and Americans were consistently trying to outwit each other in regard to the Palestine conflict. One of the most substantive diplomatic efforts made to overcome the biggest stumbling blocks—namely, the immigration issue—was undertaken jointly in 1946. It would be a significant test of Anglo-American solidarity as the counterinsurgency war raged on.

The Anglo-American Joint Committee of Inquiry

As mentioned earlier, Clement Attlee had used the report by Deputy Prime Minister Herbert Morrison to stonewall Truman's demands that the report by American lawyer Earl Harrison be implemented. In essence this meant that London had rejected the lifting of Jewish immigration quotas in favor of working more closely with Washington in finding a solution to one of the biggest issues catalyzing violence in Palestine. Morrison's keystone proposal was the establishment of a Joint Anglo-American Committee of Inquiry to investigate the movement of Jews from Europe to Palestine. This binational committee consisted of prominent politicians and lawyers who visited Palestine and the DP camps for Jews scattered across postwar Europe.[63] The committee took testimony from prominent Jewish exiles from Europe, including Albert Einstein, who was in no doubt about who was to blame for violence in the Middle East: "Difficulties between the Jews and the Arabs are artificially created by the English."[64]

Reaction to the committee's final report was different on either side of the Atlantic when it was published in April 1946.[65] President Truman pronounced himself "very happy" that many of his own views regarding the lifting of immigration levels had been heeded.[66] Conversely, reaction in London focused on how the disbanding of Zionist insurgent groups had not been made a prerequisite for immigration caps being abandoned. The British Chiefs of Staff considered the report's findings to be "disastrous to British interests" and said that they would provoke "a general Arab uprising in Palestine" while "Jewish terrorists will seek every occasion to continue their campaign of violence." This, they felt, would necessitate army reinforcements to the tune of two infantry divisions, and one armored brigade. Acknowledging the strain this would place on the armed forces, the Chiefs of Staff did suggest that "the only alternative is to ask the Americans for assistance."[67] This view was shared by Bevin, who, on the eve of the report's publication, told the cabinet that "the United States Government could not continue to offer advice without being ready to share some of the responsibility."[68] A furious Attlee vented to Richard Crossman, a British member of the committee and a Labour member of Parliament, that his "annoyance is with the Americans who forever lay heavy burdens on us without lifting a finger to help."[69]

The report itself had gone through several iterations before final publication. Negotiations on the content between the British and American delegates hammered out compromises, especially on the thorny issue of immigration. The united front that the committee was eventually able to show was a relief to many. American committee member Bartley Crum, a California attorney, felt that a failure to have secured unanimity would "have been very bad for the future of Anglo-American relations."[70]

The publication of the committee's report coincided with an upsurge in violence inside Palestine, which was met by a crackdown by British security forces. The new British general officer commanding Palestine, Sir Evelyn Barker, coordinated these counterinsurgency operations. On Saturday, June 28, 1946, he launched Operation Agatha, involving over one hundred thousand troops and police officers, who were used to seal off dozens of large Jewish settlements across the mandate. The offices of the Jewish Agency were raided, curfews were imposed on major cities, and three thousand people were arrested. The Jewish community would come to call this day "Black Sabbath."

Interestingly, Attlee telegrammed Truman with a last-minute warning of the imminent start of Operation Agatha.[71] But this advance alert was very much for information, not consultation. Truman replied to Downing Street, stating that he was in a state of mind "regretting that drastic action is considered necessary."[72] Indeed, the White House went out of its way to issue a press release explaining that the US government had no forewarning of the crackdown and that the president had talked about the situation with Zionist leaders in Washington.[73]

Almost a month after Operation Agatha was launched, the Irgun blew up the King David Hotel. The bombing—labeled an "inhuman crime" by Attlee[74]—prompted a wave of counterinsurgency operations across the mandate. The biggest of these was Operation Shark in Tel Aviv. Over twenty thousand troops cordoned off the city for nearly four days. Tens of thousands of homes were searched and their occupants interrogated in an effort to flush Irgun members out of this particular stronghold.[75] This aggressive counterinsurgency approach was in part due to an intervention by the chief of the Imperial General Staff, Field Marshal Bernard Montgomery. The hero of El Alamein was appalled by the deteriorating situation in Palestine and the seeming imperviousness of the insurgents to the authority of the British. "Monty" was also angered by what he perceived to be an overly cautious approach on behalf of British commanders in the mandate and was incredulous that civilian leaders were not prepared to authorize a greater use of force at a time when, on average, two British soldiers were being killed by insurgents each day.[76]

Diplomatic efforts to bring violence to an end occurred late in 1946 and early 1947 with two sets of conferences that took place in London. In the end, the Jewish delegation refused to attend, leaving the British government to only talk with the Arab delegation. Despite the boycott of the Jewish Agency, the Truman administration announced that it was "keenly interested" in the conference, and the embassy in London kept abreast of developments.[77] But the lack of headway made in the London Conference was a prelude to Britain deciding in February 1947 to pass off responsibility for Palestine to the United Nations (UN), as the political will within Parliament to maintain control and the ability of the military to enforce authority in the mandate began to crumble.[78] Although authority passed to the UN, the British still remained responsible for law and order until the official partition of the mandate in May 1948.

The End of the Mandate and the Creation of Israel

As the British Mandate drew to an end, insurgent and counterinsurgent found themselves caught in an action-reaction cycle of repression and revenge. In March 1947, the Irgun bombed the British Officers' Club in Jerusalem, killing fourteen military personnel. Six weeks later the British executed four Irgun prisoners found guilty of acts of terrorism. The prospect of further prisoner executions in July led the Irgun to take two British soldiers hostage. The executions took place as scheduled, and the hostages were duly killed in reprisal.[79]

It was hoped inside Whitehall that the decision to hand the mandate over to the UN would dampen the pro-Zionist criticism emanating from Washington.

Yet it actually triggered major transatlantic disagreements over the viability of partition and the withdrawal of British troops.[80] When Loy Henderson of the State Department and the US ambassador, Lewis Douglas, met with Bevin in September 1947 to discuss the winding down of the mandate, the foreign secretary could not resist launching into a large broadside against American interference and came close to implying US complicity with the insurgents:

> Again and again, when I have been endeavouring to make progress in the solution of the delicate Palestine problem, your Government has thrown us off balance by making public statements regarding the necessity of the admission of 100,000 Jews or regarding other aspects of the problem that have a destructive effect on our negotiations. Furthermore, it is no secret that the terrorists in Palestine have received the bulk of their financial and moral support from the United States; most of the ships which have endeavoured to smuggle illegal immigrants into Palestine have been purchased, outfitted and financed in the United States; organisations based in the United States have carried on extensive publicity campaigns with the purpose of encouraging the Palestinian terrorists and smugglers of illegal immigrants and of discrediting the attempts of the British Government to maintain law and order. The American Government has to an extent subsidized these activities by exempting from income tax donations to organisations so engaged. For a period of nearly two years, the British Government, without success, has been trying in a friendly way to prevail upon the American Government to take steps to prevent American encouragement of terrorists and illegal activities in Palestine.[81]

Despairing at the seemingly intractable violence, Britain turned the Mandate of Palestine over to the UN in February 1947. Three months later, the UN created a Special Commission on Palestine (UNSCOP) to decide the fate of the territory. After hearing testimony from both Jews and Arabs and extensive travel across Palestine, the UNSCOP panel recommended in September 1947 that Palestine be partitioned into separate Jewish and Arab states with Jerusalem placed under an international trusteeship. A General Assembly vote in November (thirty-three votes to thirteen, with ten abstentions) ratified the partition and set in motion not only the creation of a Jewish state but also, consequentially, the outbreak of intense Jewish-Arab violence as the antipartition Arabs resisted the split of territorial control. Against this backdrop of growing intercommunal violence, it was decided that Britain would remain in nominal control of Palestine until the partition occurred—initially thought to be August 1948 but soon brought forward to May 14. The countdown to the formal end of the British Mandate brought nervousness to the Jewish Agency leadership, which, amid a spiral of Jewish-Arab violence, feared that the arrival of a Jewish state could be derailed by Arab and international anti-Zionist opposition. Seeing the British as onlookers to violence they could not stop, Zionist leaders decided to jump the gun and seize control of their political future before any post-mandate security vacuum nullified any gains they had made in their conflict with the Arabs in early 1948. A unilateral Declaration of Independence was announced on May 14, in advance of the expiry of Britain's legal control of the mandate.[82] Out of the ashes of a complex British counterinsurgency campaign rose the new state of Israel.

Truman claimed later that he "was not committed to statehood" but was merely driven by a desire to see "the establishment of the promised Jewish homeland" that had been pledged by the British as part of the 1917 Balfour Declaration.[83] Yet when Zionist leaders unilaterally declared the creation of the state of Israel, it took Truman less than fifteen minutes to reply to the announcement with American recognition—against the recommendations of the State Department.[84] Toward the end of the British Mandate, it was becoming clear that not only were there deep divides between London and Washington but also intra-administration ructions between the White House and the State Department. Diplomats in Foggy Bottom seemed out of step with other elements within the Truman administration not only in regard to their hesitancy in favoring a separate Jewish state but also in their overall attitude toward Zionism and violence in Palestine—as typified by their 1948 issuance of an arms embargo on Palestine as a means of restricting the potency of violent Zionism inside the mandate.[85]

Conclusion

A week after the declaration of the state of Israel, Bevin let the State Department know that "the British and Americans should not drift apart" over the issue of recognition of the new nation, especially if the situation were to develop in such a way that the Americans were giving increased support to one party and the British to the other."[86] But it was quite clear that London and Washington had drifted apart long before 1948 over the issue of Palestine. Driven by a desire to alleviate the horrors of the Holocaust on the Jewish people, Truman and his closest advisers consistently sought to undermine Britain's Palestine policy over immigration caps and the constitutional future of the mandate. This was in large part fueled by a relentless push for the support of the sizeable electoral bloc of Jewish American voters behind the Democratic Party. British Palestine policy was therefore caught between the rock of American domestic politics and the hard place of Zionist violence. The result was British failure on two fronts: the failure to construct a coherent military strategy in the face of the insurgency and the failure to outmaneuver the political machinations of Washington in regard to the look of postmandate governance.

The counterinsurgency campaign in Palestine created a series of "firsts" in regard to Anglo-American cooperation in such types of warfare. It was the first time, given the seismic shifts that had occurred to the world order in the wake of the Second World War, that the United States and Britain approached a conflict having had their respective power statuses essentially reversed. Britain's postwar global role was much diminished and its imperial strength usurped by the rising power of the United States, which constrained London's ability to dictate its Palestine policy to Washington. Even the establishment of the Joint Committee demonstrated that despite the outward signs of common purpose, divergent opinions ultimately resulted in the Americans' willingness to unilaterally push for their favored policies regardless of British control over the mandate.

The new realities of post-1945 Great Power politics also enabled Palestine to provide another first: the first time that Britain deliberately played on American fear of Soviet expansionism in order to garner greater American support for a colonial counterinsurgency campaign. Raising the specter of communism as the only alternative to colonial rule would, as we shall see later, become a classic British tactic when London wanted to soften American criticism of operations against insurgents in different corners of the empire.

Another first was the nature of the insurgency facing the British. The myriad Zionist groupings were well networked among Jewish diasporas across Europe and, crucially, the United States. The Zionist cause received global publicity. The insurgency was also able to remain well supplied by a flow of arms and money from political sympathizers, creating an unprecedented situation for British commanders, who had hitherto not faced such a well-connected insurgency with international connections.

This American link provided the Palestine campaign with a final distinctive first: It was the first time that the political management of a British counterinsurgency war had been significantly affected by American political interference—itself the product of potent lobbying groups. White House concerns about electoral mathematics and ethnic voting blocs created a situation whereby Washington's pro-Zionist line was constructed as much, if not more, for domestic consumption as it was for diplomatic conduct.

Collectively these antagonistic Anglo-American interactions during the Palestine conflict—including imagined fears of communism, the friction created by the large power shift between the two capitals after 1945, and the burgeoning influence of American domestic politics on British foreign policy—would not remain exclusive to this particular counterinsurgency war. A month after America had unilaterally recognized the self-declared Israeli state, a state of emergency was declared in Malaya, allowing a new counterinsurgency conflict to strain the purported special relationship.

Notes

Epigraph: Cunningham, "Palestine," 490.

1. *Bee*, Danville, VA, December 6, 1946, http://www.newspapers.com/newspage/12280866/.
2. Louis, "British Imperialism and the End of the Palestine Mandate," in Louis and Stookey, *End of the Palestine Mandate*, 10; and Hyam, *Britain's Declining Empire*, 123.
3. Cunningham, "Palestine," 490.
4. Bullock, *Ernest Bevin*, 427.
5. Truman, *Years of Trial and Hope*, 163.
6. Ovendale, *Britain, the United States*, 2.
7. "Edward Stettinius to Harry S. Truman," April 18, 1945, Harry S. Truman Presidential Library Digital Archive Collection, www.trumanlibrary.org/whistlestop/study_collections/israel/large/index.php?action=docs.
8. "Joseph Grew to Harry S. Truman," May 28, 1945, Truman Presidential Library, www.trumanlibrary.org/whistlestop/study_collections/israel/large/index.php?action=docs.
9. Truman, *Years of Trial and Hope*, 140.
10. "Cabinet: Palestine—A Report by the Lord President of the Council," October 10, 1945, The National Archives, UK (hereafter TNA), CAB 129/3/16.
11. "The British Prime Minister (Attlee) to President Truman," September 14, 1945, in *Foreign Relations of the United States* (hereafter *FRUS*), *1945, Vol. 8*, 739.
12. "Extract from the Conclusions of the 40th (45) Meeting of the Cabinet," October 11, 1945, TNA, WO 32/10260.
13. "Telegram from Washington to the Foreign Office," November 7, 1945, TNA, PREM 8/627/1.
14. "Memorandum of Conversation between Secretary of State and Lord Halifax," October 29, 1945, US National Archives and Records Administration (hereafter NARA), Record Group (RG) 59, 867N.01/10 2945, microscopy #M1390, reel 4.
15. "Memo to Mr Byrnes, from NEA. Subject: Troops for the Maintenance of Peace in the Near East," October 9, 1945, NARA, RG 59, 867N.01/10-945, microscopy #M1390, reel 4 (replicated in *FRUS, 1945, Vol. 8*, 742).
16. "Secret: Subject—Present Political Situation in Palestine, from American Consulate General, Jerusalem, Palestine," October 6, 1945, NARA, RG 59, 867.00/10-645, microscopy #M1390, reel 4.
17. "Telegram from Prime Minister to President," May 9, 1946, NARA, RG 59 867N.01/5-1046, microscopy #M1390, reel 5.
18. Cesarani, *Major Farran's Hat*, viii.
19. Wagner, "British Intelligence and the Jewish Resistance Movement," 651.
20. Charters, "Jewish Terrorism and the Modern Middle East," 81.
21. Gilbert, *Israel*, 132, 135.

22. “Statement by the President Condemning Acts of Terrorism in Palestine,” July 23, 1946, Harry Truman public papers, document #175, Public Papers of the President, http://www.presidency.ucsb.edu/ws/index.php?pid=12462.
23. Rose, *Senseless, Squalid War*, 125.
24. Quoted ibid., 123.
25. Ibid., 199–200.
26. Cesarani, *Major Farran's Hat*, 150–51.
27. Ovendale, *Britain, the United States*, 149.
28. Evensen, “Story of ‘Ineptness,’ ” 347.
29. Quoted in Ovendale, “Palestine Policy,” 413.
30. Cohen, *Palestine and the Great Powers*, 64–65.
31. “Memorandum of Conversation between Secretary of State and Lord Halifax,” October 29, 1945, NARA, RG 59 867N.01/10-2945, microscopy #M1390, reel 4.
32. Davidson, *America's Palestine*, 175.
33. “Telegram from Washington to Foreign Office, 9 August 1946,” TNA, FO 371/52551.
34. “The Secretary of State to Rabbi Stephen S. Wise,” August 17, 1946, in *FRUS, 1946, Vol. 7*, 686.
35. Quoted in McCullough, *Truman*, 598.
36. “Harry S. Truman to Eddie Jacobson,” February 27, 1948, Harry S. Truman Presidential Library Digital Archive Collection, www.trumanlibrary.org/whistlestop/study_collections/israel/large/index.php?action=docs.
37. “Prime Minister's Personal Telegram to President Truman,” October 4, 1946, TNA, PREM 8/627/5.
38. “Telegram: American Embassy, London—from the President for the Prime Minister,” October 10, 1946, TNA PREM 8/627/5.
39. Truman, *Years of Trial and Hope*, 164.
40. “Record of Conversation between Mr Truman and Mr Bevin,” December 8, 1946, TNA, FO 371/61762.
41. Cohen, *Palestine and the Great Powers*, 109.
42. “President Truman to the British Prime Minister (Attlee),” August 12, 1946, in *FRUS, 1946, Vol. 7*, 682.
43. “The Department of State to the British Embassy, Written Oral Statement,” n.d., in *FRUS, 1947, Vol. 5*, 1014.
44. “The Under-Secretary of State (Acheson) to the Director of the Office of Near Eastern and African Affairs (Henderson),” February 15, 1947, in *FRUS, 1947, Vol. 5*, 1049.
45. “The Director of the Office of Near Eastern and African Affairs (Henderson) to the Under-Secretary of State (Acheson),” February 17, 1947, in *FRUS, 1947, Vol. 5*, 1051.
46. Hansard, House of Commons debates, February 25, 1947, vol. 433, col. 1906-8.
47. “Statement Issued by the White House,” February 26, 1947, in *FRUS, 1947, Vol. 5*, 1057.
48. “The British Secretary of State for Foreign Affairs (Bevin) to the Secretary of State,” June 27, 1947, in *FRUS, 1947, Vol. 5*, 1112–13.
49. Ovendale, *Britain, the United States*, 2, 113.

50. "Anglo-American Conversations—Palestine," December 4, 1947, TNA, FO 371/75337.
51. "Telegram: From Moscow to Foreign Office," August 8, 1946, TNA, FO 371/52551.
52. "Joint Chiefs of Staff to State-War-Navy Coordinating Committee," June 21, 1946, Harry S. Truman Presidential Library Digital Archive Collection, www.trumanlibrary.org/whistlestop/study_collections/israel/large/index.php?action=docs.
53. "Cabinet Memorandum: Review of Soviet Policy," January 6, 1948, TNA, CAB 129/23/7.
54. Jeffrey, *MI6*, 693.
55. "Confidential Annex: Circulation of JIC Reports to the Central Intelligence Agency," JIC (48) 15th Meeting (O), 20 February 1948, TNA, CAB 159/3.
56. CIA, "The Consequences of the Partition of Palestine, ORE 55, 28 November 1947," Freedom of Information Act Electronic Reading Room (hereafter FOIA ERR), www.foia.cia.gov/sites/default/files/document_conversions/89801/DOC_0000256628.pdf.
57 CIA, "The Current Situation in Palestine, ORE 49, 20 October 1947," FOIA ERR, www.foia.cia.gov/sites/default/files/document_conversions/89801/DOC_0000256621.pdf.
58. "From John Edgar Hoover to Jack D. Neal. Subject: Brith Trumpeldor of America, Inc.," January 2, 1947, NARA, RG 59 867N.01/1-247, microscopy #M1390, reel 8.
59. Ibid.
60. Aldrich, *Hidden Hand*, 265.
61. Jeffrey, *MI6*, 691–92.
62. Walton, "British Intelligence and the Mandate of Palestine," 436.
63. For a detailed account of the personalities involved in the committee's machinations, see Dinnerstein, "America, Britain and Palestine," 283–301.
64. "Hearing before the Anglo-American Committee of Inquiry," January 11, 1946, NARA, RG 59, 867N.01/1-1146, microscopy #M1390, reel 5.
65. A full copy of the report can be found in TNA, PREM 8/627/2.
66. "Statement by the President on Receiving Report of the Anglo-American Committee of Inquiry," April 30 1946, Harry Truman public papers, document #92, Public Papers of the President, http://www.presidency.ucsb.edu/ws/index.php?pid=12643&st=&st1.
67. Chiefs of Staff Committee: "Palestine: Anglo-US report—Military Implications," n.d., TNA, PREM 8/627/3.
68. "Extract from the Conclusions of the 38th (46) Meeting of the Cabinet," April 29, 1946, TNA, WO 32/10260.
69. Quoted in Rose, *Senseless, Squalid War*, 101.
70. "Letter from Bartley C. Crum to Secretary of State James F. Byrnes," May 29, 1946, NARA, RG 59, 867N.01/5-2946, microscopy #M1390, reel 5.
71. "The British Prime Minister (Attlee) to President Truman," in *FRUS, 1946, Vol. 7*, 642.
72. "President Truman to the British Prime Minister (Attlee)," in *FRUS, 1946, Vol. 7*, 642.
73. "Press Release by the White House," July 2, 1946, in *FRUS, 1946, Vol. 7*, 642.
74. "Telegram from Prime Minister to President," July 25, 1946, NARA, RG 59, 867N.01/7-2646, microscopy #M1390, reel 6.

75. Rose, *Senseless, Squalid War*, 118.
76. Segev, *One Palestine, Complete*, 476–77.
77. “Palestine Conference 1946/47: Record of Administrative and Secretarial Arrangements,” n.d., TNA, CAB 133/85.
78. Shepherd, *Ploughing Sand*, 228.
79. Gilbert, *Israel*, 142, 148.
80. Ovendale, *Britain, the United States*, 217.
81. “Memorandum of Conversation, by the Director of the Near Eastern and African Affairs (Henderson), London,” September 9, 1947, in *FRUS, 1947, Vol. 5*, 498–99.
82. For a comprehensive narrative of the end of the mandate, UNSCOP, and the creation of the Israeli state, see Gilbert, *Israel*, 142–85, and Segev, *One Palestine, Complete*, 495–519.
83. Truman, *Years of Trial and Hope*, 140, 167.
84. For a detailed insight into American policy debates over recognition of Israel, see *FRUS, 1948, Vol. 5 (Part II)*.
85. Slonim, “1948 American Embargo on Arms,” 496.
86. “Memorandum of Conversation by the Under Secretary of State (Lovett),” May 21, 1948, in *FRUS, 1948, Vol. 5 (Part II)*, 1019.

4

The Malayan Emergency

Changing America's Asian Cold War

> It is perhaps preferable that British troops remain in Malaya as long as communism menaces the South East Asian area lest by their withdrawal a power vacuum be created which communist aggression would seek to fill.
>
> —Hendrik Van Oss, US consul general in Kuala Lumpur, October 1952

The counterinsurgency war fought by the British in Malaya from 1948 to 1960 has attained vaulted status in the history of irregular war-fighting. But there were many mitigating circumstances surrounding the conflict that have allowed for positive interpretations of the outcome to become manifest. One of these was the heavy political investment that the Americans made in supporting the British in their strategic objectives in Malaya because of how it fit under Washington's new Cold War rubric in Southeast Asia.

Despite this, it still took the British twelve years to officially call an end to the insurgent-induced state of emergency. This protracted campaign was beset with tactical errors and strategic torpor. Indeed, it was not until May 1950—nearly two years into the campaign—that a comprehensive strategy, in the form of the Briggs Plan, was conceived. The essence of the plan was the belief that the insurgency could be defeated if the guerrillas were cut off from their support base. This could be achieved via a more coherent and systematic resettlement campaign. By mid-1951, progress in "clearing" areas of insurgents (via the adoption of the so-called ink spot strategy[1]) was slow, and political hopes of a military success had faded.

However, the campaign was given a confidence boost by the appointment as joint civil-military leader of Gen. Sir Gerald Templer. Upon his arrival in Malaya, he openly committed himself to the central tenets of the Briggs Plan as the mainstay of his own tenure in office. Despite the continuity of policy, a cult of personality surrounded Templer and his no-nonsense, high-profile leadership style. Yet inspirational leadership has its flip side, and Templer's blunt approach in some quarters created a negative backlash as some communities resented the increasingly stringent food rations, curfews, and detentions that he instigated. Malaya was to represent an unequal distribution of carrot and stick.

By the time the state of emergency was declared in Malaya in 1948, American attention was firmly on continental Europe as the early Cold War took shape. The new grand strategic challenge of boxing in communist expansion had given rise to the "Truman Doctrine," a policy that had been immediately tested during the Berlin Blockade. The attempts of the Marshall Plan to use financial aid as a bulwark against communism was challenged by the Soviet coup against the Czechoslovak government in the same year that the Malayan Communist Party (MCP) initiated its uprising against the British. But it was the rapidly drawing "Iron Curtain" across Europe that dominated the minds of American foreign policy makers in the late 1940s—and has indeed dominated the academic literature on the forging of the "special relationship" at this time. Asia was on the periphery of Washington's strategic radar at this point in the Cold War. But Mao Zedong's victory in the Chinese Civil War, American intervention in the Korean War, and the French colonial collapse in Indochina would change all that, along with the way that the Harry S. Truman administration came to view Britain's counterinsurgency war in Malaya.[2] The Malayan Emergency became contextualized strongly within a Cold War framework as anticommunism took over as the predominant American foreign policy propellant. Any anticolonial rhetoric surrounding the counterinsurgency effort in Malaya faded as the conflict became important to Washington's Cold War "pivot to Asia." Hendrik Van Oss, the US consul general in Kuala Lumpur, summed up the new hardheaded American thinking regarding Malaya when he asserted to the State Department in October 1952 that "from a purely strategic point of view it is perhaps preferable that British troops remain in Malaya as long as communism menaces the South East Asian area lest by their withdrawal a power vacuum be created which communist aggression would seek to fill."[3]

American support for the British campaign removed any significant diplomatic obstacles to the prosecution of the counterinsurgency war, thus permitting an essentially colonial campaign to be openly interpreted by Washington as a fundamental battle against communist expansionism. Such a view was reinforced by Secretary of State Dean Acheson's comments in his report to the National Security Council (NSC) in July 1949 that if Southeast Asian countries such as Malaya are "swept by communism we [the United States] shall have suffered a major political rout the repercussions of which will be felt throughout the rest of the world."[4]

This shift in perspectives on the conflict in Malaya worked both ways. The Clement Attlee administration soon came to reframe the counterinsurgency war as a way of trying to demonstrate to the Americans that Britain was a reliable and capable partner in the nascent Cold War.[5] Whitehall came to downplay the colonial implications of retaining control of Malaya in favor of playing to Washington's anticommunist sympathies. This was not to be a war to prevent the fragmentation of Britain's empire in Asia but, rather, London's contribution to the West's new Cold War imperatives. It was an act of subtle political manipulation. All the key British players in the Malayan Emergency, from prime ministers to high commissioners, made all the right noises when they thought Washington was listening.[6]

Washington did open its ears at the first mention of communist involvement. The emergency itself was the product of communist insurrection against a new set of political arrangements that Britain introduced once the colony was returned from the Japanese after the end of the Second World War. A new Federation of Malaya was inaugurated in February 1948 that cemented the social dominance of the majority ethnic Malays and denied full citizenship rights to the minority ethnic Chinese population. This pushed many into the fold of what was predominantly (but not exclusively) an ethnic Chinese Malayan Communist Party (MCP), which had organized a guerrilla war against the invading Japanese forces in the early 1940s. The new federation's constitution, imbued with racial bias, combined with a crackdown by the colonial authorities on the activities of leftist groups and trade union organizations to trigger the MCP into action. The MCP created the Malayan People's Anti-British Army (MPABA) as its insurgent wing to undertake attacks against vulnerable, but economically vital, rubber and tin plantations in the countryside. This unrest grew throughout the spring and early summer of 1948 to such an extent that on June 19 the high commissioner, Sir Edward Gent, declared a federation-wide state of emergency.[7]

Part of the British response to this emergency was the implementation of sweeping legislation that permitted the authorities to undertake mass detentions of suspected insurgents or their sympathizers (known as the Min Yuen) in communities on the fringes of jungle where the insurgents (who in late 1948 renamed themselves the Malayan Races Liberation Army, or MRLA) were hiding.[8] The British military also undertook the large-scale relocation of these communities as a means of depriving the insurgents of their support base and logistical help.[9]

British security preparedness for the outbreak of the insurgency was woeful. Just two days before the emergency was declared, Lt. Col. John Dalley, head of the Malayan Security Service (MSS), wrote a memo stating, "At the time of writing there is no immediate threat to internal security in Malaya."[10] The army, police, and intelligence agencies in the colony were underequipped and had a poor sense of the size and strategy of the insurgent enemy. With both the MRLA and the British Army each totaling a force size of around four thousand at the outbreak of the emergency, the British resorted to large-scale sweeps through the jungle in an effort to flush the insurgents out. The effect of these sweeps was contradictory. They did break MRLA units down into smaller groups as they attempted to evade the British; however, the sweeps simultaneously aroused the anger of rural communities and increased insurgent recruitment.[11] Such paradoxes became symptomatic of a strategic malaise at the heart of the British response to the violence. It was not until April 1950 that the authorities, under pressure from the British expatriate community that controlled much of Malaya's lucrative rubber and tin industry, decided to appoint a separate director of operations to galvanize the military campaign and demonstrate to the outside world that Britain had control of the situation. That man was Gen. Sir Harold Briggs.

America and Malaya in the Briggs Era, 1950–52

The appointment of Briggs was not the reason that the Truman administration began taking an interest in the British counterinsurgency campaign in Malaya. His arrival in 1950 coincided with the outbreak of the Korean War and the fallout from Mao's victory in China. Against this shifting regional dynamic that worried the Americans, Briggs was tasked with bringing a belated strategic cohesion to the British war effort. It was desperately needed. By the end of 1949, MRLA attacks had increased fourfold from the beginning of the year to an average of four hundred a month.[12]

Briggs immediately undertook a nationwide security review that culminated in a report known simply as the Briggs Plan. At the heart of the plan was an understanding that the insurgency could be defeated if it was cut off from its support base. By severing the link between the guerrillas in the jungle and the Min Yuen, the insurgent campaign would be isolated from its food and information supply. This could be achieved through the creation of so-called resettlement areas, which eventually saw over four hundred thousand people forcibly relocated to newly constructed communities away from insurgent strongholds.[13] What would follow, Briggs hoped, was victory in the intelligence war as the population placed greater faith in the security that the authorities could provide, thus diminishing the flow of information and recruits to the MRLA.

Malcolm MacDonald, the commissioner general for Southeast Asia, went out of his way to market the Briggs Plan to American diplomats in the region. He invited the US consul general in Singapore, Charles Baldwin, to attend meetings of the British Defence Co-ordination Committee and granted him clearance to see intelligence material. It had the intended effect, with Baldwin urging the State Department to provide greater levels of support to the British campaign.[14]

This was symptomatic of wider transatlantic lobbying efforts. In August 1950, the Foreign Office requested that the embassy in Washington make representations to the State Department regarding the purchase of American military and communication equipment for the military of the Federation of Malaya (not British forces). This request included police radio equipment, fifty thousand shotguns, two thousand sheets of armor plate, seven hundred and fifty tons of barbed wire, and five Chinese-speaking interpreters.[15] The same request was made through two visiting survey missions of US aid administrators that were in Malaya at the same time.[16]

As the request was being mulled over in Washington, the US vice-consul in Singapore, Karl Sommerlatte, enunciated a fear held by diplomats in Asia that unless the Briggs Plan came to significantly reverse the security situation in Malaya, the British ran the risk of "a repetition of the debacle of '42"—namely, the loss of the colony to enemy forces.[17] The State Department's eventual decision to not honor this request (which did not formally come until two years later[18]) reveals a schism in American attitudes toward the counterinsurgency campaign in Malaya, with diplomats in the region pressing for more active assistance while the State Department in Washington cautiously avoiding the need to send military supplies. The Truman administration was arguably waiting to see if the Briggs Plan facilitated a turnaround in the British campaign that would nullify the need for America to get sucked into the effort to prevent another Asian "domino" from falling.

Results were slow in coming under Briggs's leadership. The year 1951 saw the highest number of insurgent attacks as the MRLA fought back against the large-scale resettlement program Briggs had initiated. Yet in October of that year the MCP issued what would be known as the "October Directives," which demonstrated an appreciation on behalf of the party hierarchy that victory would not be possible, given the existing strategy. The directives subordinated military operations in favor of aggressive political activity among members that attempted to be inclusive of non-Chinese ethnicities. In short, it attempted to "expand and consolidate the mass organisations" to complement the MCP's acts of terrorism.[19] The subsequent reduction in insurgent attacks, which was not necessarily evident until the following year, was capitalized on by Briggs's successor.

American and Malaya in the Templer Era, 1952–54

The retirement of Harold Briggs offered the government of Winston Churchill the chance to galvanize the counterinsurgency campaign even further. They made the rare step of unifying the civilian and military command of Malaya under one man. In 1952, Gen. Sir Gerald Templer, a soldier of extraordinary enthusiasm with a forthright leadership style, took over as the joint high commissioner and director of operations in the federation. Gen. J. Lawton Collins, the chief of staff of the US Army, declared Templer, shortly before his arrival in Malaya, to be "the best man in the British Army."[20] It was clearly London's hope that should this supposition be true, Templer could turn the counterinsurgency effort in Malaya around.

Soon after Templer took over, he met with the US consul general in Kuala Lumpur, Hendrik Van Oss. According to Van Oss's record of the meeting, which he telegraphed back to the State Department, Templer felt that "US-UK coop [cooperation] is most important factor in anti-Commie struggle," even if he did reveal he was "appalled at US ignorance [about] Malaya."[21] Ever aware of the need to shape public perceptions about the counterinsurgency effort, Templer urged Van Oss to get more American newspaper correspondents out to cover the emergency in order to increase domestic US knowledge of the conflict. The high commissioner acquiesced to the continuation of American consular receipt of Malayan government intelligence documents and invited Van Oss to attend briefing sessions that would be "most useful for US purposes"[22]—presumably an allusion to gathering a stronger picture of communist activity in the wider region.

The American consul was left with a strong impression of the imposing British general. Van Oss informed his superiors in the State Department that Templer was "very cordial, frank, informed, [and] determined," even if his conversation was "liberally sprinkled with salty expletives."[23] A few weeks after this first meeting with Van Oss, Templer met his counterpart in Singapore, Charles Baldwin. The high commissioner again took the opportunity to push an American diplomat for, Baldwin recalled, "not soldiers or money but . . . a manifestation of United States' support of the British policy towards Malaya."[24] Templer went one step further with Baldwin beyond the request to encourage more journalists that he made of Van Oss. He stated his desire for Washington to send a military liaison officer ("preferably of the rank of Colonel") who would be "shown and told everything" in order to foster greater US-UK cooperation in Malaya.[25] When this request reached Acheson, the secretary of state promised he would consult with the army and "give every consideration" to the idea, although he did concede that his "tentative and informal view" was that a "temporary assignment [is] a greater possibility than permanent assignment."[26] By July 1952, Templer had still not witnessed any movement by the Americans on his liaison officer appeal. He continued to press Baldwin, bluntly promising him that there would be no Anglo-American rifts among his personnel: "If I have anyone who can't work with Americans I'll fire him."[27] Templer's persistence eventually paid off. It would take nine months, but, in April 1953, the Americans announced the temporary four-month secondment of Dr. Lessing Khan of the Pentagon's Psychological

Warfare section to Kuala Lumpur. Khan was to be placed within the Operations Research Office in order to contribute to work on the propaganda campaigns the British were formulating to encourage insurgent surrenders and discourage popular support for the MRLA.[28]

In the autumn of 1953, Templer also had the opportunity to press his interpretation of the situation on senior members of the White House. In October, President Dwight Eisenhower sent Vice President Richard Nixon on a major tour around Asia and the Far East. The visit lasted just over two months, involved stopovers in a dozen countries, and entailed an estimated hundred thousand handshakes.[29] The purpose of Nixon's epic trip was to shore up support for the United States along the new fault lines of Asia's Cold War created by the communist victory in China. Nixon was intent on seeing for himself what the anticommunist struggle looked like, including that of a counterinsurgency variety. Malaya was the fourth leg on Nixon's itinerary, and he spent just two days there (October 26 and 27), with a crammed schedule. He was taken on a tour of a rubber plantation and a "New Village"—the physical embodiment of the Briggs Plan in action—to talk to relocated citizens. Political discussions with provincial sultans were followed by talks with General Templer at King's House, the high commissioner's residence in Kuala Lumpur.[30] Nixon was clearly impressed with the direction Templer was taking the British war effort, noting later (with fairly crude reductionism) that "the British were not making the mistake . . . of trying to fight a guerrilla war with conventional tactics and traditional strategy."[31] The following day, Templer accompanied Nixon to inspect troops from the First Battalion of the Somerset Light Infantry in the Ulu Langat area who were recently returned from jungle-bound counterinsurgency operations.

Clearly drawn in by Templer's forceful personality, Nixon swallowed the line that Templer pressed on him in their meeting that this was a Malayan fight, not a British one, with Nixon perceiving that "the British trained the natives and enlisted their wholehearted support in the fight against the insurgents."[32] Such an ability to foster benign American perceptions of this colonial war is perhaps an underappreciated aspect of Templer's legacy—and one that deviates from the orthodox assessment of his success in neutralizing the MRLA. During Templer's time in post from 1952 to 1954, insurgent incidents fell from five hundred a month to fewer than one hundred.[33] But one of the main questions is the extent to which Templer can personally take the credit for this outcome. His bold leadership style and his appreciation that there should be an intricate marriage between normal and emergency government activities strengthened British confidence and helped build a more coherent counterinsurgency campaign. One of Templer's biggest American fans, the leading "COINdinista" John Nagl, has argued that "it is difficult to overstate the impact that Templer . . . had on the course of the Emergency."[34] His high profile and blunt style may have created an impression of him single-handedly turning the campaign around.

However, Templer was to a large extent merely implementing the core tenets of the Briggs Plan, albeit with more vigor. Templer has been given more credit than he deserves. For example, the MCP's strategic overhaul, enunciated in its October Directives, which reverted insurgent tactics away from guerrilla attacks to political education in October 1951, were not made public until December 1952. The subsequent dip in insurgent violence between these dates (from six thousand incidents in 1951 to thirty-seven hundred in 1952) was incorrectly seen as a consequence of Templer's dynamic leadership.[35]

But Templer did help shape American perceptions of the war. Files in the US National Archives show that during his tenure as joint high commissioner and director of operations in Malaya, Templer was providing semiregular updates to American diplomats, taking meetings with the US consul general from either Kuala Lumpur or Singapore approximately every two months. Stemming from these meetings, one of Templer's lasting legacies on Anglo-American relations over Malaya was to encourage local American diplomats to see the conflict from a Cold War perspective. He impressed on Van Oss in October 1952 that "the MCP movement in Malaya received its policy directives from Peking."[36] Playing on fears of malign Chinese influence over the direction of the communist insurgency in Malaya was a way by which key British political and military figures aimed to maintain American support for the ongoing campaign.

Malaya, Mao, and the Chinese Challenge

The triumph of the communist "long march" to victory in China in 1949 distinctly impacted both British and American interpretations of the dynamic of the insurgency in Malaya. The Chinese had been immigrating to Malaya since the sixth century, and by the mid-twentieth century formed nearly 40 percent of the total Malayan population of 6.3 million.[37] Yet they remained socially and politically ostracized and thus prime for manipulation by the predominantly ethnic Chinese Malayans who made up the MCP. The demographic spread of Chinese Malays was of strategic concern to the British authorities considering that they were the majority ethnic group in ten of Malaya's fifteen largest cities, housing 43 percent of Malaya's entire Chinese population.[38]

American reluctance to immediately recognize communist China contrasted with the swiftness of British acknowledgment in January 1950. To a large extent this can be put down to London's dual imperative of preserving economic influence in China (based around the lucrative commercial foothold of Hong Kong) and managing the political consequences of expanding communist influence over its colonies—not to mention the hope that China could be drawn away from the Soviet Union in due course if treated respectfully.[39] Specifically in Malaya, British recognition of the People's Republic of China (PRC) presented diplomats with the difficult situation of trying to persuade the ethnic Chinese population in Malaya that recognition of the new state should not lead them to support their communist brethren within the colony.[40] A line needed to be drawn between respect for the PRC as a sovereign entity and zero tolerance for communist agitation within Malaya. It was a precarious balancing act that was designed to quell further unrest.

The UK's commissioner general for Southeast Asia, Malcolm MacDonald, cautioned the Foreign Office against recognizing the PRC for fear that it would "land us in some difficult consequences in Malaya." His main concern was the possibility of newly arrived Chinese communist consuls whose "instructions from their government would be to do everything possible to stimulate anti-British Chinese nationalism amongst these Chinese [in Malaya]."[41]

The influence of China also loomed large in American perceptions of Malayan security. As early as July 1949, Secretary of State Acheson had come to the conclusion that the British needed to be fully backed in their counterinsurgency efforts in Malaya because "the only alternative to British rule visible at this time is Chinese domination, which would be unacceptable not only to Malaya but also to us."[42] Such fears of Chinese expansionism were rife within the US diplomatic corps. Two years after Acheson's assessment, the director of the Philippine and Southeast Asian Affairs Office at the State Department, William S. B. Lacy, laid out his fears of a regional "domino effect": "Malaya is likely to be invaded whenever the Chinese feel that they have digested Indo-China and Thailand."[43] Anger that China was directing the politics and violence of the region, specifically in Malaya, was manifested by Vice President Nixon, who commented on his return to Washington from visiting the country that "if China had not gone communist . . . there would be no war in Malaya."[44]

The Permanent Under-Secretary's Committee (PUSC) of the most senior civil servants in Whitehall was quick to point out the economic imperatives that Washington would inevitably draw from Mao's victory in relation to Malaya. In its 1949 report on the state of Anglo-American relations, the PUSC noted that "the loss of China increases the threat to areas in which the USA has a special concern ... [and] from which she draws valuable raw materials such as Malaya."[45] A Central Intelligence Agency (CIA) assessment of the situation in Malaya a few weeks later confirmed the PUSC interpretation of American attitudes by depicting American interest in the outcome of the counterinsurgency campaign in explicitly economic terms: "Primarily, Malaya is of importance to the US because it is the world's greatest producer of rubber and tin." It goes on to examine how up until that moment in time the insurgency had been "fairly well contained" by the British—a fact that was welcomed as it ensured "continued US access to Malaya's strategic commodities."[46]

So fearful was Washington of Chinese support bolstering the communist insurgency in Malaya that the NSC produced a staff study in February 1952 that outlined a possible scenario in which American troops could be deployed alongside British forces in Malaya to ensure victory in the counterinsurgency campaign. Resting on an assumption of massive communist gains across the rest of Southeast Asia, the NSC paper hypothesized that "if Indochina, Burma and Thailand should fall to massive Chinese communist intervention, it may be in the US interest to provide direct contribution of US army, air, and naval units to help the British [in Malaya]."[47] While it remained a localized war of decolonization, the Americans were willing to let the British fight the MRLA alone, but should the regional dynamics negatively turn against American Cold War priorities, this declassified report reveals just how much consideration was given to making the counterinsurgency war in Malaya a joint US-UK military effort.

But the utter absence of any Chinese weapons or funding filtering through to Malaya forced even the CIA to admit in late 1949 that it had "no evidence of material support from the Chinese Communist Party," referring only to CCP "interest" in the emergency.[48] Yet this did not blunt American suspicion that Mao was orchestrating some of the insurgent violence in the colony. As the emergency entered its fifth year and more countries around the globe recognized the new Chinese state, key American diplomatic figures in Southeast Asia were more wary of Peking than Moscow in terms of how communist support for the MRLA was manifest. A report in June 1953 by Charles Baldwin, the US consul general in Singapore, argued that the Americans needed to show utter solidarity with the British in their counterinsurgency war, stating that "the influence of the United States added to that of the United Kingdom . . . will be required to counter the future influence upon Malaya of mainland China."[49] At the end of that year, a State Department intelligence note mentioned the delicate regional politics that hinged on the outcome of the war. It also came to some pessimistic conclusions about the state of the British counterinsurgency campaign in the face of such region-wide subversion: "So long as the threat of Chinese Communist aggression in Southeast Asia exists, the British probably will be unable to eradicate the guerrillas [in Malaya]."[50] Such negative interpretations of the British war effort made Washington all the more uncomfortable as the counterinsurgency campaign took on a more important regional dimension with the outbreak of the Korean War in 1950.

The Korean War and Changing American Attitudes to Malaya

The Korean War propelled the Americans into joining the colonial powers of Britain and France in taking responsibility for the security of Southeast Asia.[51] The war effort militarized the Truman Doctrine on a regional scale. The British counterinsurgency war in Malaya was henceforth seen through a Cold War lens by Washington. What was at first seen as a minor colonial skirmish became a key battleground in the effort to repel communist expansionism in Southeast Asia, especially as the war coincided with Mao's victory in China. Indeed, the relevance of Britain's counterinsurgency campaign in Malaya would not have been lost on President Truman when he spoke to Prime Minister Attlee of the necessity of immediate Anglo-American discussions in the wake of the Korean crisis and the establishment of the PRC. Such talks, Truman noted, would be "about other steps which might be taken to strengthen non-Communist Asia... [including] the intensification of economic and military assistance to encourage the organization of resistance to Communist encroachment."[52] When these talks did occur in December 1950, Attlee assured Truman of steadfast British fealty over Korea: "We are in it with you. We'll support you. We'll stand together on those bridgeheads."[53] An echo of this pledge resounded in Tony Blair's commitment to stand "shoulder to shoulder" with George W. Bush over fifty years later in the run-up to the Iraq War.

Truman gratefully received this pledge from Attlee, acknowledging swift British support for the UN mission in spite of "the fact that Communist activity in Malaya put a heavy strain on British manpower."[54] However, the economic demands of the American war effort in Korea created a fortunate side effect for the British in Malaya. American need for Malayan tin and rubber for use in military supplies proliferated massively after 1950, increasing demand within the colony for workers on the plantations. The insurgency therefore had to compete with the allure of a steady job and regular wages in the minds of the Malayan people. As Richard Stubbs has drily noted, "trying to organise a revolution is not easy in times of full employment."[55] Even before the Korean War broke out, Malayan rubber was the British Empire's best earner, totaling sales of $200 million compared to Britain's entire exported goods value of $180 million in 1947 alone.[56] The counterinsurgency campaign was imbued with an economic imperative to protect the investments made in this most lucrative of colonies. In light of this, protecting Malaya was granted additional importance in London and Washington, given lingering wariness over the ways in which Moscow would stoke economic and political unrest throughout the colony.

The Soviet Specter

American reluctance to recognize Mao's China was in large part driven by a perception throughout Washington that the new Chinese state was a Soviet puppet. A conspiratorial mind-set pervaded the Truman administration that lumped together all communist states in an automatic assumption of Soviet overlordship. A few months before the formal declaration of the PRC, Secretary of State Acheson told the NSC of his belief that "it is now clear that SEA [Southeast Asia] as a region has become the target of a co-ordinated offensive plainly directed by the Kremlin."[57] This belied the presence of Sino-Soviet ructions from the years preceding Mao's victory in 1949 that were not overcome afterward.[58] It took several years for this default perception of communist solidarity to be dismantled, especially in regard to American views on external communist interference in Malaya. Two years after Mao's rise to power in China, the State Department noticed a discernable lack of Soviet interference in Malaya: "With its very large production of gold and with what must be its huge quantities of weapons, it would seem the Soviet Union could do far more than it has done for the Communists in . . . Malaya."[59]

This American surprise at the lack of Soviet involvement was perhaps a side effect of the confidence with which Britain claimed it observed Moscow's hand in stoking Malayan violence. In May 1950, nearly two years into the emergency, the Colonial Office was still stridently asserting that the MCP was "part of the Kremlin's world-wide campaign against the Western powers."[60] The basis of this view stemmed from the MCP's involvement in the Calcutta Youth Conference for international communist parties in February 1948 where the Cominform (Communist Information Bureau) purportedly instructed the MCP to initiate an insurgency. Firm evidence to back up this interpretation is flimsy and fails to take into account the internal status and deliberations of the MCP itself. Furthermore, the international communist conspiracy argument does not consider how MCP leader Chin Peng attempted to prevent the disintegration of the MCP in the wake of the revelation that his predecessor, Loi Tek, had been a British agent.[61] If the Soviet Union had instigated the insurgency, it remains odd that no Soviet arms, funding, or military "advisers" were sent to ensure success.

In the absence of any weapon supplies being coordinated by the Kremlin, a different Soviet action concerned the Americans—namely, Moscow's attempts to illicitly exploit Malaya's significant rubber production. Attempts to reduce Moscow's access to foreign natural resources that could aid its regional economic and political influence caused the CIA to note with alarm in March 1949 that up to 70,000 tons of rubber had been covertly smuggled to the Soviet Union from Malaya on top of the 104,000 tons already formally purchased for the year ahead. American fears were based, as the CIA document bluntly states, on the fact that "rubber is of basic strategic importance for the conduct of war."[62] Restricting Soviet access to Malayan rubber was thus seen as rendering strategic harm to Moscow's future war-readiness. Furthermore, the reduction of Soviet influence over Malaya was of heightened importance to Washington, given ongoing American efforts to assist another colonial power fight a counterinsurgency campaign in the region.

French Indochina, Malaya, and the Asian Cold War

The United States was not the first Western power to attempt to stem the spread of communism in Malaya's regional neighbor, Vietnam. During the Second World War, France turned its protectorate of Vietnam into a full-fledged colonial possession. The end of the war witnessed a declaration of independence by the nationalist leader of the communist Workers' Party, Ho Chi Minh, who launched a guerrilla war against the French colonial presence in 1946.[63] An attritional counterinsurgency campaign by the French military culminated in a spectacular defeat to the Viet Minh in May 1954 at the Battle of Dien Bien Phu.[64] The story of European decolonization in Asia (unwilling though that may have been) is of fundamental importance to the formation of America's early Cold War policy, given how the insurgent threat to imperial rule served as a prelude to the unraveling of colonial control, which itself became conjoined with Washington's fervent anticommunism.

Robert Thompson, who was serving as a senior member of the Colonial Service in Malaya during Templer's leadership (and who would later go on to try to influence the direction of the American counterinsurgency effort in Vietnam) recalled how American interest in the French colonial counterinsurgency campaign in Indochina sparked awareness in American military circles of the British campaign in nearby Malaya. During the Templer years, Thompson later noted, an unspecified number of American officers who were advising the French "visited Kuala Lumpur from Saigon . . . [because they] wanted to see how we were dealing with insurgency in Malaya."[65] These fact-finding missions were to be in vain, given the defeat suffered by the French at Dien Bien Phu, which marked the moment that the United States began its long and agonizing involvement in Vietnam.

In the final year of the Truman administration, key figures in the State Department were acknowledging the link between the two colonial counterinsurgency wars and America's broader Cold War objectives in Southeast Asia. Concerns of a regional domino effect were evident in a State Department–Joint Chiefs of Staff meeting in January 1952, where it was noted that the French loss of Indochina would make it "politically harder to defend Malaya" because "all the Chinese fence-sitters [in the region] would show up on the other side."[66] There was a collective sense of gloom about the British chances of success in their counterinsurgency campaign should the French fail in theirs, mainly because of the knock-on effect this would have on American regional strategy. Charles Bohlen, counselor at the State Department, pessimistically concluded that "it is highly doubtful that Malaya could be held because of political and psychological reactions due to the loss of Southeast Asia. The number of guerrillas would rise by geometric proportions." If Malaya fell, Bohlen starkly stated, "we would have lost the cold war."[67]

The intertwined fates of American Cold War goals in the region and two colonial counterinsurgency wars were palpably observable in this meeting. It was an acknowledgment that was repeated soon afterward when the NSC constructed a policy document (which later became NSC 5405) with the aim of reinforcing American Cold War strategic commitments to Southeast Asia. Malaya was singled out as a linchpin in this strategy, given its political and economic importance. The document went on to advocate closer cooperation with Britain in securing the region as well as "covert operations designed to achieve these objectives."[68] The document explicitly advocated the need for the United States to "support the British in their measures to eradicate communist guerrilla forces and restore order." Should direct Chinese involvement in the insurgency be detected, the NSC went on, then the US "should assist in the defense of Malaya as appropriate, as part of a UN collective action or in conjunction with the United Kingdom and any other friendly governments."[69]

By late 1954, President Eisenhower was still asking his top military advisers "whether the British would defend Malaya to the bitter end" should China directly intervene in support of the MRLA.[70] The NSC consensus was that they would, but the discussion reveals how much the administration needed Britain to win its colonial counterinsurgency war in order to help maintain the regional Cold War balance of power. With such concerns in mind, four months later the US Joint Chiefs of Staff put together a top secret plan for potential American military deployments to Southeast Asia "in the event of the loss of Indo-China to the Communists." Designed to back up the anticommunist rhetoric of NSC 5405, the plan noted that a potential deployment of troops to Malaya to help defeat the "internal threat" of communism would see the United States send six brigade headquarters, twenty-three infantry battalions, two armored car regiments, one field battery, and one field squadron, as well as up to fourteen various air force squadrons, to assist the British forces already on the ground.[71]

Despite this planning it was eventually decided at the Five Power Military Conference (attended by the military leadership of the United States, the United Kingdom, France, Australia, and New Zealand) in June 1954 that British forces in Malaya at the time "are adequate to deal with the present Communist terrorist threat."[72] Although the Americans were not going to put their own "boots on the ground," the decision did not stop them from propping up the British counterinsurgency effort in other ways. In fiscal year 1954–55, the Eisenhower administration spent $1.5 million on Malaya (approximately $13 million in today's money), which went toward nonmilitary activities including "technical assistance, information services, and educational exchange."[73]

Financial assistance to the Malayan authorities was only part of the support Washington was hoping to give the British after the collapse of French rule in Indochina. Declassified documents reveal how in mid-1956 the Office of Southeast Asian Affairs at the State Department attempted to make arrangements "for close working-level consultation[s] with the UK with regard to Communist subversion in Singapore and the Federation of Malaya." But the Americans were left frustrated that these plans were scuppered by British opposition. The State Department blamed residual Colonial Office attitudes that seemed to want to keep the Americans out of decision making regarding Britain's empire.[74] Such efforts were moot anyway, given the plans already being put in place for gradual decolonization, not to mention the eventual payoffs that the counterinsurgency campaign was getting in relation to insurgent surrenders. The emergency was coming to an end.

The End of the Emergency and the Legacy of Malaya

The end of Templer's stint as joint civil-military supremo of Malaya effectively marked the end of major military operations against the MRLA. It had become a weakened and isolated insurgent force, unable to gain access to sustainable supply routes and susceptible to new forms of the propaganda war designed to induce insurgent surrenders.[75] By the end of 1955, even the Americans had become convinced that "unless assisted by a large-scale invasion force from outside [the MRLA] are not capable of overthrowing the constituted authorities."[76]

It became clear to London that political reform, in the guise of full decolonization, held the key to transitioning Malaya away from colonial control and toward indigenous governance that, crucially, would be moderate and to London's taste. The State Department expressed its "great satisfaction" at the British decision in February 1956 to grant Malaya independence by August of the following year.[77] This process was largely placed in the hands of two key political groups inside Malaya, the United Malays National Organization (UMNO) and the Malayan Chinese Association (MCA), the latter of which was of particular importance to General Templer's broader goals as it posited itself as a noncommunist alternative for the ethnic Chinese population. The UMNO and the MCA united to form the Alliance Party in 1954, and in the first federal elections, held in June 1955, they won all but one of the fifty-two seats. The new chief minister, Alliance Party leader Tunku Abdul Rahman, was a crucial figure in Malaya's transition to independence, and he duly became the state's first prime minister in August 1957. Although British operations technically lasted another three years, the emergency was all but over. The MCP had lost the battle to dictate the political future of Malaya, and the MRLA had lost the paramilitary battle, in large part due to the absence of any external support and the successful British isolation of their support network.

The US Army and US Marine Corps counterinsurgency field manual *FM 3-24*, published nearly sixty years after the outbreak of the emergency, praised the British conduct in Malaya as a historic campaign that "provides lessons applicable to combating any insurgency."[78] Yet it is a particularly American proclivity to see Malaya as some sort of counterinsurgency exemplar. Even the British military since the ending of the emergency have been reticent to use it as a firm blueprint for future campaigns.[79] The relevance of certain components of the Malayan campaign, such as the ink spot strategy and the oft-cited, but infrequently enacted, "hearts and minds" operations, to the revival of American counterinsurgency doctrine in Iraq and Afghanistan has been overhyped. A more appropriate appraisal of Malaya's legacy on American thinking is gained when looking at the years immediately after Malayan independence. The 1960 *Special Forces Manual*, for example, borrowed numerous examples and terminology from the British campaign. This included the advocacy of indigenous "civilian self-defense forces" at the community level, the recruitment of "special constables" from within the local population to act as force multipliers, and the utilization of "special intelligence personnel" to act as agents and informers in communities susceptible to insurgent infiltration.[80] In the absence of any of its own significant campaign histories to fall back on, the US military borrowed heavily from elements of the campaign plans formulated by Briggs and Templer. Seemingly there was little to be gleaned from the parallel counterinsurgency campaign the British were also fighting thousands of miles away in Cyprus.

Notes

Epigraph: "Foreign Service Despatch from AMCONSUL, Kuala Lumpur," October 25, 1952, US National Archives and Record Administration (hereafter NARA), RG 59 797.00/10-2552, box 4329.

1. The ink spot strategy involved spreading military control out of multiple small areas simultaneously that would then eventually merge to create cohesive coverage, similar to blots of ink on a page.
2. Dockrill, "Foreign Office, Anglo-American Relations," 459.
3. "Foreign Service Despatch from AMCONSUL, Kuala Lumpur," October 25, 1952, NARA, RG 59 797.00/10-2552, box 4329.
4. "A Report to the National Security Council by the Secretary of State on US Policy Towards Southeast Asia" (NSC 51), July 1, 1949, Digital National Security Archive (hereafter DNSA), www.nsarchive.chadwyck.com/nsa/documents/PD/00145/all.pdf.
5. Deighton, "Britain and the Cold War," in Leffler and Westad, *Cambridge History of the Cold War*, 127–28.
6. A. J. Stockwell, "The United States and Britain's Decolonization of Malaya," in Ryan and Pungong, *United States and Decolonization*, 188–89.

7. For a comprehensive narrative of the buildup to the declaration of emergency, see Short, *Communist Insurrection in Malaya*; Clutterbuck, *Long, Long War*; and Hack, "Origins of the Asian Cold War," 471–96.
8. Chin Peng, the MRLA leader, claimed that the British insisted on using the name Malayan *Races* Liberation Army for propaganda reasons and that the group was really called the Malayan *National* Liberation Army. See Hack, "Malayan Emergency," 383–414.
9. For an overview of this policy, see Hack, "Detention, Deportation and Resettlement," 611–40.
10. "Internal Security—Malaya," Malayan Security Service report by Director John Dalley, June 14, 1948, The National Archives, UK (hereafter TNA), CO 537/6006.
11. See Hack, "Malayan Emergency."
12. Newsinger, *British Counterinsurgency*, 45.
13. Ibid., 50.
14. Stockwell, "United States and Britain's Decolonization," 198–99.
15. "Memorandum: List of Requirements Requested from the United States Government for the Federation of Malaya," August 15, 1950, NARA, RG 59 797.00/8-1550, box 4326.
16. Stockwell, "United States and Britain's Decolonization," 199.
17. "Stability of British Malaysia," September 25, 1950, NARA, RG 59 797.00/9-2550, box 4326.
18. "Foreign Service Despatch: Conversation with Sir Gerald Templer," October 11, 1952, NARA, RG 59 797.00/10-1152, box 4329.
19. An English translation of the October Directives, made by the intelligence services in Malaya, can be found in "Captured Malayan Communist Party Documents," TNA, CO 1022/187.
20. "Memorandum on the Substance of Discussion at a Department of State–Joint Chiefs of Staff Meeting," January 16, 1952, in *Foreign Relations of the United States* (hereafter FRUS), *1952–54, Vol. 12 (Part I)*, 27.
21. "Telegraph from Kuala Lumpur to Secretary of State," February 19, 1952, NARA, RG 59 797.00/2-1952, box 4328.
22. Ibid.
23. Ibid.
24. "Foreign Service Despatch from AMCONGEN, Singapore," March 3, 1952, NARA, RG 59 797.00/3-352, box 4328.
25. Ibid.
26. "Telegram to Amconsul SINGAPORE," April 15, 1952, NARA, RG 59 797.00/4-1552, box 4328.
27. "Foreign Service Despatch from Singapore," July 15, 1952, NARA, RG 59 797.00/7-1552, box 4329.
28. "Foreign Service Despatch from Singapore. Subject: Loan of US Psychological Warfare Specialist to Malaya," April 1, 1953, NARA, RG 59 797.00/4.153, box 4330.

29. For a transcript of Nixon's postvisit address to the nation via television and radio on December 23, 1953, see Department of State, *Bulletin* 30, no. 758-783 (January 4– June 28, 1954): 10–14.
30. For a comprehensive photographic collection of Nixon's two-day trip to Malaya, see "Vice President Nixon Visits Malaya October 1953," www.nixonmalaya1953.com.
31. Nixon, *Memoirs of Richard Nixon*, 121–22.
32. Ibid., 122.
33. Ramakrishna, "'Transmogrifying' Malaya," 79.
34. Nagl, *Learning to Eat Soup*, 89.
35. Stubbs, *Hearts and Minds*, 159–60.
36. "Foreign Service Despatch from AMCONSUL, Kuala Lumpur," October 25, 1952, NARA, RG 59 797.00/10-2552, box 4329.
37. Barber, *War of the Running Dogs*, 15; and Sarkesian, *Unconventional Conflicts*, 63.
38. Newsinger, *British Counterinsurgency*, 43.
39. McLean, "American Nationalism," 27.
40. Ovendale, "Britain, the United States," 151.
41. "Letter from Malcolm MacDonald to Sir William Strang," August 19, 1949, TNA, FO 371/75814.
42. "A Report to the National Security Council by the Secretary of State on US Policy Towards Southeast Asia" (NSC 51), July 1, 1949, DNSA, www.nsarchive.chadwyck.com /nsa/documents/PD/00145/all.pdf.
43. "Memorandum of Conversation, by Mr George H. Alexander of the Economic Resources and Security Staff. Subject: Political Prospects in Southeast Asia," January 4, 1951, in *FRUS, 1951, Vol. 6 (Part I)*, 2.
44. See transcript of his address to the nation in Department of State, *Bulletin* 30, no. 758-783 (January 4–June 28, 1954): 12.
45. "Permanent Under-Secretary's Committee (PUSC) report #51: Anglo-American Relations—Present and Future," November 9, 1949, TNA, FO 371/76386.
46. CIA, "Current Situation in Malaya" (ORE 33-49), November 17, 1949, https://www.cia .gov/library/readingroom/docs/DOC_0000258390.pdf.
47. "NSC Staff Survey on United States Objectives and Courses of Action with Respect to Communist Aggression in Southeast Asia" (Annex to NSC 124), February 13, 1952, DNSA, www.nsarchive.chadwyck.com/nsa/documents/PD/00282/all.pdf.
48. "Central Intelligence Agency Report for the President of the United States: Current Situation in Malaya," November 17, 1949, Declassified Document Reference System (hereafter DDRS).
49. "Foreign Service Despatch from Singapore. Subject: An Estimate of Future US and Chinese Influence in Malaya," June 4, 1953, NARA, RG 59 797.00/6-453, box 4330.
50. "Department of State Memorandum—Intelligence Note: Malaya," December 29, 1953, NARA, RG 59 797.00/12-2953, box 4331.
51. Lowe, "Change and Stability," 141.

52. Truman, *Years of Trial and Hope*, 425.
53. Ibid., 426.
54. Ibid., 418.
55. Stubbs, *Hearts and Minds*, 126.
56. Newsinger, *British Counterinsurgency*, 41.
57. "A Report to the National Security Council by the Secretary of State on US Policy Towards Southeast Asia" (NSC 51), July 1, 1949, DNSA, www.nsarchive.chadwyck.com/nsa/documents/PD/00145/all.pdf.
58. McLean, "American Nationalism," 35.
59. "Memorandum by Mr Charlton Ogburn to the Assistant Secretary of State for Far Eastern Affairs (Rusk)," January 15, 1951, in *FRUS, 1951, Vol. 6 (Part I)*, 6.
60. "The Colonial Empire Today: Summary of Our Main Problems and Policies," Colonial Office International Department paper, May 1950, TNA, CO 537/5698.
61. Deery, "Malaya 1948: Britain's Asian Cold War?," 42.
62. CIA, "Rubber Supply Situation in the USSR" (ORE 6-49), March 23, 1949, NARA, https://research.archives.gov/id/6924337.
63. For a discussion of the French war in Vietnam, see chapters 5 and 6 of Karnow, *Vietnam*.
64. For a detailed account of the battle and the end of French rule in Vietnam, see Windrow, *The Last Valley*.
65. Thompson, *Make for the Hills*, 103.
66. "Memorandum on the Substance of Discussion at a Department of State–Joint Chiefs of Staff Meeting," January 16, 1952, in *FRUS, 1952–54, Vol. 12 (Part I)*, 27.
67. Ibid., 32.
68. "Statement of Policy Proposed by the National Security Council on United States Objectives and Courses of Action with Respect to Communist Aggression in Southeast Asia," n.d., in *FRUS, 1952–54, Vol. 12 (Part I)*, 47–48.
69. Ibid., 51.
70. "Memorandum of Discussion at the 180th Meeting of the National Security Council," January 14, 1954, in *FRUS, 1952–54, Vol. 12 (Part I)*, 363.
71. "Memorandum by the Joint Chiefs of Staff to the Secretary of Defense (Wilson)," May 21, 1954, in *FRUS, 1952–54, Vol. 12 (Part I)*, 517.
72. "Five Power Military Conference of June 1954," n.d., in *FRUS, 1952–54, Vol. 12 (Part I)*, 561.
73. "Note to the National Security Council by the Executive Secretary (Lay)," August 20, 1954, in *FRUS, 1952–54, Vol. 12 (Part I)*, 774.
74. "Memorandum from the Director of the Office of Southeast Asian Affairs (Young) to the Assistant Secretary of State for Far Eastern Affairs (Robertson)," May 23, 1956, in *FRUS, 1955–57, Vol. 22*, document #459, 774.
75. For a comprehensive assessment of the propaganda war in Malaya, see Carruthers, *Winning Hearts and Minds*.

76. “Staff Study Prepared by an Interdepartmental Committee for the Operations Coordinating Board,” December 14, 1955, in *FRUS, 1955–57, Vol. 22*, document #448, 748.
77. Editorial note, *FRUS, 1955–57, Vol. 22*, document #452, 762.
78. Department of Defense, *FM 3-24*, 235.
79. Strachan, “British Counter-Insurgency,” 8.
80. McClintock, *Instrument of Statecraft*, 214–15.

5

Mayhem in the Mediterranean

Counterinsurgency in Cyprus

Compromise would have all the better chance of success . . . if it could be given the full and active support of the American administration.

—Sir John Harding, governor of Cyprus

Despite Sir John Harding's assessment that American support for any political settlement to bring the insurgency on Cyprus to an end was essential, no useful assistance was offered by Washington. Instead, the Dwight Eisenhower administration spent much diplomatic energy working to undermine the British position as counterinsurgency operations took place on the island from 1955 to 1959. Similarly to the ongoing campaign in Malaya, the conflict in Cyprus was taking place in a strategically sensitive location, with the Mediterranean island being at the juncture of Southern Europe, the Middle East, and North Africa. Washington's perception of the conflict was therefore colored not by the intercommunal tensions that were catching the British up in a cycle of reactive violence, but by the regional implications of a postconflict settlement. This made for an incredibly strained "special relationship," especially given the ways in which covert American diplomatic efforts seemed to be working against British objectives to bring the insurgency to a close. It is therefore surprising that this episode features so little in the broader literature on the special relationship.

The British first occupied Cyprus in 1878 by agreement with the Ottoman government. At the outbreak of the First World War and the Turkish alliance with Germany, Britain changed its governance of Cyprus from a protectorate to an officially annexed colony.[1] A series of decisions by London taken after the Second World War were made to secure Britain's position in Cyprus. It would be this seemingly intransigent British overlordship of Cyprus that by the 1950s would spark a vicious insurgency instigated by elements of the island's Greek Cypriot community in the name of *enosis*—union with Greece. The spearhead of this violent undertaking was a group known as the EOKA (Ethniki Organosis Kyrion Agoniston—the National Organization of Cypriot Fighters).

As W. Byford-Jones pointed out at the time, the "precise origins of EOKA are lost in the low whispers of conspiracy."[2] It was led by a retired Greek army colonel, the Cypriot-born George Grivas, whose right-wing demagoguery, military experience (he had led a pro-Nazi collaborationist movement in Greece during the Second World War), and links to powerful Cypriot church leaders made him a potent insurgent leader.[3] Using his connections to the Orthodox Church and the Greek military hierarchy, Grivas went about securing funds, weapons, and sympathy for the EOKA's struggle for *enosis*, which was launched with a violent cacophony of bomb attacks on British political and military targets across the island on April 1, 1955.[4] The EOKA's insurgency would present significant operational dilemmas for the British military, which had to spread scarce resources over sprawling mountain ranges and densely packed city backstreets.

Playing Cat and Mouse in Town and Country: EOKA Violence and the British Response

Grivas began to accelerate the EOKA's readiness for an outright insurgency in early 1955. The first major arms shipment the group organized from Greece occurred in January of that year when a boat called the *Ayios Georghios* left Athens loaded with ten thousand sticks of dynamite, over two thousand detonators, and an assortment of guns. But a tip-off to the police resulted in the shipment and its recipients being arrested dockside.[5] Unperturbed, Grivas continued to solicit weapons from sympathizers in Greece, writing letters pleading for more weaponry to be transported to the island in order to arm the EOKA units that had been set up across Cyprus. All members of the group were required to adopt a nom de guerre to avoid leaks, as well as actively encouraged to infiltrate the civil service and security forces. Assassination squads were formed on an ad hoc basis to silence vocal opponents of *enosis* as 1955 drew on, ratcheting up the level of violence on the island to such an extent that the US consul general in Nicosia, Raymond Courtney, ruefully informed the State Department of the "grimness and tension" that was gripping the island as the EOKA appeared intent on prosecuting an "all-out battle to force the British—and their allies—to capitulate."[6]

An eventual formal declaration of an open insurgency came on the first day of April after much buildup. By this time, Grivas had set up a headquarters in a house in a suburb of Nicosia, the capital. But he alternated between this and numerous mountainside hideouts in the Troodos mountain range in the center of the island, where the EOKA had set up rural training camps to prepare its various cells for an urban campaign of assassination and bombing. Indeed, Grivas spent the rest of this insurgency shuttling between various city and mountain locations in order to avoid arrest and to personally undertake meetings or oversee training.[7]

The British authorities on the island soon had to change their view of the EOKA. By late 1955, the group could no longer be perceived as a minor irritant, given the proliferation of attacks on British military targets. Therefore, on November 26, a state of emergency was officially declared on the island and a formal counterinsurgency campaign launched. But the colonial authorities' state of preparedness for tackling an insurgency was woeful. The novelist and poet Lawrence Durrell, who spent much of the Cyprus Emergency as the director of information services within the island's colonial bureaucracy, noted how his own agency was "in pitiable shape," while the police force at the outbreak of violence was in a "deplorable" state.[8] Adaptation to the situation had to happen quickly. One of the most significant changes had occurred a month before the state of emergency had been declared. The need for strong leadership in the crisis resulted in the former chief of the Imperial General Staff, Field Marshal Sir John Harding, being coaxed out of retirement to replace Sir Robert Armitage as governor. The appointment of such a senior ex-military figure to take the lead in restoring civil order to Cyprus sent a clear message about British intent. Even the US embassy in London felt compelled to report back to the State Department that "if anyone can restore law and order in Cyprus, he [Harding] is the man to do so."[9]

One of Harding's biggest headaches when he assumed leadership was caused by the lacuna of intelligence on the insurgent enemy. Given this scarcity, a joint civil-military Cyprus Intelligence Committee was established to coordinate the flow of information streaming in from across the island on suspected EOKA hideouts and members.[10] One of the largest intelligence problems the British had to handle was understanding the relationship between the EOKA's mutual presence in town and country. Urban assassinations were proving a favorite tactic of the EOKA. Indeed, one of the most popular shopping districts in Nicosia, Ledra Street, came to be nicknamed "the Murder Mile" because of the high number of EOKA assassinations there of off-duty British soldiers and, in some cases, their wives.[11] At the same time it was becoming apparent that rural communities were hiding the presence of EOKA leaders and playing host to training camps. The British responded to this in December 1955 by launching Operation Foxhunter as a means of undermining EOKA's rural network and exposing the group's link to religious leaders. The British had deduced that Greek Orthodox monasteries nestled on tree-covered mountainsides had become favorite EOKA hideouts. Foxhunter involved sweeping every monastery on the island for weapons. Yet the potency of the operation was stunted because the searches were not undertaken simultaneously due to shortages of military personnel, therefore allowing EOKA informers within the ranks of the police to tip off other monasteries in advance of an impending search.[12]

The links between the EOKA and the Greek Orthodox Church were perceptibly close, especially given that the formal face of *enosis* was the leader of the church on the island, Archbishop Makarios III. His quasi-political role as ethnarch (leader of the Greek-Cypriot community at large) made the British especially nervous, given his parallel religious role as influential archbishop of Cyprus. Even Grivas had called Makarios "the real leader of the National Liberation struggle."[13] It was exactly this influence that Harding aimed to harness in favor of reducing EOKA violence when he invited the archbishop to a series of talks from October 1955 to February 1956. These talks were designed to move forward the discussions about political obstacles, such as the constitutional future of Cyprus, as a means of dampening the impetus to violence. But according to John Reddaway, a senior civil servant in Cyprus involved in the talks, the negotiations were "doomed from the start because neither side had in substance modified its stance.... The Archbishop was unwavering in his determination to procure *enosis* without delay, the British in their conviction that *enosis* was impracticable in the foreseeable future."[14] The ultimate breakdown in talks between Harding and Makarios in early 1956 led the governor to bitterly condemn the archbishop for being in league with insurgents and convinced him that the only way to end violence on Cyprus was to defeat the EOKA militarily.

One of the first steps to achieving this, Harding thought, was to physically remove the spiritual figurehead of the *enosis* movement as a means of deflating insurgent morale. A month after his last fruitless meeting with Makarios, Harding authorized the detention and subsequent deportation of the archbishop to the Seychelles in the Indian Ocean. Harding's decision was in part influenced by intelligence pertaining to the archbishop's sourcing of foreign money to fund EOKA activities, especially from America. The governor became convinced that "a large sum of the money which the Archbishop collected from Greek communities in the USA was handed over by him in Athens for the purchase of the explosives in the captured caïque *Ayios Georghios*.[15] The Makarios deportation can therefore be conceived not just as an act of draconian counterinsurgency but also as a defiant stance against the role played by American influences on the violence in Cyprus. Exasperation among those on the right wing of Anthony Eden's new Conservative government at American interference on the Cyprus issue certainly stoked Harding's feelings.[16] Yet the effect of the deportation was almost entirely counterproductive for the counterinsurgency effort. The resentment within the Greek Cypriot community toward the colonial authorities at Makarios's removal from the island was near total and resulted in an outpouring of solidarity with the EOKA and the undermining of any potential "hearts and minds" operations by the British military, given the Orthodox Church's ability to cast opposition to colonial rule in moral terms that resonated with the population.[17]

Forging a Constitutional Settlement (with American Approval)

In July 1956, Eden appointed Lord Radcliffe as constitutional commissioner for Cyprus. Radcliffe's task was to draw up plans for the future political governance of the island, which he published on December 19. Based on the idea of double self-determination for Greek and Turkish Cypriots, the Radcliffe plan allowed for both minority Turkish and majority Greek votes on the issue. The British were so keen to garner American support over Cyprus that plans were made for Lord Radcliffe to visit the United States himself in order to push London's "line of attack," as British ambassador to Washington Sir Harold Caccia put it, and ensure "maximum impact" in the American media for the new constitutional proposals.[18] Caccia had come to this conclusion after noticing "the deleterious effect which their [American] silence about the Radcliffe proposals is having in Athens." He was worried that this was a tacit sign by the White House to the Greek government to knock back the plans. Washington had been leaning on Athens to accept the proposals but only after a belated diplomatic pause.[19]

Constitutional wrangling over the future of Cyprus continued long after the Radcliffe proposal had been effectively torpedoed by Washington. In 1958, a plan named after Prime Minister Harold Macmillan was tabled, offering shared Greco-Turkish sovereignty of the island. Sir Hugh Foot, the new governor of Cyprus who had replaced Harding in October 1957, was unequivocal in his opinion that the Macmillan Plan was a spark to a "civil war between the Greek and Turkish communities on the island."[20] Although initially cold toward the plan, Washington came to realize that the political inertia needed to be broken and encouraged Athens to consider the proposal on the table. In the meantime, Foot's fears of communal strife were being realized. Washington interpreted this violence as a Turkish effort to ensure outright partition, resulting in greater American pressure on Athens to agree to a plan for joint sovereignty, not complete independence.[21]

With Greco-Turkish negotiations over the political future of Cyprus stifled, the British government made direct efforts to stem the political impetus behind the insurgency. In February 1959, talks between the British, Greek, and Turkish foreign ministers, along with Greek and Turkish Cypriot representatives, were held at Lancaster House in central London. These talks finally resulted in an agreement as to the future constitutional makeup of Cyprus, which would see the separate ethnic communities on the island vote for their own representatives. This would eventually pave the way for independence the following year. After Makarios accepted the principles of the London Conference, Grivas ordered the cessation of the insurgency.

Upon receiving news of the agreement in February 1959 that brought the conflict to an end, President Eisenhower sent Macmillan his "sincere felicitations" at the sealing of "a peaceful and equitable solution" to the violence.[22] Eisenhower's relief was undoubtedly genuine, given the significant political capital that Washington had invested in engineering a specific political outcome to this particular counterinsurgency conflict.

America and Counterinsurgency in Cyprus

The problem of Cyprus's political future was attracting broad international attention even before the EOKA insurgency broke out. It was an issue that the British government was keen to avoid being dragged into the spotlight at the United Nations (UN). In large part this rested on the acquiescence of Washington.[23] As early as August 1954, over a year before the declaration of a state of emergency on Cyprus, key Eisenhower administration officials were staking partisan stances on the future of the island. Ambassador to the UN Henry Cabot Lodge was keen to use Cyprus as leverage with the British by hinting at putting it on the UN agenda should the United Kingdom prove uncooperative in debates about restricting Chinese representation on key bodies within the organization. Lodge suggested that "if necessary we point out to Scott [minister at the British embassy in Washington] that there is a great preponderance of opinion in this country that Cyprus should be turned over to Greece and that we will have to take this into account in our position on this question."[24] Wise to the American strategy, the Foreign Office thought that American policymaking was actually in more of a quandary than Lodge was letting on. London recognized the dilemma of the American position: avoid exposing rifts in the North Atlantic Treaty Organization (NATO)—Turkey, the other major player in the Cyprus problem, was an important NATO regional ally—that could be exploited by the Soviet Union, while at the same time maintain "reverence for the idea of self-determination." Despite acknowledging the American conundrum, the Foreign Office was reluctant to do anything to ease it.[25] Unperturbed, Lodge continued to lean on the British delegation at the UN to ensure a trade-off between the by now linked issues of China and Cyprus by appealing to "the interests of Anglo-American harmony."[26] As the EOKA's violent insurgency got under way in 1955, these interests would become increasingly divergent.

The Foreign Office knew that accommodating American opinion was important if international attitudes were to not swing against the British on the Cyprus issue. R. W. L. Wilding of the Foreign Office's Southern Department (who had responsibility for covering Cyprus) felt that the Americans' position on Cyprus was "of cardinal importance," particularly given their influence over the Greek position. Thus, Wilding told Foreign Secretary Anthony Eden, future policy should "be formulated with one eye on American opinion" because otherwise "progress in Cyprus [would be] virtually impossible and the resulting unrest would be bound to weaken our hold on the island and perhaps endanger the security of our troops there."[27] London's concern at the American hold over Athens was well founded. Soon after the formal beginning of the EOKA insurgency, Secretary of State John Foster Dulles attempted to placate Greek anger over continuing British rule in Cyprus by hinting to the Greek ambassador to Washington that America was toeing the British line over Cyprus and implied that the special relationship was merely a veneer: "Our actions are not due to favoritism. It is incorrect to assume that our actions are dictated by the UK. *Some things go on beneath the surface*."[28]

Despite his barely concealed Anglophobia, Dulles continued to politely request that the British embassy continue to pass any information on the UK government's policy on Cyprus, possibly only so this could be passed on to his Greek counterparts to give Athens a head start on opposition to the policies.[29] But the Foreign Office stonewalled Dulles's request. Orders were issued from Whitehall to embassies in Washington, as well as the other key capitals, Athens and Ankara, not to inform the Americans about any plans for Cyprus. The British ambassador to Turkey, Michael Stewart, let his bosses at the Foreign Office know that on three occasions he had "played the idiot boy" when his American opposite number in Ankara had inquired as to British proposals.[30] But the Foreign Office was more than happy to keep the Americans in the dark, especially in the run-up to the tripartite London Conference of British, Greek, and Turkish foreign ministers in September 1955.

Amid recrimination, the London Conference ended without any settlement being reached on the future of Cyprus. The new foreign secretary, Macmillan, wrote to Dulles after the talks not only to vent his frustration at the intransigence of the other parties but also to encourage the Americans to prevent the Greeks from tabling another motion about Cyprus at the UN as it would only "encourage further disorder and terror in Cyprus."[31] A noncommittal reply from Dulles a few weeks later served only to remind Macmillan that the Eisenhower administration "need not emphasize the traditional and popular feelings in the United States on colonial questions."[32] But behind the scenes Dulles continued to push the Greek government down particular paths. When, for example, plans for the constitutional future of Cyprus that met with the approval of Washington were rejected by Athens in December 1955, Dulles fired off an angry telegram to the US embassy in Greece that revealed both his partisanship and his frustration: "I have done my best to urge the UK to bring its policy more in line with Greek and

Cypriot desires. . . . However it will be difficult for me to continue to argue the Greek case with conviction if Greek Government is unable accept a formula."[33]

As the British counterinsurgency campaign got into full swing in 1956, the Americans remained unconvinced of any discernable military progress. Having held discussions with Colonial Office mandarins in April 1956, the first secretary of the US embassy in London, Peter Rutter, reported back to the State Department that the British security efforts on Cyprus "have not met with any appreciable success"—even if Whitehall officials continued to "strongly assert" things were on the right track.[34] Indeed, the State Department had come to the conclusion that the British were actually the major obstacle to a settlement on Cyprus, not the EOKA. They perceived that British refusal to reopen negotiations on the future of Cyprus during a lull in EOKA violence in August 1956 would actually exacerbate the insurgency in the long run by hardening Greek Cypriot attitudes against a settlement.[35] Downing Street quickly sensed American disquiet on the Cyprus front. In June 1956, Prime Minister Eden wrote to President Eisenhower, filling him in on the latest developments in the counterinsurgency campaign. But this telegram was more than just an update. Eden was attempting to curry American favor for the latest constitutional settlement created by Lord Radcliffe, which proposed granting both Greece and Turkey decision-making powers regarding the future of Cyprus. Eisenhower's reply to Eden poured cold water on the Radcliffe Plan, reflecting what British ambassador Sir Roger Makins felt were the "immoveable" and "unhelpful thoughts" of Dulles.[36]

The simmering hostility between Dulles and Eden spilled over into wider Anglo-American tensions during the Suez Crisis in the autumn of 1956. This had a significant knock-on effect in American engagement with the Cyprus conflict and their willingness to assist the British in ending EOKA violence. Eden became increasingly loath to adapt his Cyprus policy in the face of American disapproval, especially after the Suez debacle. The passage of time did not dim Eden's resentment toward the Americans, and his post-Suez ire extended toward Washington's interference over Cyprus too. His memoirs are littered with coded criticisms of Eisenhower and Dulles's perceived meddling: "Too many thought our troubles [over Cyprus] due to old fashioned colonialism. . . . I was convinced that the Cyprus problem would only be resolved between the three Governments, British, Greek and Turkish."[37]

Chastened by the Suez Crisis, Eden's successor in Downing Street, Harold Macmillan, sought to be more accommodating toward American desires.[38] Yet the new government, especially new foreign secretary Selwyn Lloyd, still faced the obstinacy of John Foster Dulles as the Cyprus conflict moved into 1957. Ahead of a crucial UN debate on Cyprus in February that year, Lloyd sent Dulles a personal message stating his worry at the impact that a US vote against the United Kingdom could have on Anglo-American relations: "If the United States vote against a resolution calling for the cessation of Greek activities, it will be regarded here as an unfriendly act."[39] The United States did not fully commit this "unfriendly act" and decided to abstain from the vote, resulting in no motion being carried. But it left Dulles brimming with anger at Lloyd's temerity at using such a phrase.[40] From that round of talks at the UN, the British delegation, headed by Sir Pierson Dixon, reported to the Foreign Office that Dulles's perpetual talk about the need for "self-determination" in Cyprus "seemed directed at making our flesh creep."[41]

Efforts to smooth over the entire special relationship, as well as hammer out some common ground over Cyprus, were undertaken at the bilateral Bermuda conference in March 1957. With the repercussions of Suez still hanging in the air between Eisenhower and Macmillan as they sat down at the Mid-Ocean Club on the North Atlantic island, conversation between the leaders touched on several key issues relating to Cyprus. The president told the prime minister that he felt the British "were not gaining much" by keeping Makarios in exile in the Seychelles—a perception that Macmillan agreed with.[42] Macmillan's promise to release the archbishop was a big stride in reconciling Anglo-American relations over Cyprus.[43] But the prime minister was fully aware of the political pitfalls of both releasing Makarios and of permitting overt American influence over attempts at conflict resolution. Macmillan later warned Eisenhower: "My right-wing [of the Conservative Party] assume that we released the Archbishop at your request, so private pressure by you would be better than public statements."[44] The attempt to drive American opinion on Cyprus below the radar of public awareness was sweetened by Macmillan revealing more of his intentions to Eisenhower. Macmillan intimated that the primary reason for persisting with the counterinsurgency campaign was to secure the long-term future of the British military bases on the island. The State Department memorandum of this part of Bermuda Conference records that "the Prime Minister confirmed that the British are not greatly interested in Cyprus except for the military importance of the island."[45] Even the British government came to perceive the conflict not as another installment of decolonization but as a struggle to protect Britain's long-term strategic foothold in the region—an issue with increasingly important international consequences. Even the new US consul general in Nicosia, Taylor Belcher, had observed that the "British authorities here do not view this as a colonial problem any longer and they believe Britain is being made the whipping boy in a situation which is certainly now . . . an international problem."[46] Such perceptions of the Cyprus conflict certainly created a permissive environment for the United States to play a greater role in proposing diplomatic solutions to violence on the island. Two of the most significant American efforts are worth considering in more detail, especially because they were conducted covertly. They highlight the quietly influential approach that the Americans came to take in the middle of yet another protracted British counterinsurgency war.

Covert Diplomacy: US Secret Cyprus Talks and the Holmes Mission

In August 1956, American efforts to intercede in the Cyprus conflict reached their zenith. The State Department authorized the undertaking of "secret, high level talks" to be undertaken with British, Turkish, and Greek representatives to hasten a settlement. The envoy sent to carry out these discussions was Julius Holmes, a special assistant to Dulles for NATO affairs. Prior to the talks, Holmes sent Dulles a memo outlining his negotiating position, stating that he wanted the British to accept a plan for elections, Cypriot self-government (limited for a ten-year period, pending a future plebiscite), and the preservation of sovereign UK military bases.[47] A month later Dulles gave Holmes the green light to conduct these talks with the proviso they be kept secret. Dulles suggested that Holmes "use NATO cover as appropriate" to dissuade observers that this was a unilateral or formal American intervention.[48]

The talks began in late September, with the British ambassador to Turkey, Michael Stewart, mirthfully noting how "nothing would please us better than that the Americans would succeed where we have so far failed."[49] On the eve of Holmes's arrival in London, a briefing memo for Foreign Secretary Harold Macmillan written by his civil servants cautiously asserted that "American intervention on Cyprus can only be effective if the US Government can do two things: a) persuade the Greek Government to withdraw the support which it gives to EOKA through Athens Radio, etc; and b) to take a more positive line over self-government for Cyprus."[50] Macmillan met Holmes later the same day he received this memo. The American envoy opened discussions on a tentative note, wondering whether his objective to actively seek a settlement on the Cyprus issue, and indeed the stance of the American government, would be adversely affected by the rapidly unfolding events in the Suez Canal.[51] The Suez Crisis cast a long shadow over the Holmes mission. Holmes himself was convinced that the British had "not thought through" the relationship between the Cyprus conflict and the Suez Crisis and their mutual impact on regional security and American interests.[52] The deepening of the Suez Crisis in October coincided with Holmes's travels to Athens and Ankara on the next leg of his mission. Anthony Eden's rage at the Americans was fueled by reports that emerged from Athens that the publication of the Greek government's proposals for *enosis* had been drafted with the help of Holmes himself.[53] *Enosis* was clearly now the primary diplomatic option the United States wanted to pursue. Eden fumed in a message to the Foreign Office: "I am bewildered by this Holmes negotiation. . . . I do not understand on what grounds the Americans are in this special position. It could not be by virtue of any help they have given us over Suez."[54]

It was because of, and not despite the Suez Crisis that the Holmes mission on Cyprus got nowhere. In his final report back to the State Department outlining the progress of his covert tripartite talks, Holmes observed that the outbreak of the Suez Crisis in the middle of his mission was "the principal element which handicapped progress" because, he felt, the British had become so obsessed with humbling Egyptian leader Col. Gamal Abdel Nasser that they "have not put their minds to the possibility of a negotiated settlement in Cyprus."[55] The British had become distracted from the conduct of their own counterinsurgency war.

The failure of the Holmes mission in 1956 did not entirely dissuade the Eisenhower administration from the notion that secret American intervention in the Cyprus conflict was at an end. Just over a year after the Holmes talks, the State Department renewed its tactic of covert diplomacy in order to resolve the conflict, but this time on a bilateral basis with the British. Designed to "establish more adequate exchanges with [the] British on [the] Cyprus problem," the US delegation was led by State Department official Walworth Barbour.[56] His objectives were to fathom the endgame of Britain's counterinsurgency war on the island and to explore the possibilities of numerous temporary and permanent constitutional solutions. The new prime minister, Harold Macmillan, wrote to Dulles expressing how he was "very glad" that the United States had agreed to the secret talks as well as how Anglo-American solidarity (and secrecy) was integral to ending the conflict on Cyprus.[57] The US consul general in Nicosia, Taylor Belcher, struck a note of caution, however, when he suggested that the solidarity of the special relationship should not come at the price of increasing tensions between Greece and Turkey in a strategically important region for US Cold War strategy: "A joint US-UK position would be a great help in solving the problem but success only seems possible only if the US decides that the danger of further rift in Greco-Turkish [*sic*] warrants the full use of its credit and influence in Athens and Ankara."[58] With Taylor's caution ringing in its ears, the American delegation began nine days of talks in London on September 10, 1957. During the meetings Foreign Office officials promised not to "scuttle" from Cyprus but insisted that an orderly departure, accompanied by the maintenance of key military bases, was possible. The US delegates agreed that the idea of a UN trusteeship of Cyprus was a bad one as "it might give an opening to the Russians." The Americans seemed more open to the British idea for a "condominium solution" that would give the British, Greeks, and Turks responsibility for governing the island.[59] It was agreed by the end of these secret talks that the British would put the condominium solution unilaterally to the NATO secretary-general, Paul-Henri Spaak, and the US would subsequently "inform Spaak that it finds the proposal interesting and would like to see it developed more fully." The Americans would then encourage Spaak to sell the proposal to Ankara and Athens rather than do it themselves and compromise any leverage they may have had.[60] These Anglo-American machinations are a prime example of how the special relationship needed to be utilized covertly in order to be effective.

Yet by early October, the State Department had cooled on the idea. Dulles instructed the embassy in London to inform the British that "after further consideration of the condominium proposal, we felt it would be unwise seek persuade [*sic*] Spaak to advocate a particular solution." Dulles went even further by criticizing what he saw to be "serious problems" with the plan, especially the issue of "ultimate authority."[61] Below the surface Dulles's argument was toeing a decidedly pro-Greek line and perhaps reflected insistence from Athens that anything short of *enosis* would be unacceptable. It was therefore clear to the British that secret talks with the Americans did not mean that other national interests were precluded from the room.[62] This confirmed to Whitehall that if the United States were to be brought more in line with British policy on Cyprus, a tried and tested method needed to be utilized—lest fears of communism nullify fears over colonialism.

Cyprus and the Cold War Dimension

Uncertain of how the Eisenhower administration would react to Britain's latest "small war," the governments of Winston Churchill and then, after April 1955, Anthony Eden attempted to dampen American enthusiasm for a UN debate on Cypriot self-determination by talking up the potential negative consequences of such a move. High on this list was the creation of a deepening rift between Greece and Turkey—a key NATO ally, whose dissatisfaction could be exploited by the Soviet Union. As seen in Palestine, the British sought to exploit American fears of communist expansionism. Similarly to Malaya, American concerns over Cyprus were contextualized within wider regional concerns. Greco-Turkish schisms over Cyprus had repercussions for NATO's vulnerable southern flank, while the British withdrawal from Suez had connotations for the shape of Middle Eastern politics in the face of aggressive pan-Arab nationalism pushed by Nasser.

Cyprus was a strategically important asset to the British. As Lawrence Durrell noted, "Cyprus was not only Cyprus; it was part of a fragile chain of telecommunication centres and ports, the skeletal backbone of an Empire striving to resist the encroachments of time."[63] The island was Britain's foothold to the wider Middle East and for this reason held significant strategic importance for all three armed forces. It also proved to be a vital staging post for British intelligence capabilities, enabling the monitoring of Soviet action in the region. As if to cement the strategic necessity of Cyprus to Britain, in the early 1950s MI6 had shifted its regional headquarters from Suez to Nicosia, while in 1954 the military transferred its Middle East Command headquarters from Egypt to Cyprus as well.[64] If Cyprus was of that much strategic importance to the British, then the Americans certainly felt they held a vested interest in maintaining the island as a useful resource.

But American concerns were motivated predominantly by concerns over preserving NATO solidarity in the area and not creating any conditions that would grant the Soviets any leeway in the region. Typical of the American attitude was John Foster Dulles's comments to British ambassador Sir Harold Caccia in February 1957. When discussing Cyprus, Dulles downplayed the localized colonial aspect of the insurgency and instead placed it in a bigger picture by emphasizing "the grave dangers to the whole Western world. . . . Unless some kind of solution can be found Greece may be lost to NATO. This would breach the southern flank of NATO and might permit the communists to cut across the Mediterranean."[65] Yet this made for divergent Anglo-American priorities. The Americans' reading of the regional scene led them to think that placating the Greek position over Cyprus was the best bulwark to communism, whereas the British felt that handing Cyprus over to Greece would stoke more violence on the island, which in itself would be the crucible for communist exploitation. The British therefore tried to convince the Americans of their way of thinking by openly linking Cyprus to communism. British security sources tried desperately hard to persuade their American counterparts that the EOKA's cell structure was evidence of communist mimicry.[66] Soon after stepping down as governor of Cyprus, the newly minted Lord Harding pushed a line regarding potential communist influence on the island. In a speech in London in January 1958, Harding argued that there was a real "danger of political penetration and infiltration and of subversion."[67] This was another colonial counterinsurgency war fought as if it were a "hot" conflict of the Cold War. Even the former chief of the Imperial General Staff, Field Marshal Bernard Montgomery, tried to persuade his old wartime friend President Dwight Eisenhower to personally intervene in the Cyprus conflict because the protracted insurgency "is having awkward repercussions in the contest between the free world and the onward march of international communism."[68] A year earlier Anthony Eden had tried a different tack with Eisenhower in a letter to Washington in which the soon-to-be disgraced prime minister flagged up the wider regional problems that could arise through disruptions to oil supplies if the situation on Cyprus was not adequately resolved through a maintenance of a British presence in the region: "I do not think that either of our countries would be really happy if we were only able to counter a threat to vital oil supplies in the Persian Gulf from landing grounds in Arab lands."[69]

The American willingness to see the Cyprus conflict through a predominantly regional lens can in part be explained by the relative absence of any pressing domestic political agenda being pushed by a powerful set of lobby groups. The Greek American ethnic diaspora was fairly large but was dwarfed by other electoral blocs that had or would play a large role in shaping American policies toward British counterinsurgency wars, such as the Jewish and Irish American populations. Most departments within the Eisenhower administration had developed a broadly pro-Greek policy platform, something that a bitter Eden felt was the result of "no Turkish lobby in the United States."[70] However, despite the presence of a discernable Greek American community, it was not concentrated in specific states (especially ones with a large number of Electoral College votes) and therefore held little political leverage.[71] Cyprus was to be a counterinsurgency war that the Americans placed within the broader jigsaw of regional Cold War grand strategy, not domestic politics. Either way, they ensured that the outcome of the conflict served their own geopolitical aims. Once the emergency in Cyprus was over, the Americans came to review their position on the island. The National Security Council Planning Board highlighted the importance of US communication facilities there in a 1959 report. Further attention was paid to ensuring continued American access to military bases, where an expanded force of signals intelligence officers, mainly attached to the US Naval Security Group, could be located. In short, the Americans engineered Cyprus to become their own "intelligence watchtower" from which to observe the wider region.[72] It was a win-win for Washington, as the British left Cyprus with a niggling sense of strategic underachievement in yet another counterinsurgency war.

Conclusion

The concomitant events in Suez and Cyprus in the mid-to-late 1950s put the British government in an impossible bind. Retreat from both outposts was strategically unthinkable, not to mention publicly embarrassing. Even the US ambassador to the United Kingdom, Winthrop Aldrich, felt a modicum of sympathy for the British position when he admitted to the State Department that "no British Government could have given up both Suez and Cyprus simultaneously and successfully faced a general election."[73] Instead, the British tried to cling to both, in the face of significant American consternation. Washington's vested interest in the outcome of the British counterinsurgency campaign on Cyprus was predicated on securing a broadly pro-Greek settlement, which contrasted with Britain's antipathy toward Athens, given the Greek-Cypriot violence of the EOKA. But the protracted ethnic violence that simmered beneath the surface of the British-EOKA fight was inescapable when it came to seeking a long-term solution.

A telegram from the US consulate in Nicosia back to the State Department toward the end of the counterinsurgency campaign in 1958 concluded that the British "now consider themselves in a virtual Palestinian situation."[74] It was an astute observation. The fight against the EOKA was heavily couched in terms of trying to find a postcolonial settlement amid ethnic conflict within the indigenous population. Despite the withdrawal of British troops and the resultant independence granted Cyprus, these ethnic tensions caused increasing political friction that in 1963 resulted in the de facto partition of the island between a Greek south and Turkish north, which remains in place to this day.

Sir John Harding, who had spent the worst years of the counterinsurgency campaign as governor of Cyprus, was in no doubt when he left his post of who harbored a significant portion of the blame for the failure to foster peace efforts: America.[75] Instead, the Eisenhower White House and, more potently, the State Department of John Foster Dulles were never fully supportive of British attempts to quell EOKA violence on Cyprus due to their conflicting desire to help Athens attain a favorable postconflict settlement. Washington's endeavor to recalibrate the regional balance of power in the Mediterranean resulted, once more, in a reluctance to support the British in a counterinsurgency campaign. Washington's collaboration with Athens took Cyprus's independence as an eventuality, with ongoing British counterinsurgency operations being viewed as little more than a minor hindrance to the attainment of this outcome. Covert diplomatic missions sent by Washington were used to strengthen Athens's negotiating position, to the detriment of British efforts to balance both political talks on constitutional arrangements and counterinsurgency operations designed to weaken the elusive EOKA. The outcome was ultimately satisfactory to neither party. The EOKA was never militarily defeated, and another British colony was granted independence, only for it to be hamstrung by internecine ethnic conflict. The Cyprus conflict demonstrated just how deeply divergent British and American priorities were in regard to the transition to independence of British colonies, especially ones in the grip of insurgent violence. Such schisms were reinforced a few years after the Cyprus pullout, this time in South Arabia.

Notes

Epigraph: Harding, "Cyprus Problem," 296.

1. Reddaway, *Burdened with Cyprus*, 3.
2. Byford-Jones, *Grivas and the Story of EOKA*, 52.
3. Dimitrakis, "British Intelligence and the Cyprus Insurgency," 377.
4. Robbins, "British Counter-Insurgency in Cyprus," 722.
5. Byford-Jones, *Grivas and the Story of EOKA*, 64.
6. "Foreign Service Despatch from Am.Consulate Nicosia to Department of State," September 29, 1955, US National Archives and Records Administration (hereafter NARA), Record Group (RG) 59, 747C.00/9-2955, box 3273; and "Foreign Service Despatch from Am.Consulate Nicosia to Department of State," June 30, 1955, NARA, RG 59, 747C.00/6-3055, box 3273.
7. Byford-Jones, *Grivas and the Story of EOKA*, 103.

8. Durrell, *Bitter Lemons of Cyprus*, 158, 164.
9. "Foreign Service Despatch, from Am.Embassy London to Department of State," September 28, 1955, NARA, RG 59, 747C.00/9-2855, box 3273.
10. Aldrich, *Hidden Hand*, 372.
11. Byford-Jones, *Grivas and the Story of EOKA*, 127.
12. Aldrich, *Hidden Hand*, 372.
13. Quoted in Byford-Jones, *Grivas and the Story of EOKA*, 145.
14. Reddaway, *Burdened with Cyprus*, 44.
15. Quoted in Byford-Jones, *Grivas and the Story of EOKA*, 97.
16. Markides, "Britain's 'New Look,'" 498.
17. Reddaway, *Burdened with Cyprus*, 58.
18. "Confidential: From Washington to Foreign Office," January 19, 1957, The National Archives, UK (hereafter TNA), FO 371/130099.
19. Hatzivassiliou, "Blocking Enosis," 258.
20. Foot, *Start in Freedom*, 169.
21. Evanthis Hatzivassiliou, "The Cyprus Question and the Anglo-American Special Relationship," in Aldrich and Hopkins, *Intelligence, Defence and Diplomacy*, 162.
22. "Message to Prime Minister Macmillan of the United Kingdom on the Cyprus Agreement," February 20, 1959, document #39, Dwight D. Eisenhower papers, Public Papers of the President, http://www.presidency.ucsb.edu/ws/index.php?pid=11662&st=&st1=.
23. Johnson, "Britain and the Cyprus Problem," 113–30.
24. "Memorandum of Conversation, by the Assistant Secretary of State for United Nations Affairs (Key)," August 17, 1948, *Foreign Relations of the United States* (hereafter *FRUS*), *1952–54, Vol. 3*, 753.
25. "The United States Government and the Cyprus Issue and Tactics at the United Nations," August 18, 1954, TNA, FO 371/112855.
26. "Telegram: From United States Representative at the United Nations (Lodge) to the Department of State," September 9, 1954, *FRUS, 1952–54, Vol. 3*, 780.
27. Wilding minutes on "Confidential: Sir Roger Makins (British Embassy, Washington DC) to Anthony Eden (Foreign Office)," January 12, 1955, TNA, FO 371/117621.
28. "Memorandum of a Conversation between Secretary of State Dulles and the Greek Ambassador (Melas), Department of State, Washington DC," May 25, 1955, document #117, *FRUS, 1955–57, Vol. 24*, 272 (emphasis added).
29. "Secret: From Washington to Foreign Office," August 2, 1955, TNA, FO 371/117647.
30. "Secret: British Embassy, Ankara to Foreign Office," July 27, 1955, TNA, FO 371/117647.
31. "Confidential: To John Foster Dulles," September 15, 1955, NARA, RG 59, 747C.00/9-1555, box 3273.
32. "Secret: From John Foster Dulles to Harold Macmillan," October 5, 1955, NARA, RG 59, 747C.00/9-1955, box 3273.
33. "Telegram from the Department of State to the Embassy in Greece," December 23, 1955, document #153, *FRUS, 1955–57, Vol. 24*, 326.

34. "Foreign Service Despatch from AmEmbassy London," April 17, 1956, NARA, RG 59, 747C.00/4-1756, box 3275.
35. "Telegram from the Department of State to the Embassy in the United Kingdom," August 24, 1956, document #189, *FRUS, 1955–57, Vol. 24*, 393.
36. For Eisenhower's reply, see "Top Secret: From Washington to Foreign Office," June 23, 1956, TNA, FO 371/123901. For Makin's thoughts, see two telegrams "From Washington to Foreign Office," June 21 and 23, 1956, TNA, FO 371/123900.
37. Eden, *Full Circle*, 400–402.
38. Hatzivassiliou, "Cyprus Question and Anglo-American Special Relationship," 150.
39. "Confidential: From Foreign Office to Washington," February 8, 1957, TNA, FO 371/130128.
40. "Confidential: From Washington to Foreign Office," February 12, 1957, TNA, FO 371/130128.
41. "Confidential: From New York to Foreign Office," February 8, 1957, TNA, FO 371/130099.
42. Eisenhower, *White House Years*, 124.
43. Hatzivassiliou, "Cyprus Question and Anglo-American Special Relationship," 160.
44. "Message from Prime Minister Macmillan to President Eisenhower," March 31, 1957, document #237, *FRUS, 1955–57, Vol. 24*, 470.
45. "Memorandum of a Conversation, Mid-Ocean Club, Bermuda," March 21, 1957, document #232, *FRUS, 1955–57, Vol. 24*, 465.
46. "Foreign Service Despatch from AmConsulate Nicosia, Subject: A Cyprus Solution—Some Problems We Must Face," September 6, 1957, NARA, RG 59, 747C.00/9-657, box 3281.
47. "Memorandum from the Assistant Secretary of State for Near Eastern, South Asian and African Affairs (Rountree) to the Secretary of State," August 13, 1956, document #188, *FRUS, 1955–57, Vol. 24*, 384–92.
48. "Telegram from the Department of State to the Embassy in France," September 8, 1956, document #194, *FRUS, 1955–57, Vol. 24*, 403–4.
49. "Secret: British Embassy, Ankara to Sir John Ward (Foreign Office)," September 18, 1956, TNA, FO 371/123298.
50. "Secret: Cyprus—The Visit of Mr Julius Holmes," September 25, 1956, TNA, FO 371/123928.
51. "Secret: Record of Meeting Held in the Secretary of State's Room at 6pm," September 25, 1956, TNA, FO 371/123928.
52. "Telegram from the Embassy in the United Kingdom to the Department of State," September 26, 1956, document #198, *FRUS, 1955–57, Vol. 24*, 408–9.
53. "Top Secret: From Foreign Office to New York," October 9, 1956," TNA, FO 371/123929.
54. "Prime Minister's Personal Minute: Minister of State, Foreign Office," October 9, 1956, TNA, FO 371/123929.
55. "Memorandum from the President's Special Representative (Holmes) to the Acting Secretary of State," November 19, 1956, document #211, *FRUS, 1955–57, Vol. 24*, 434.

56. "Telegram from the Department of State to the Embassy of the United Kingdom," September 5, 1957, document #259, *FRUS, 1955–57, Vol. 24*, 497.
57. "Eyes Only Ambassador. Department of State Telegram," September 4, 1957, NARA, RG 59, 747C.00/9-457, box 3281.
58. "Foreign Service Despatch from AmConsulate Nicosia. Subject: A Cyprus Solution—Some Problems We Might Face," September 6, 1957, NARA, RG 59, 747C.00/9-657, box 3281.
59. "Secret Office Memorandum. Subject: Cyprus—US-UK Talks in London," September 16, 1957, NARA, RG 59, 747C.00/9-1657, box 3281.
60. "Telegram from London to Secretary of State," September 19, 1957, NARA, RG 59, 747C.00/9-1957, box 3281.
61. "Telegram from Department of State to AmEmbassy London," October 7, 1957, NARA, RG 59, 747C.00/10-157, box 3281.
62. For the British files on the talks, see "Secret: Cyprus," TNA, FO 371/130102.
63. Durrell, *Bitter Lemons of Cyprus*, 205.
64. Aldrich, *Hidden Hand*, 567–68.
65. "Memorandum of a Conversation, Department of State, Washington," February 11, 1957, document #221, *FRUS, 1955–57, Vol. 24*, 449.
66. Aldrich, *Hidden Hand*, 575.
67. A reproduction of the text of the speech delivered on January 22, 1958, at Draper's Hall, London, appears as Harding, "The Cyprus Problem in Relation to the Middle East," 291–96.
68. "Letter from Viscount Montgomery to President Eisenhower," November 1957, NARA, RG 59, 747C.00/12-957, box 3282.
69. "Top Secret: From Foreign Office to Washington," June 7, 1956, TNA, FO 371/123894.
70. Eden, *Full Circle*, 414.
71. Hatzivassiliou, "Cyprus Question and Anglo-American Special Relationship," 151.
72. Aldrich, *Hidden Hand*, 579.
73. "Telegram from the Embassy in the United Kingdom to the Department of State," September 9, 1955, *FRUS, 1955–57, Vol. 24*, 283.
74. "Telegram from the Consulate in Nicosia to the Department of State," June 9, 1958, document #207, *FRUS, 1958–60, Vol. 10 (Part I)*, 623.
75. Harding, "Cyprus Problem," 296.

6

Middle Eastern "Winds of Change"

Counterinsurgency in South Arabia

> [Britain] would leave behind it only two monuments [in South Arabia]. One was the game of Association Football, the other was the expression "fuck off."
>
> —Richard Turnbull, British high commissioner to South Arabia

Prime Minister Sir Alec Douglas-Home was not among the most famous (or indeed influential) of Brits to have crossed the Atlantic in February 1964 when he arrived at the White House for talks with President Lyndon Johnson. Beatlemania was sweeping the United States, and the "British Invasion" of the American music charts was clearly weighing on the president's mind. "I like your advance guard," Johnson quipped to Douglas-Home, "but don't you think they need haircuts?"[1] But the mop-tops of the Fab Four were not the most pressing point of discussion at this transatlantic visit. A key area of foreign policy debate was to be the conduct of British counterinsurgency operations amid the civil war in South Arabia.

The campaign in South Arabia, containing both covert and overt strands from 1963 to 1967, was a formative moment in British counterinsurgency learning. It was arguably the most politicized campaign of its sort that the military had been asked to fight. Douglas-Home sought to maintain British sovereignty over the military base at Aden within a newly independent federal state, but Harold Wilson decided to withdraw from the country before the strategic goals had been attained. This saw the balance tip significantly away from the military in favor of Whitehall in terms of strategic formulation. This shift was compounded by the fact that the counterinsurgency campaign was politically motivated not solely by unfolding events on the ground but by a political thirst for revenge. The shadow of the Suez Crisis hung over the campaign in South Arabia. Much of the "special relationship" literature has focused on how the Suez debacle affected US-UK relations, yet the legacy of Suez on Britain's conduct of future military operations in the Middle East is frequently overlooked. Suez provided an omnipresent spur for operations in South Arabia, given Col. Gamal Abdel Nasser's heavy involvement in aiding enemy insurgents. In this context it is important to remember that the British Army had not tackled an insurgent group with such a high level of supplies and solidarity from an external source. Egyptian influence, munitions, and troops molded the political and military nature of the conflict. Against this background, the Americans sought to reconcile their Cold War priorities in the Middle East in light of pervasive Soviet interest in the Yemeni conflict with their frustration at the British conduct of their campaign. It was the first time that the British had conducted a significant amount of their counterinsurgency operations covertly, with Downing Street trying to maintain plausible deniability in the early stages of British involvement. This chapter will chart how this led to Anglo-American friction, resulted in a British foreign secretary lying to the face of an American president in the Oval Office, and ended in the British massively scaling back their imperial presence in the Middle East and Asia, to the horror of Washington.

British involvement in the Arabian Peninsula has a long history. The port of Aden was sequestered as a trading post by the East India Company in 1839. Since then, it was held as a Crown colony until January 1963, when it merged with the tribal amalgam that was the protectorates to create the Federation of South Arabia (FSA). This was not a formal British colony and was led by a tribal Federal Council, which permitted the British to keep their military bases.[2] This was a crucial facet to the broader functionality of the British military because in 1960 Aden replaced Cyprus as the British Army's General Headquarters (GHQ) of Middle East Land Forces (MELF) in the wake of the EOKA insurgent campaign discussed in chapter 5. After London and Singapore (GHQ of Far East Land Forces), Aden was one of three locations vital to Britain's global military presence.[3] It was also of value to the British, given the large economic stakes at play with the sizeable British Petroleum refinery in Aden.

The counterinsurgency campaign the British waged did not stand in isolation. It must be placed in the wider context of the Yemeni Civil War. On September 26, 1962, a coup by a group of army officers, motivated by the pan-Arab nationalism espoused by Nasser, overthrew the imam of Yemen, Mohammed al-Badr, sparking a civil war between the royalist tribes who remained loyal to the deposed imam, and the republicans behind the newly established breakaway Yemen Arab Republic (YAR). This conflict would provide the first cover for British intervention, given London's desire to support the pro-British royalists against the Egyptian-backed republicans. Yet it was not until 1963 that republican dissidents within the FSA initiated an insurgent campaign inside the federation itself. This was the pretense used to instigate a broader counterinsurgency campaign, which itself was distinctly split into two parts. There was an urban campaign in Aden against the YAR and an Egyptian-sponsored insurgent group, the National Liberation Front (NLF), and a rural campaign against YAR forces. British efforts to defeat the NLF represented the overt plank of the counterinsurgency campaign, triggering the deployment of troops to the streets of Aden. Yet it was the parallel rural campaign in the Arabian hinterland that formed the covert plank of British involvement. The secret deployment of mercenary units to train, equip, and fight alongside royalist troops in the civil war, as well as the more aggressive use of air power, was designed to undermine the Egyptian influence over the YAR. But all of this came at the price of driving a wedge between London and Washington as American opposition to British management of the conflict intensified.

British commitment to the conflict in South Arabia was cemented on December 10, 1963, when a lone insurgent linked with the NLF attempted to assassinate the British high commissioner to the FSA, Sir Kennedy Trevaskis, in a grenade attack at the Khormaksar airport. The attack convinced a previously skeptical Douglas-Home, who had become prime minister a few months earlier, of the need to tackle republican aggression both within and outside the borders of the FSA. A state of emergency was declared within the federation, and Trevaskis stepped up efforts to pressure London into expanding the existing covert program of arming friendly tribal groups and committing to more overt uses of counterinsurgent force.[4]

Despite maintaining the need for a transatlantic Cold War alliance, British actions in the Middle East, unlike Asia, troubled the Americans. The divergent British and American reactions to the 1962 Yemeni coup encapsulated the opposing regional interests the two nations had. Washington was keen to isolate the wider region from similar military coups that could be manipulated by Moscow, while London was more immediately concerned with securing its interests within the borders of the FSA and Aden in particular.[5] But as Eden's private secretary, Guy Millard, pointed out, in the wake of the 1956 Suez Crisis, Britain "could never again resort to military action outside British territories without at least American acquiescence."[6] The result of this situation was consistent British attempts to shroud the use of covert mercenary groups in South Arabia at the same time as urging Washington not to recognize the YAR. First John F. Kennedy and then Lyndon Johnson hoped that Yemen could be nurtured into the wider body politic of independent democratic capitalist states along with other third world nations. This conflicted with London's desire to shepherd its Middle Eastern protectorate down its own path to independence (which included continued British influence). The resulting policy clash was fueled by Washington's inability to reconcile the ingredients of anticolonialism and anticommunism and Britain's desire to maintain long-range economic interest in a lucrative oil-rich region.[7] The first major Anglo-American spat this provoked was over recognition of the new Yemen Arab Republic at the start of Britain's counterinsurgency campaign.

Recognizing the YAR and Anglo-American Friction

Debates over whether to recognize the new Yemen Arab Republic provided for some sharp divisions of transatlantic opinion. The British were keen to maintain the primacy of the royalist Federation of South Arabia and bastardize the separatist republic in an effort to protect key strategic assets in the country. The Americans, conversely, were reluctant to ignore the new breakaway state that had shunned feudal rule.

Prime Minister Harold Macmillan admitted that he had a "prolonged argument with Washington" over the issue of YAR recognition,[8] which the Americans had already granted in December 1962, a few months after the coup. The British governor in Aden, Sir Charles Johnston, argued that he shared the view of ministers within the FSA that American recognition of the YAR was "incomprehensible" and motived by "an underlying wish to keep Nasser on his throne and save him from the consequences of his Yemeni adventure."[9] Johnston's rationale was typical among British diplomatic hands in the region who continued to feel aggrieved at American conduct over the Suez Crisis and Washington's de facto maintenance of Nasser's rule in Egypt. Earlier that month Macmillan had noted with exasperation that British recognition of the YAR "may seem to have been forced on Her Majesty's Government by the Americans."[10] But the resistance continued for some time despite heavy pressure from the White House. Kennedy telegrammed Macmillan in late January 1963 openly questioning the British stance, wondering aloud to the prime minister "whether non-recognition still has value."[11]

But the Macmillan government was determined that withholding recognition did have value to the legitimacy of the nascent counterinsurgency campaign. In a paper presented at the prime minister's behest in January 1963, the Cabinet Office noted that although early British recognition of the YAR "would facilitate continued close co-operation with the US Government in restraining the Republicans causing trouble in Aden," such a decision would leave an impression that "the independent British role in Arabia had been swallowed up in the Pax Americana." It went on to posit that Britain "can in fact be more use to the Americans themselves if we pursue an independent policy in Arabia than if the Arabs conclude that we are their satellites."[12] British prestige in the region was at stake and would be irreparably ruined if London were seen as Washington's puppet.

There were many within the Kennedy administration who were frustrated by British obstinacy over the recognition issue. Senior National Security Council

(NSC) member Robert Komer, who was acting as a key point man within the administration on the Yemeni conflict, wrote to the president in February 1963, stating that it was "regrettable but understandable" that London had decided not to recognize the YAR. But Komer was concerned that this would unnecessarily alienate the northern Yemenis, "thus exacerbating the very threat to Aden it would like to damp down."[13]

On the same day that Kennedy took receipt of that memo from Komer, he also received a message from Macmillan setting out the British rationale for refusing to acknowledge the new republican state. The prime minister asked the president to understand that the British have "a difficult hand to play in Aden" because of its importance "to our military position in the Gulf." Macmillan acknowledged that recognizing the YAR would have its benefits, but the priority was defending assets and allies in the federation, who, the prime minister assured Kennedy, would be moved toward independence "under a moderate regime" in due course. Macmillan ended his note by recognizing, with regret, that "you and we should now seem to be somewhat out of step in our Yemen policy, but as I see it this due [*sic*] more to differences in our circumstances than to divergence in objectives."[14] But such a rationale did not wash with many in Washington. Toward the end of the year, American annoyance with the British position in Yemen was palpable. Komer was among the first to lose his cool by advocating in September 1963 that Washington start to "beat up [the] UK to stop shafting us and recognize [the] YAR."[15] Soon after Komer's annoyance at British conduct in Yemen started to boil over, there was a change of leadership in London with Douglas-Home replacing Macmillan in 10 Downing Street. This brought with it new American suspicions about exactly how much support the British were giving to their royalist allies in Yemen in the name of counterinsurgency.

Covert Operations, British Lies

Members of the British cabinet harbored a deep obsession with Nasser. The more hawkish members of the Macmillan government were determined to reap revenge for his actions during the Suez Crisis. Nasser's position as the self-styled bête noire of the British in the Middle East ensured that the right-wing "Suez Group" of Tory ministers who had actively pushed for his overthrow in the mid-1950s reconvened to form the "Aden Group" a decade later when the Yemeni conflict began to draw significant Egyptian interest.[16] The group, including Defense Secretary Peter Thorneycroft, Colonial Secretary Duncan Sandys, Aviation Minister Julian Amery, and backbench MP-cum–Yemen emissary Neil "Billy" McLean, saw the protection of British political, military, and economic interests in South Arabia as a critical means of stemming the influence of Nasser-inspired Arab nationalism in the region. They lobbied Macmillan and then Douglas-Home to initiate direct support for mercenary operations and successfully shut the Foreign Office out of the policymaking process over Yemen with their aggressive anti-Nasser, proroyalist agenda. Indeed, it is unclear as to how much Foreign Secretary Rab Butler (who took over from Douglas-Home in October 1963) actually knew about mercenary activities. In a memo to the new prime minister, Butler appeared oblivious to ongoing covert operations when he cautiously urged that "we should not as a Government, either overtly or covertly, get involved with the internal Yemeni situation."[17]

Neil McLean made several trips to Yemen in late 1962 and early 1963. These visits were causing headaches at the American embassy in London. US diplomats expressed their concerns to the Colonial Office that McLean was vastly overstepping the mark by making secret trips to the YAR to assist royalist fighters. McLean's visits, the embassy felt, "obstruct efforts to achieve some constructive stabilization" in the area.[18] This observation had a ring of truth to it. McLean's reports depicted imperiled royalist allies in desperate need of British assistance and proved influential in forging a consensus to withhold recognition of the YAR. McLean urged Macmillan to authorize the secret shipment of British weapons and, crucially, to agree to the deployment of covert operations by a group that came to be known as the British Mercenary Organisation (BMO). Crucially, Macmillan refused to authorize direct British assistance to mercenary operations, but the presence of British nationals in the midst of the civil war gave Washington cause for concern.

The BMO was forged out of a secret meeting in April 1963 at White's Club in London attended by key members of the Aden Group, the founder of the Secret Air Service (SAS) Col. David Stirling, and, crucially, Foreign Secretary Douglas-Home, whose very presence at the meeting would come back to haunt him six months later when sat in the Oval Office with President Kennedy.[19] Under the leadership of colonels Jim Johnson and David Smiley, the BMO secretly deployed to South Arabia not long after the White's Club meeting. Bankrolled and supplied by the neighboring Saudi Arabian authorities, the BMO operated separately from the formal British military structure, allowing Downing Street to maintain plausible deniability of its activities.

The BMO was small but effective and relied in part on recruitment from their disgruntled Suez Crisis allies, the French. Smiley himself noted that "at the height of the mercenary effort, when I was commanding them, they [the BMO] never numbered more than 48, of whom 30 were French or Belgian and 18 British." Yet it is significant, as Smiley went on to point out, that the BMO was there purely to "advise the commanders (of the royalist forces), train their troops and provide communication and medical services.... It is important to realise that none of the mercenaries actually fought in the war."[20] This advice and training under Smiley's leadership paid dividends. By 1965, the royalists had recaptured large swaths of territory lost over the past year. Priority was given to severing or disrupting the Egyptian supply lines to their republican allies. This prompted Nasser to significantly escalate Egyptian involvement in 1964, blunting the potency of several dozen mercenaries.

The two distinct elements to the British military campaign in South Arabia, the public and the private wars, made for two distinct strategies and ultimately two distinct outcomes. With a restricted purview, the BMO can perceivably be held to have met its goal of helping stem the military tide of the Egyptian-backed army of the YAR in the South Arabian hinterland. Their regular army comrades fighting the overt counterinsurgency campaign in Aden and the troublesome tribal regions of the FSA could point to only partial successes amid the complexities of parallel urban and rural counterinsurgency campaigns. However, the undiminished insurgent strength, fueled by external support from Egypt, ensured that British counterinsurgency strategy never attained a level of effectiveness.

Eventually the very presence of a covert mercenary organization run by British nationals (albeit without the support of the British government) in South Arabia was exposed by an Egyptian newspaper and subsequently the *Sunday Times*, which reproduced five letters written by members of the BMO operating in Yemen. The cover was blown, and the mission ended. But the year-long existence of the BMO, which the British had felt was a well-maintained covert action, had been surmised by the Americans. This led to some tense diplomatic exchanges at the very highest level.

In one of his last major overseas trips as foreign secretary before becoming prime minister, Douglas-Home met with President Kennedy in the White House in early October 1963, a few weeks after Komer accused Britain of "shafting" the United States over Yemen. The president pressed Douglas-Home on levels of support royalist forces inside Yemen were receiving from London. Sitting across from Kennedy, the foreign secretary replied curtly that London was "giving them nothing."[21] Kennedy had deliberately caught the next British prime minister in a web of lies. American intelligence had already deduced that British nationals were engaged in covert operations in South Arabia. Declassified documents reveal that in the weeks immediately after the revolution in Yemen in 1962, at the time Macmillan was sanctioning weapon shipments to the royalists, the NSC notified Kennedy that Britain "seems to be covertly in the play" in Yemen.[22] The State Department noted as early as October 9, 1962—almost a year before Douglas-Home's White House lies in the Oval Office—that covert British action "*which can hardly be concealed for long*, is likely to lead to a sizeable commitment of UAR [Egyptian] forces in Yemen and conceivably to a Yemeni-UAR invitation to the Soviet Union to increase its participation."[23] Not only was Washington secretly aware of Britain's covert operations but its refusal to make London aware of this knowledge reveals something about the power dynamics of the special relationship in this instance. Britain was clearly unwilling to bring the Americans into their plans to help engineer a particular outcome to the Yemeni Civil War, the result of a residual feeling in London that British power was still able to be wielded with a certain degree of autonomy in the Middle East. Washington's refusal to let this occur was manifested in hiding its own intelligence about its supposedly close ally's (albeit secret) military operations. Anglo-American interactions over the war in Yemen were marked by their mutual duplicity.

The cat had nearly been let out of the bag long before President Kennedy offered Douglas-Home the chance to come clean at their meeting in October. Hinting at the possibility of British covert action inside Yemen, Kennedy urged Macmillan in January 1963 that "disengagement from Yemen . . . is in both our interests." Kennedy interpreted that civil war as intractable (it "may seesaw back and forth almost indefinitely") and tried to warn Britain off backing the royalists to the hilt, given what he interpreted to be their slim chance of winning outright ("they may occasionally cut the roads, but they show little capability for seizing the major towns").[24] In September 1963, Robert Komer of the NSC appraised for key administration officials what, for the United States, would be "The Next Round in Yemen." When pondering why the US had not managed to engineer a truce among the warring factions in the civil war, he fathomed that the worst-case scenario was that "the UK may at least be covertly encouraging the Saudis and the royalists."[25] Komer's fears were well placed. Some small effort was made by Washington to keep closer tabs on British policymaking inside Aden itself. In 1963, an agreement was reached between London and Washington that saw a US naval liaison officer being seconded to work with the British military commanders in Aden.[26] But the British were still reluctant to let the Americans inside policymaking on South Arabia, and, as late as May 1964, Douglas-Home was still peddling the discredited line in the House of Commons that "our policy towards the Yemen is one of non-intervention."[27]

But America's increasing involvement in Vietnam coupled with the assassination of Kennedy, who had taken a personal interest in the Yemeni conflict, ensured that Britain's war in South Arabia became dimmer on the Washington radar.[28] As a result the Americans came to see the conflict as another piece in a global anticommunist game, ignoring the more regional role the British saw for themselves as guarantor of political and economic stability.[29] Inevitably, this led the conflict to be interpreted to a large extent through the lens of Soviet involvement and fears (real and imagined) that Nasser was Moscow's conduit to wider Middle Eastern infiltration.

Nasser, the Soviets, and the Middle East Cold War

Not since Palestine had Anglo-American tensions over the conduct of a counterinsurgency campaign spilled over into broader diplomatic hostilities. Washington seethed at what it perceived to be renewed British imperialist behavior in the Middle East, while the British were left frustrated that the Americans did not share their loathing of Nasser, thus legitimizing their desire to undermine Egyptian intervention in South Arabia. Intelligence agencies in London and Washington did actively float the idea that Nasser was a Soviet stooge and that Egyptian troops in Yemen were to be the first wave of forces used to destabilize the entire Arabian Peninsula.[30] This conclusion stemmed from the knowledge that the Soviets had been selling arms to nationalist forces in Yemen since 1956.[31] The containment of, and retribution against, Nasser is a vein that ran through British policy in this war, and the British were unabashed in letting the Americans know this. In a meeting with Dean Rusk in August 1964, Denis Greenhill, the interim chargé d'affaires at the British embassy in Washington, argued that Britain "felt that it was time for him [Nasser] to suffer a setback; Yemen appeared to be the suitable place."[32]

Despite Anglo-American fears that the Soviets would use Yemen as a Trojan horse into the wider Middle East, no significant direct intervention was staged by the Kremlin to support the YAR. This was the result of strategic sensitivities in relation to the fragile politics of the region that cast aside ideological expedience in the medium term.[33] The Soviets offered no communist alternative to the existing appeal of pan-Arab nationalism espoused by Nasser, given Nikita Khrushchev's acknowledgement of the Egyptian leader's broad regional influence at the time.[34] Indeed, the paucity of British intelligence in the wake of the 1962 revolution generated particular worry within Whitehall when it got wind of a CIA estimate that within a week of the coup, Abdullah al-Sallal's new regime would be receiving support from up to twelve thousand Egyptian troops in the spirit of pan-Arab nationalist solidarity.[35] However, CIA reports were distrusted by the British intelligence community as exaggerating the strength of the Egyptian influence in order to discourage British involvement in the civil war.[36] It emerged that only a hundred Egyptian troops were deployed to Yemen in the weeks after the revolution, but this was still enough to set alarm bells off in Whitehall.[37] The buildup, however, was swift. Nasser sent fifteen thousand troops to Yemen by the end of the year. The Egyptian strategy during their intervention in the Yemeni Civil War conceivably had three priorities: to support the YAR in the name of pan-Arab nationalism; to manipulate the Yemeni situation to foster instability inside its regional rival, neighboring Saudi Arabia; and to drive the British out of the FSA.[38] Although the first and third of these goals were met, it is questionable as to the extent to which it was the Egyptian presence that guaranteed the outcome. At best, the Egyptians were conduits through which the Yemeni republicans, northern regulars, and southern insurgents alike could achieve their own goals thanks to Egyptian arms and training. As a third-party intervention, it can be seen as a success. As an outright military deployment, it cannot. The large Egyptian forces in the YAR, some fifty thousand by 1965, left themselves open to militia ambushes on a terrain they knew little about and failed to adequately devise a strategy capable of countering small, speedy royalist fighters whose British sponsors had trained in the ways of guerrilla combat. In short, they sent a regular army to fight an irregular war with conventional tactics and unwieldy operational perspectives.[39] But it still made for a complex political dynamic within the broader region that gave Washington cause for concern.

A policy review of the Yemeni conflict by the State Department in the spring of 1963 depicts large regional interests at play and problematizes the role played by the British. It acknowledged the presence of large numbers of Egyptian forces in the country and that they were being used as a conduit for "Soviet military [and] technical assistance." From this document it appears that the United States seemed more intent on maintaining a balance of friendship with both the pro-YAR Egyptians and the pro-FSA Saudis over the Yemen issue. The State Department noted how one of the main causes of "costly delays" in formulating a coherent US policy toward the Yemeni conflict was "deference to [the] UK." Britain was clearly being lined up as an obstacle to effective American policymaking, given the dilemma of trying to encourage both the Saudis and the Egyptians to disengage at the same time as the British continued their intervention. The policy review urged the need for the US to "press [the] UK to 1) exert caution in dealing with Yemen border problems; 2) recognize [the] YAR."[40] Presumably the first request is a euphemism for warning the British about continued covert cross-border raids, which were being carried out by the BMO.

In March 1963, Komer underlined to Kennedy the need for the United States to "damp down the Yemen affair before it blows up" into a wider regional conflict.[41] The key appeared to be prompting Riyadh and Cairo to withdraw all help from their respective Yemeni proxies in the civil war. But American concerns were realigned in early 1964 with news of reconciliation between Nasser's Egypt and the Saudi government. The secretary of state, Dean Rusk, called Lord Harlech, the British ambassador to Washington, to "reassess" the situation in Yemen "in light of the changing regional political picture."[42] After this particular meeting, the counselor at the British Embassy, John Killick, told State Department officials that American "expressions of interest and concern regarding Yemen helped strengthen the forces of realism and reason in the British Government." He was, however, taken to task on his assessment by State Department Near East Affairs diplomat Harrison Symmes, who pointed out that although American and British "objectives are the same" regarding Yemen, there was a significant difference in approach.[43] The State Department indicated its own displeasure at revelations about connections between the British government and private mercenaries. Although Egypt was the problematic common denominator in US-UK policymaking during the conflict, the State Department warned the British that their conduct was counterproductive: "We [the US] are prepared again to take up the cudgels with Nasser but our ability to influence Nasser to lay off Aden is directly affected by the British ability to provide proof and assurances that they have no designs on the Yemen republic." Again, broader Cold War concerns were rife. Intelligence reports indicated that Abdullah al-Sallal, the president of the breakaway YAR, had planned a trip to Moscow for late 1964 but that this visit was "not unconnected with YAR concern at reports of a British build-up in Aden."[44] The American strategy had become about trying to encourage the British to diminish their involvement as much as possible in the YAR for fear of stoking Soviet involvement in the region. It was the first time in a colonial British counterinsurgency war that the British presence acted not as a bulwark against but as an incentive for communist agitation. At the end of 1964, the US chargé d'affaires in Taiz, Harlan Clark, asserted to the State Department that "the time has surely come for the UK to show its readiness to deal with responsible Yemeni leaders and to explore the possibilities for a settlement in the south"—but only after Egyptian troops had withdrawn. Clark went on to argue that "what we are facing in the south is a British-Arab problem, whose satisfactory solution is clearly in the US interest"—namely because successful Egyptian penetration into the FSA would "in the end benefit only the communists."[45] Cold War priorities were never too far from American thinking in this particular counterinsurgency conflict.

There was one anti-Nasser sentiment in particular that had the potential to unite British and American attitudes during the conflict. In 1963, reports began to emerge out of Yemen that indicated that Egyptian forces had been behind poison-gas attacks on FSA forces. Komer noted that such claims were "having considerable impact, especially on Capitol Hill," that could change the tone of American policy on the entire Yemeni conflict.[46] When the US ambassador to Cairo pressed Nasser on the poison-gas accusations, the Egyptian leader said the reports were mistaken and that napalm was being used to destroy crops, which had led to some confusion.[47] The Egyptian ambassador to the United States went even further by claiming in discussions with State Department officials that if poison gas had been used, he "suspected it to be [the] work of either British intelligence or Saudis."[48] In order to verify the origin of chemicals used in the attacks against royalist tribes, the British Ministry of Defence sent samples back to the government scientific facility at Porton Down for testing. They also sent samples to CIA laboratories in the US to double-check the veracity of any claim.[49] In the end, the British and American results came to different conclusions as to the origins and content of the chemical cocktail, with the Americans casting doubt on deliberate Egyptian intent. This led the Ministry of Defence to disregard the CIA's analysis, citing Langley's use of new and unproven analytical techniques.[50]

Despite their clear frustration at the British handling of the conflict in South Arabia, it is interesting the Americans never fully utilized the United Nations (UN) as an additional lever to admonish or cow the British. It appeared that Washington wanted to unilaterally encourage the British to change their course of action in the country and not have such influence dissipated by the UN. This decision by Washington is an important one, given the way in which the UN had played no role in any other British counterinsurgency campaign until Yemen. This conflict, for yet another reason, would be a turning point.

As soon as Britain began to reconstitute the political structure of South Arabia and conduct counterinsurgency operations, the UN pursued an active role in curtailing London's actions. The UN Committee of 24, the group established to review decolonization procedures, published a report in July 1963 condemning Britain's constitutional machinations that had created the FSA.[51] After Britain's declaration of a state of emergency in South Arabia on December 10, 1963, the UN General Assembly passed Resolution 1972 six days later, which called for the British to end their policy of deportation and imprisonment of suspected insurgents.[52] Britain denounced the resolution as one-sided, yet the support with which it passed through the General Assembly demonstrated the international scrutiny that British actions in South Arabia (the overt military operations at least) would be under from the beginning.

This scrutiny would increase after the condemnation wrought on Britain after civilians were killed during a Royal Air Force bombing raid in March 1964 on the fort town of Harib. After this event Douglas-Home's government could no longer resist attempts by the UN to increase its presence on the YAR-FSA border for fear of losing face on the international stage. A United Nations Security Council resolution condemning the Harib attack was eventually passed 9–0 in April 1964.[53] It is worth noting that the only other country to abstain from the vote other than the United Kingdom was the United States. This came about after a significant amount of intragovernment wrangling within the Johnson administration over how to handle the response: Hang the British out to dry in the court of world opinion but risk the Soviets taking advantage of diminished British influence? Or avoid stinging the UK with too much opprobrium and attempt to shepherd London in a new direction of Washington's own making? The latter argument won out.[54]

In June 1963, the British acquiesced to the deployment of the UN Yemen Observation Mission (UNYOM). Coercive American pressure was instrumental in securing British agreement to this mission. Robert Komer intimated in a memo to National Security Adviser McGeorge Bundy in October 1963 that British acquiescence had been secured "because of our thinly veiled threat to withdraw our jets [from neighboring Saudi Arabia], leaving them to field inevitable Saudi requests to provide air defense."[55] The threat of noncooperation over Yemen by the Americans was to create an unfeasible burden on London of more Middle Eastern commitments that Britain could ill afford. But UNYOM, which cost $2 million and only ever posted twenty-five observers on the ground, ceased its activities in September 1964, citing British obstinacy in aiding the task assigned them and failing to bring the warring parties together to broker a peace deal to end the civil war.[56] The Americans did nothing to help prop UNYOM up, but neither did they assist Britain in extracting itself from an increasingly vicious insurgency. This middle path that Washington seemed to tread—avoiding the distinct options of civil-military assistance (as seen in Malaya) or utter condemnation—meant that the Johnson administration was thoroughly surprised by the high-stakes gamble London took to get itself out of this particular counterinsurgency imbroglio.

The Withdrawal from East of Suez and the Legacy of Counterinsurgency in South Arabia

Whitehall was preparing to step down from its political commitment to the FSA as early as mid-1964. A conference held in London in June that year brought together the Douglas-Home government and tribal representatives of the federation. It settled on an agreement that the FSA would be granted full independence by 1968.[57] Four months later Harold Wilson's Labour Party attained a narrow parliamentary majority, but this changed very little in terms of how Britain dealt with the Yemeni conflict.[58] Wilson maintained the Tories' line of withholding recognition of the YAR, agreed that withdrawal from South Arabia was necessary, and shared their predilection for sanctioning covert operations when required.[59] Initial Labour intentions to maintain a military base in Aden even after a large-scale withdrawal were abruptly halted with the sudden announcement in a February 1966 Ministry of Defence white paper that the Aden base would be abandoned, as would all British military commitments east of Suez. This was the cause of horror in Washington. The plan to withdraw from Aden was brought forward a year to late 1967, marking a political acceptance that the need for a major forward operating post in the Middle East at the height of decolonization was anachronistic.[60]

The abandonment of the Aden base by the Wilson government is not as strategically shortsighted as it may appear when seen in the context of the newly obtained base on Diego Garcia. The British Indian Ocean Territory, acquired in November 1965, had been transformed into a military base of key Cold War strategic value, as it was capable of launching British (and later American) aircraft within flying range of both the Middle East and the Far East. This dual function of Diego Garcia must understandably have alleviated fears in the Ministry of Defence (and the Pentagon) of losing strategic reach should Aden be abandoned. Defence Secretary Denis Healey would later admit that the maintenance of the military base in Aden was "out of all proportion to the gain" and defended the political decision to withdraw without defeating the insurgency by stating that "all alternatives would have been worse," given the inability to find a constitutional compromise between the seemingly irreconcilable tribes of the federation.[61]

The influence of the sterling crisis of the late 1960s on Wilson's decision to withdraw from east of Suez is inescapable. The British military presence and operations east of Suez, including Aden, were costing £35 million per year by 1966, at a time when the government was close to deciding to devalue the pound.[62] This was as much a pragmatic economic decision as it was politically expedient.[63] Overall, the Wilson government executed a politicized exit strategy from a counterinsurgency campaign on a scale not seen before. Domestic considerations, combined with a politically advantageous desire to relieve Britain of expensive and seemingly prolonged duties in one of the last troublesome colonial campaigns, witnessed politics trump strategy. This left the Americans furious, despite previous indications that they wanted the British out too.

According to Foreign Secretary Rab Butler, who met with Lyndon Johnson in April 1964, the president "seemed to be determined to get us out of our base in Aden."[64] Despite this high-level pressure, the CIA was confident enough to predict in late 1965 that it was "highly unlikely that Britain will decide to abandon the base [Aden] completely."[65] However, when London announced its east-of-Suez withdrawal in 1966, the Americans felt betrayed and thought it would leave a political vacuum at the center of a volatile region susceptible to the appeals of communism.[66] The timetable for departure set out in the 1966 white paper did indeed spark an increase in activity in the Middle East by the Soviet Union, which multiplied its cohort of military advisers in Egypt and Syria in 1967, although crucially not deploying them to Yemen itself.[67] Indeed, the Americans considered, although ultimately dismissed, the possibility of launching their own covert operations through Yemeni dissidents to destabilize Nasser and prevent a total Egyptian takeover of South Arabia. On July 14, 1967, the 303 Committee, a cross-departmental body that oversaw American covert operations, discussed a plan for sponsoring covert paramilitary operations by antirepublican groups in Yemen with the purpose of bogging down Egyptian forces—much along the same lines as Macmillan's initial covert supply of weapons to the royalist forces. Four days later in a meeting with President Johnson, key cabinet divisions on this proposal were made evident, with Secretary of State Dean Rusk opposed to the idea and Secretary of Defense Robert McNamara extolling its virtues. [68] In the end, Johnson parked the idea of the American military having to plug the gap left by British forces, but its very consideration reveals American unwillingness to let postcolonial vacuums left by failed British counterinsurgency wars be filled by Cold War enemies.

British defense secretary Denis Healey later revealed his cynicism toward American anger at the east-of-Suez withdrawal, citing a need to hide domestic political blushes and a reluctance to publicly accredit any upside to the British colonial legacy: "The United States, after trying for thirty years to get Britain out of Asia, the Middle East, and Africa, was now trying desperately to keep us in; during the Vietnam War it did not want to be the only country killing coloured people on their own soil. Moreover, it had at last come to realise that Britain had an experience and understanding in the Third World, which it did not possess itself."[69]

Although perhaps privately perplexed at American anger at the white paper, the British were keen to utilize American help in making the withdrawal as smooth as possible. In a joint US-UK meeting in Washington in January 1966 to discuss the implications of the east-of-Suez timetable, the foreign secretary, Michael Stewart, suggested that the American government might wish to "use its influence with Nasser to encourage him to refrain from making difficulties for the British in connection with their withdrawal from Aden."[70] But Washington did not go out of its way to alter Nasser's behavior. The news of the British withdrawal was having its own impact on the Egyptian leader's actions. Indeed, it led him to rethink his entire Yemen strategy. Secure in the knowledge of a protracted British pullout, Nasser devised in the week after the British announcement a so-called Long Breath strategy, which constituted the redeployment of the bulk of the Egyptian forces in the YAR from the north closer to the southern border with the FSA, ready to exploit the impending military vacuum.[71] But this came at a high cost for Nasser. When Israel launched its offensive against Egypt, Syria, and Jordan in June 1967, up to one third of Egypt's military was deployed in Yemen.[72] The humiliation Egypt suffered during the Six-Day War prompted a chastened Nasser to initiate a withdrawal from Yemen in October of that year—a process complete by mid-December, a month after the British had departed.

By the time the Six-Day War broke out, the British Army had already passed security responsibility for the FSA interior to the South Arabian Army (SAA). The British retreated to form a defensive perimeter around Aden as troops became sitting targets for reprisal attacks by insurgents. Their impending withdrawal had created an environment of lawlessness that would find echoes forty years later in Basra, Iraq. Fears over the dependability of the post-transition SAA were realized on the eve of British withdrawal when the SAA declared allegiance to the NLF insurgents. The ignominy of the retreat of the British forces was compounded by the knowledge that the fundamental strategic goal of the Aden military mission, to secure the protectorate for the FSA, was not achieved. The indigenous army it had trained to aid it in this mission had mutinied and left the city in the hands of the insurgents it had spent the last four years battling against. The swift collapse of the FSA soon after the British departure (an event the CIA had predicted in a September 1966 national intelligence estimate[73]) sealed the ostensible failure of the British military mission. Three years after the British withdrawal, the republicans eventually subjugated the FSA to form the Marxist state of the People's Democratic Republic of Yemen (PDRY) in November 1970. The PDRY became a haven for Middle East and European terrorist groups seeking a sanctuary, while Aden became a significant port for the Soviet and Chinese fleets, which gained naval footholds there.[74]

South Arabia was arguably the first counterinsurgency "defeat" since Palestine, with the British unable to achieve any of its major objectives. Subjugated to political demands, up against a well-supplied insurgent enemy, and lacking any political support from Washington, the British military was unable to fulfill the grand strategic mission set before it. Haunted by the specter of Suez, British policymakers had been willing to initiate a program of covert operations to facilitate an intervention that was outweighed from the outset by the sheer quantity of Egyptian forces augmenting the Yemeni republicans. In the face of international pressure and confusing signals from the Americans, the British government crossed the counterinsurgency Rubicon in 1966 by committing to a protracted withdrawal in the absence of a neutered insurgency. The international community, friends and foes alike, was able to use this blow to British military and political esteem to its own advantage: The Egyptians got a Middle East free from British interference, and a sizeable portion of UN member states were placated by the eventual relinquishment of British colonial control, while the Americans were able to extend their sphere of influence and fill the breach left by the British as self-championed guarantors of regional security and oil supplies in the Middle East. We are still living with the results of this final consequence of this failed counterinsurgency campaign and the subsequent British withdrawal from commitments east of Suez in 1967.

Notes

Epigraph: Quoted in Healey, *Time of My Life*, 283.

1. Brown, *One on One*, 127.
2. Balfour-Paul, *End of Empire*, 49, 78.
3. Mockaitis, *British Counter-Insurgency*, 45.
4. Mawby, "Clandestine Defence of Empire," 121.
5. Smith, "Revolution and Reaction," 198.
6. Quoted in Adamthwaite, "Suez Revisited," 449.
7. Fain, "Unfortunate Arabia," 130; and Louis, "American Anti-Colonialism," 414.
8. Macmillan, *At the End of the Day*, 270.
9. "Telegram to the Secretary of State for the Colonies from Aden (Sir C. Johnston)," December 29, 1962, The National Archives, UK (hereafter TNA), PREM 11/4356.
10. "Top Secret: United Kingdom Recognition of the Yemen Regime," December 12, 1962, TNA, PREM 11/4356.
11. "Telegram from President Kennedy to Prime Minister Macmillan," January 26, 1963, document #142, *Foreign Relations of the United States* (hereafter *FRUS*), *1961–63, Vol. 18*, 324.
12. "Secret: The Yemen," n.d., TNA, PREM 11/4356.

13. "Memorandum for the President," February 14, 1963, John F. Kennedy Presidential Library, Digital Archive Collection (hereafter JFK DAC), www.jfklibrary.org/Asset-Viewer/Archives/JFKPOF-128-018.aspx.
14. "Message from: Prime Minister Macmillan, London, England. To: President of the United States, WashDC," February 14, 1963, JFK DAC, www.jfklibrary.org/Asset-Viewer/Archives/JFKPOF-128-018.aspx.
15. "Paper by Robert W. Komer of the National Security Staff," September 20, 1963, document #329, in *FRUS, 1961–63, Vol. 18*, 711.
16. Jones, "Where the State Feared to Tread," 719.
17. "Secret: From Foreign Secretary to PM," November 21, 1963, TNA, PREM 11/4928.
18. "Telegram from AmEmbassy London to Department of State," May 29, 1964, US National Archives and Record Administration (hereafter NARA), RG 59, POL 27 YEMEN, Military Operations, box 3026.
19. Walker, *Aden Insurgency*, 55.
20. Smiley, *Arabian Assignment*, 154.
21. "Extract from Record of a Conversation between the President of the United States and Lord Home, at the White House, Washington, 4 October 1963," TNA, PREM 11/4928.
22. "Memorandum from Robert W. Komer of the National Security Council Staff to President Kennedy, 4 October 1962," document #68, in *FRUS, 1961–63, Vol. 18*.
23. "Memorandum from the Assistant Secretary of State for Near Eastern and South Asian Affairs (Talbot) to Secretary of State Rusk," October 9, 1962, document #76, in *FRUS, 1961–63, Vol. 18* (emphasis added).
24. "Telegram from President Kennedy to Prime Minister Macmillan," January 26, 1963, document #142, in *FRUS, 1961–63, Vol. 18*, 324.
25. "Paper by Robert W. Komer of the National Security Staff," September 20, 1963, document #329, in *FRUS, 1961–63, Vol. 18*, 710.
26. For the files that document the planning for this secondment, see TNA, FO 371/168656.
27. *Hansard*, House of Commons Debates, May 14, 1964, vol. 695, col. 605.
28. Jones, *Britain and the Yemen Civil War*, 85.
29. Pieragostini, *Britain, Aden and South Arabia*, 88.
30. Jones, "Where the State Feared to Tread," 718.
31. Fain, "Unfortunate Arabia," 129.
32. "Department of State Memorandum of Conversation. Subject: Saudi Arabia and UAR with Respect to Yemen," August 21, 1964, NARA, RG 59, POL 27 YEMEN, Military Operations, box 3026.
33. John T. Ducker, "The International Context of South Arabia and British Policy," in Hinchcliffe et al., *Without Glory in Arabia*, 72.
34. For a comprehensive analysis of Soviet-Egyptian relations in relation to early proxy involvement in Yemen, see Ferris, "Soviet Support for Egypt's Intervention," 5–36.
35. Dorril, *MI6*, 679.
36. Ibid., 682.

37. "Top Secret: From CINI MIDEAST, to MoD, London," October 15, 1962, TNA, DEFE 13/398.
38. Witty, "Regular Army in Counter-Insurgency Operations," 410.
39. Ibid., 418.
40. "Policy Review of the Yemen Conflict [1963]," enclosure to "Memorandum from the Department of State Executive Secretary (Brubeck) to the President's Special Assistant for National Security Affairs (Bundy)," document #163, *FRUS 1961–63, Vol. 18.*
41. "Memorandum from Robert W. Komer of the National Security Council Staff to President Kennedy," March 11, 1963, document #188, *FRUS 1961–63, Vol. 18.*
42. "Department of State Memorandum of Conversation. Subject: Yemen," March 17, 1964, NARA, RG 59, POL 27 YEMEN, Military Operations, box 3026.
43. Ibid.
44. Ibid.
45. "Airgram from AmEmbassy, Taiz, to Department of State," December 5, 1964, NARA, RG 59, POL 16 YEMEN, Independence/Recognition, box 3026.
46. "Memorandum for the President," July 18, 1963, JFK DAC, www.jfklibrary.org/Asset-Viewer/Archives/JFKPOF-128-018.aspx.
47. "Telegram From the Embassy in the United Arab Republic to the Department of State," July 11, 1963, document #294, *FRUS, 1961–63, Vol. 18* www.jfklibrary.org/Asset-Viewer/Archives/JFKPOF-128-018.aspx.
48. "Outgoing Telegram from Department of State," July 18, 1963, JFK DAC, www.jfklibrary.org/Asset-Viewer/Archives/JFKPOF-128-018.aspx.
49. "Memo: Samples from Yemen," n.d., TNA, DEFE 55/418.
50. "Yemen: Gas Warfare. Technical Notes on Meetings Held at the Central Intelligence Agency, Langley, Virginia, USA, 11–12 March 1968," TNA, DEFE 55/418.
51. Pieragostini, *Britain, Aden and South Arabia*, 52.
52. Chang, "United Nations and Decolonisation," 45.
53. To appreciate the British diplomatic maneuverings during the UN Security Council debate in response to the Harib attack, see TNA, FO 371/174628.
54. "Memorandum from the President's Special Assistant for National Security Affairs (Bundy) to President Johnson," April 9, 1964, document #326, in *FRUS, 1964–68, Vol. 21*, 623–24.
55. "Memorandum from Robert W. Komer of the National Security Council Staff to the President's Special Assistant for National Security Affairs (Bundy)," October 19, 1963, document #344, in *FRUS, 1961–63, Vol. 18*, 748.
56. O'Ballance, *War in the Yemen*, 100–105.
57. For the full text of the conference report, see "South Arabia Conference Report," June 29, 1964, TNA, DEFE 13/570.
58. Halliday, *Arabia without Sultans*, 201.
59. Jones, *Britain and the Yemen Civil War*, 188.
60. For a detailed analysis of the implications and consequences of British withdrawal from east of Suez, see Louis, "The British Withdrawal from the Gulf," 83–108.

61. Healey, *Time of My Life*, 284.
62. Hanning, "Britain East of Suez," 253.
63. Darby, *British Defence Policy*, 304.
64. "Top Secret: From Washington, to Foreign Office," April 29, 1964, TNA, DEFE 13/569.
65. "Central Intelligence Agency, Special Memorandum, Subject: Outlook for Aden and the Federation of South Arabia," November 5, 1965, Declassified Document Reference System (hereafter DDRS), 9.
66. Louis, "British Withdrawal from the Gulf," 84.
67. Walker, *Aden Insurgency*, 227.
68. "Editorial Note," in *FRUS, 1964–68, Vol. 10*, 841.
69. Healey, *Time of My Life*, 280–81.
70. "Memorandum of Conversation," January 27, 1966, document #255, in *FRUS, 1964–68, Vol. 12.*
71. O'Ballance, *War in the Yemen*, 156.
72. Jones, "Where the State Feared to Tread," 733.
73. "National Intelligence Estimate (30-1-66)," September 8, 1966, DDRS, 1.
74. Walker, *Aden Insurgency*, 296.

7

The Counterinsurgency Phoenix

Britain and America's War in Vietnam

> The Americans are too apt to think that quantity is a substitute for quality and method.
>
> —Secret Foreign Office memo, July 3, 1961

> If failure comes to Vietnam, it is bound to cause profound dismay and recriminations in the United States. There will be a general search (as there was after the Communist victory in China and the invasion of Korea) for someone to blame and British intervention at the present stage could all too easily make us the principal scapegoat.
>
> —Secret Foreign Office memo, February 9, 1965

All relationships have their crisis moments. Ones that claim they are "special" are particularly vulnerable to lasting damage when issues of mistrust creep in. The American war in Vietnam proved to be one such crisis in the "special relationship." What started as a military advisory mission under John F. Kennedy expanded under Lyndon Johnson to become one of the longest and bloodiest conflicts in American military history. Nixon's lip service to "peace with honor" saw the war secretly extend into Laos and Cambodia. All the while, America's supposed closest ally oscillated between timid peacemakers and acquiescent partners in Vietnam—a picture more complex than the image depicted in much of the literature on the special relationship that depicts a stoic Harold Wilson refusing to allow British troops to join America's war effort. This uncomfortable middle path that Britain tried to tread during this particularly brutal counterinsurgency war took two distinct paths. The first was direct capital-to-capital diplomacy, especially during Wilson's premiership, which coincided with Johnson's crescendo of operations in the mid-1960s. The second was the creation of the British Advisory Mission to Vietnam (BRIAM) under the leadership of fabled counterinsurgency guru Robert Thompson. Both of these paths were taken by London in the hope of rendering some influence over the direction and character of America's war. Yet on both fronts it became clear that any British sway over Washington's strategy was minimal.[1] While Thompson's ideas were highly valued in Washington, his policy recommendations were met with a decidedly cooler reception by American military commanders on the ground in Vietnam, the result, perhaps, of his grating optimism about what could be achieved if only the Americans adopted a more British-style approach. All the while, Wilson's efforts to mitigate what he saw to be Johnson's impulsive hawkishness would end in frustration and recrimination, including from the backbenchers of his own party.[2] This chapter will explore how this dual-track approach unfolded and assesses the evolution of the special relationship at work from the early days of the Kennedy administration through to Thompson's futile attempt to shape Richard Nixon's curtailment of the conflict. The outcome showed Britain as a neutered ally, a minor irritant to America's ruthless prosecution of its war against communist expansionism in Southeast Asia. There was nothing particularly special about Britain's role in America's last major counterinsurgency war of the twentieth century.

American involvement in Vietnam started almost as soon as the involvement of France had been brought to an end by the humiliating defeat of its colonial forces at the Battle of Dien Bien Phu in May 1954. The Geneva Accords, signed in July, brought the French colonial presence in Indochina to an end and fatefully established a demarcation line along the seventeenth parallel between a communist north, run from Hanoi by the Workers' Party leader Ho Chi Minh, and the south, under the control of former emperor Bao Dai in Saigon. Keen to destabilize the communist Democratic Republic of Vietnam and prop up the nominally anticommunist State of Vietnam, President Dwight Eisenhower immediately instigated a covert program of paramilitary assistance and psychological operations under the auspices of the newly formed Saigon Military Mission, led by Col. Edward Lansdale, who had made his name offering counterinsurgency assistance to the Philippine leader Ramon Magsaysay during the communist Hukbalahap uprising. Lansdale and the CIA began to work closely with the South Vietnamese prime minister, Ngo Dinh Diem, who in 1955 declared himself president of a new Republic of South Vietnam. Diem's nepotistic regime received the support of Washington in lieu of any realistic alternative bulwark to the expansion of communism in the region. American support was hardened by the emergence of a communist insurgent group, known as the Viet Cong, inside the borders of the new republic in 1957. In the face of growing violence by the turn of the decade, the newly installed Kennedy administration felt duty-bound to assist the Army of the Republic of Vietnam (ARVN) in preparing for this burgeoning counterinsurgency campaign. Kennedy duly bolstered the levels of military and economic aid to Diem's government in line with the recommendations of a report compiled by National Security Council (NSC) member Walt Rostow and ex-army chief of staff Maxwell Taylor. Eager to prevent the fall of another Southeast Asian "domino" to communism, Kennedy took the central fears of the Rostow-Taylor report to heart. He created a new organization, the US Military Assistance Command, Vietnam (USMACV), to be run by a four-star general and augmented by the presence of a large number of US military advisers who would train the ARVN. The proliferation in numbers of these counterinsurgency advisers was swift. By mid-1962, there were around nine thousand American troops fulfilling noncombat duties in the country.[3] The stage had been set for a comprehensive counterinsurgency intervention that would draw America into a protracted conflict that soon lost its pretense as an advisory mission. But it would not take long for allies to offer the Kennedy administration assistance.

Counterinsurgency in Camelot: Kennedy and the Establishment of BRIAM

From the very earliest days of the Kennedy administration, London was sending overtures to Washington that displayed a keen readiness to aid the Americans in their nascent intervention in Vietnam. In advance of a meeting between the British ambassador, Sir Harold Caccia, and Secretary of State Dean Rusk in February 1961, the Foreign Office briefed its man in Washington to demonstrate to Rusk that Britain "would be very willing to join with the Americans in any action they thought our assistance would be helpful."[4] Caccia took that meeting with Rusk, leaving the State Department with the impression that "the British, on the basis of their Malayan experience, hoped to be able to cooperate."[5] But the receptiveness to such British eagerness by American officials on the ground in Vietnam was low. British diplomatic personnel in Saigon got the feeling from their American counterparts that the Americans "are not prepared to take us into their confidence."[6] But a request from the prime minister of Malaysia would force a shift in that perception.

Tunku Abdul Rahman wrote to Duncan Sandys, the secretary of state for Commonwealth relations, on April 19, 1961, urging Britain to send assistance to help prop up the government of Diem. Rahman personally recommended the deployment of Robert Thompson, who had served as a permanent secretary of defense in Malaysia after the country achieved independence from Britain in 1957.[7] In Washington, Caccia leaped on this plea as further evidence of British usefulness to the Americans.[8] However, the Foreign Office instructed the Washington embassy that the contents of Rahman's letter "should not at this stage be revealed to the Americans," and it was decided that London would continue to press the case for offering assistance unilaterally.[9] This strategy seemed to pay off. Caccia reported in early May that the State Department "say they strongly favour assistance by third countries particularly the United Kingdom." His cable back to the Foreign Office alluded to the nature of potential British involvement when he made a pointed reference to how "there are certain sections of the Pentagon which still favour the United States carrying out all counter-insurgency training on their own."[10]

The Foreign Office's trumpeted announcement to all relevant embassies in mid-May 1961 that consultations with the Americans "in the counter-insurgency field" would allow the Americans to utilize elements of "the [British] experience acquired in Malaya . . . to good effect" was a little premature.[11] A week earlier Kennedy's new Presidential Task Force on Vietnam had met, resulting in a welter of opposition to permitting any British military presence on the ground. Gen. Charles H. Bonesteel, the secretary of the General Staff, argued that the British would use any deployment to Vietnam "as a means for exercising control over our freedom of action." Seymour Weiss, an undersecretary of state, concurred, adding that "the British contribution would be quite limited in number and size, thereby hardly warranting a major voice in policy formulation." This position was challenged by the Task Force Chairman, Roswell Gilpatric, who "did not see why we should keep the British out"—a thought echoed by Deputy National Security Adviser Walt Rostow, who argued that "the problem was not in keeping the British out but rather getting them in and sharing the problem with us."[12]

Some of the strongest opposition to British involvement actually came from within the American contingent of military advisers already on the ground in Vietnam as part of the Military Assistance Advisory Group (MAAG). Lt. Gen. Lionel McGarr, the MAAG chief, wrote to the outgoing chairman of the Joint Chiefs of Staff, Gen. Lyman Lemnitzer, in June 1961, warning him off sanctioning British counterinsurgency "trainers." He not only questioned the commitment of third-party assistance to MAAG but went on to disparagingly assert that he was "unable here to pin down 'Thompson group' qualifications and, more important, its authority." The idea of using Robert Thompson to spearhead a small group of British advisers inside Vietnam was clearly treading on the toes of certain members of the US military. The need to "show the flag" of allies in this counterinsurgency war, McGarr asserted, was "political expediency" and "militarily counter-productive."[13]

But this did not stop the snowball effect of political will behind Thompson. After it was revealed that the Vietnamese foreign minister, Vu Van Mau, had also made it known his preference for a British mission to be sent, the British embassy in Saigon interpreted this as "effectively a vote of no confidence by the Viet Namese [*sic*] Government in MAAG."[14] Even the foreign secretary, Alec Douglas-Home, pressed the case for Thompson's appointment to Rusk personally by telling him that "there is nothing that Thompson doesn't know about counter-insurgency methods."[15] The pressure seemed to work. The Foreign Office was given the nod by Washington to substantiate the plans for a four-man British Advisory Mission to Vietnam. It was envisaged that the task of BRIAM would be to establish "close contacts with the Vietnamese Government and to advise and assist them over the whole counter-insurgency field."[16] Thompson himself saw his remit a little more specifically to include advising on "intelligence, police, surrender policy . . . and strategic hamlets."[17] Thompson handpicked a small team of people with direct experience of either the police or civil service during the campaign in Malaya to aid him in this task. This would include Desmond Palmer, Jock Hindmarsh, and Dennis Duncanson.[18] Before arriving in Saigon to formerly start the work of BRIAM in September 1961, Thompson stopped off in Washington for consultations with officials from the State Department, the CIA, General Lemnitzer, and a host of counterinsurgency experts brought in from the RAND Corporation.[19] The Americans were clearly keen to keep Thompson on message.

On the surface it might appear that American acquiescence toward the establishment of BRIAM was an act of alliance solidarity designed to strengthen US-UK relations in the crucial Cold War crucible of Southeast Asia.[20] Yet BRIAM was more the result of British persistence than American proactivity. Indeed, Washington's ambivalence toward a British mission was epitomized by the State Department's decision to devolve all planning for BRIAM's arrival to embassy staff and the MAAG in Saigon.[21] BRIAM was kept decidedly out of the loop. Even Kennedy's national security adviser, McGeorge Bundy, later admitted that during the early years of the Vietnam War, although he himself did not believe "that there was any major misleading of the British . . . there may have been some delays in informing them."[22]

Upon arriving in Vietnam in September 1961, Thompson and his team immediately embarked on a weeklong tour around the Mekong Delta, a hot spot of Viet Cong violence, as a means of getting "the Americans and South Vietnamese to work out and adopt an overall strategic plan of campaign."[23] His subsequent report, titled "Appreciation of Vietnam," became known simply as the Delta Plan.[24] It represented Thompson's blueprint for avoiding the deployment of ground troops in Vietnam and involved plans for changes to the civil-military command structure and an expansion of the strategic hamlet program that forcibly relocated villages vulnerable to Viet Cong influence.[25] For British officials, the Delta Plan represented a Malaya-style road map for counterinsurgency success, and the Foreign Office duly passed Thompson's report on to Washington.[26] The new British ambassador to Vietnam, Harry Hohler, felt the flushes of "a 'special relationship' . . . developing here between the Americans and ourselves . . . based on growing confidence and arising from direct co-operation in a common enterprise."[27] But for key American officials, BRIAM was already seriously overstepping the mark. Frederick Nolting, the American ambassador in Saigon, telegrammed the State Department to report that he felt that the "Thompson Mission is badly off rails from standpoint US-UK coordination [*sic*]." He detailed what he perceived to be the "procedural and substantive" difficulties caused by BRIAM's activities, including Thompson's habit of unilaterally advising President Diem without consulting the Americans first.[28] Serious Anglo-American tensions over Vietnam were already present at the creation of BRIAM.

But for all the resentment that BRIAM was stoking in some corners of Washington and Saigon, there were some within the Kennedy administration who not only appreciated Thompson's ideas but used them to mold their own thinking. One such person was Roger Hilsman, the State Department's director of the Bureau of Intelligence and Research. In presenting his "Strategic Concept for South Vietnam" plan at the request of the president in February 1962, Hilsman acknowledged his indebtedness to Thompson's calls for a combined focus on civil-military and socio-economic measures.[29] Soon after Hilsman's plan crossed Kennedy's desk, Thompson himself was called to Washington to take part in discussions with the president's Task Force on Vietnam. Thompson was blunt with his hosts. He felt it would take three to six years to defeat the Viet Cong and revealed his discomfort that "the numbers of Americans in SVN [South Vietnam] is growing too large" and that this would be exploited by insurgents who would inevitably depict the Americans as neocolonialists.[30] Other Thompson-inspired ideas began to percolate through some agencies involved with the war. In May 1962, the United States Information Service ran a competition for its staff, with a $50 prize for the person who could "coin a new phrase which would describe the communists as foreign puppets," because Thompson felt that "there should be a new name for the Viet Cong" as reference to the term "Viet" implied some form of legitimacy.[31]

Although the newly established MACV decided to share its weekly intelligence reports with BRIAM in July 1962, Anglo-American friction in Vietnam was rife.[32] One of the main areas of contention was the issue of where to target "pacification programs." Thompson had argued that the priority should be areas of low Viet Cong infiltration and spread out from there. Conversely, the Americans, Thompson recalled, "of course preferred to tackle the toughest areas first and were impatient for action and results."[33] Thompson felt protective of his recommendations for changes to the Strategic Hamlet Program. Although the concept was not his (indeed, population relocation programs had been used by the British in Malaya with the creation of so-called New Villages and implemented in Vietnam before Thompson's arrival as part of the Rural Community Development Program), Thompson felt that the Strategic Hamlet Program was "haphazard" and needed to be transformed into something more "organised and directed."[34] One member of Thompson's BRIAM team, Dennis Duncanson, felt that observations tracing the American Strategic Hamlet Program to the British New Villages implemented in the 1950s in Malaya were "misread." In fact, Duncanson argued, they were deliberately designed to cynically secure British "moral support" for the program (and, thus, potentially a scapegoat should it go wrong).[35]

Regardless of BRIAM's use to the Kennedy administration's war effort, it was demonstrating a certain utility to London, not least of which was its use as a fig leaf to hide British reluctance to provide large amounts of direct military support. Foreign Secretary Alec Douglas-Home gave the game away in a letter to the Treasury in February 1963 requesting that BRIAM's funding be extended. Clearly pleased with the "respect and influence" that Thompson had in Washington, Douglas-Home went on to state how BRIAM's existence was important "in relieving us from American pressure to contribute in more expensive ways to the assistance of Vietnam."[36] But Washington was wise to London's game. Over a year earlier, the Vietnam Task Force had concluded that the British were "very circumspect about supplying military aid" and concluded that "a 'hard sell' is likely to be needed at a high level" to get the British on board.[37] Such efforts would intensify significantly under President Johnson, but to no avail.

By the spring of 1963, Robert Thompson was brimming with optimism. He reported back to London in March that year that the Vietnamese government "is beginning to win the shooting war against the Vietcong." His secret memo chronicled the improvements to the Strategic Hamlet Program that had allowed, in his opinion, the government to regain the initiative. This memo is instructive not just as a glimpse into the buoyant confidence that Thompson had regarding the war effort but also for the way in which he ended the memo with a strategic maxim that would not look out of place in debates about counterinsurgency wars half a century later: "If we plan for a long haul we may get quick results. If we go for quick results, we may at best get a long haul."[38] Regardless of the results he achieved, Thompson was nothing if not eminently quotable. Sound bites about counterinsurgency remain his legacy.[39]

A month after sending this memo to London, Thompson was given the opportunity to present his interpretation of events to the key players in Washington. He met with Averell Harriman—a man Thompson later described as having a "baleful influence on the war" and being "one of the architects of his country's defeat"[40]—just days before Harriman took over as chairman of the president's Special Group for Counterinsurgency. That same week in early April 1963, Thompson was summoned to the White House for a meeting with Kennedy himself, followed by an invitation to become the first Briton to attend a meeting of the NSC, where he participated in discussions on policy and strategy in Vietnam—in a clear sign of how highly his experience and judgment were valued in Washington.[41] Touching on the same theme of political stability in Vietnam he had raised with Harriman, Thompson warned Kennedy that "if Diem disappeared there would be a risk of losing the war within six months since there was no other leader of his caliber available."[42] Seven months later

Kennedy would disregard this advice and agree to the removal of Diem. In a few more prescient comments to the president, Thompson also warned Kennedy not to use chemical defoliants (as it would create "automatic aversion" among the Vietnamese population) and to carefully consider the use of tactical air power ("Thompson was dead against strafing and bombing occupied villages as this would leave an indissoluble legacy of bitterness").[43] But on the whole, Thompson painted Kennedy what would become a stock picture of optimism pertaining to the long-term landscape of the American war effort. On a personal note Thompson revealed that after his meeting with the president he found Kennedy to be "a great disappointment," striking him as "a bit of a dilettante and not nearly hard-headed enough."[44] Clearly unaware of how Thompson felt about him, Kennedy continued to show his faith in his British counterinsurgency mentor. He asked Bundy to pass on a request to British ambassador David Ormsby-Gore in September 1963 that all reports by Thompson for BRIAM be passed to Washington because of "how much weight the President attached to Mr Thompson's views" and a residual skepticism about the nature of American intelligence reports coming out of Vietnam.[45] Subsequently aware that his reports would get attention at the highest level in Washington, Thompson changed his tone by the autumn of 1963 to one that was more guarded. Although citing decent progress across some security areas, the BRIAM chief wrote in his next major report in October 1963 that "we must expect a vastly increased Vietcong activity" as the Strategic Hamlet Program was being further rolled out across the country. Despite forecasting "a decisive military improvement in twelve months and certainly within two years," Thompson closed this report with a summation clearly crafted to catch the president's eye and steel his resolve: "We have got to face the reality that we are in for a protracted war. . . . The stakes are far too high for the West to baulk at the cost in time, money or effort. . . . The holding of Vietnam will, in my view, be vital both physically, politically and psychologically to our global strategy against communism (and especially China) over the rest of this century."[46]

However, this report was not sent to President Kennedy by the Foreign Office. Officially Thompson was told that this was because US defense secretary Robert McNamara and chairman of the Joint Chiefs of Staff Gen. Maxwell Taylor had in the meantime visited Vietnam and produced their own report for Kennedy. Yet the inclusion in the archival files of a briefing note outlining fundamental differences of opinion between Thompson and the British ambassador to Vietnam, Gordon Etherington-Smith, regarding the prognosis for the war effort (the former more optimistic, the latter much more pessimistic) at the very least implies that the British were using the McNamara/Taylor report as a fig leaf to hide deep divisions within the British diplomatic contingent on the ground in Vietnam.[47]

John F. Kennedy's assassination in Dallas in November 1963 marked the end of British hopes at having a direct line of influence over American policy in Vietnam.

Indeed, the entirety of 1963 had signaled changes to the British perception of the Vietnam War. London's attention in Southeast Asia was diverted back to its old colony Malaysia, which had become engaged in an undeclared war (the "Konfrontasi") with Indonesia.[48] All the time, London and the BRIAM members had become increasingly disillusioned, first with Washington's handling of the "Buddhist crisis" and then by the decision to back Diem just before tacitly endorsing the fatal coup against him.[49] Thompson had become frustrated with the American military briefings he attended in Saigon, feeling that they presented "a worthless indication of the situation" because of the reliance on "bare statistical facts" and the absence of a qualitative appreciation of the situation.[50] This would not be the last time in a counterinsurgency war that a key British liaison figure would express bafflement and frustration at US military briefings.

Thompson's disillusionment with the American military evolved into a pervasive pessimism about the whole war effort in his reports to Washington. In a memo to McNamara in March 1964, all signs of Thompson's optimism from the year before had diminished considerably, as he warned the defense secretary that the "prospects of winning the war in South Vietnam outright are now gloomy."[51] By August it was clear to the BRIAM chief that, since the beginning of 1964, his advice "has been far more directed towards the Americans" than toward the Vietnamese who were supposed to be the main recipients of his counsel.[52] Despite some suggestions that Thompson became an informal member of the NSC team working on Vietnam policy (made so by the NSC's Michael Forrestal in February 1964[53]) or that he become a fully integrated member of Gen. William Westmoreland's command in Saigon (made so by the secretary of state's special assistant for Vietnam, William Sullivan, in May 1964[54]), Thompson began the process of winding BRIAM down. He himself admitted that the mission had been relegated to the position of "an observer and commentator." As far as the counterinsurgency campaign was concerned, Thompson felt that "the mission's work has been more or less completed and we are now largely under-employed."[55] The Foreign Office was in agreement, noting to the British embassy in Saigon that "it seems clear that BRIAM must be disbanded about next April. . . . [I]ts usefulness has come to an end."[56]

It was also clear to the State Department in mid-1964 that BRIAM was being routinely ignored by US military commanders in Vietnam. William Sullivan noted how the US Mission in Saigon was keeping Thompson at arm's length and urged presidential intervention to remind commanders of the value of British advice.[57] In his comparative study of Anglo-American counterinsurgency cultures in Malaya and Vietnam, John Nagl argued that we should not be surprised by the way in which BRIAM was ignored by US military leaders because of what he cites as the pervasive American "organizational culture that accepted military victory through annihilation as the only way to win a war."[58] Thompson's nuanced and patient view of counterinsurgency clashed with an American military organizational culture that valued swift victory and kinetic solutions to most problems. The war in Vietnam was the first opportunity in the post–Second World War period for the British to observe American counterinsurgency doctrine up close. It revealed a stark gulf in culture, theory, and practice. Political approaches to the war were no closer, as the tense relationship between Lyndon Johnson and Harold Wilson revealed.

The Special Relationship under Strain: Johnson, Wilson, and Vietnam

Lyndon Johnson initially showed dismay at rumors that London was shutting down BRIAM, feeling it would "have a most unfortunate effect" on the war effort.[59] But, as with most of Johnson's dealings with the British over Vietnam, his concern was primarily for maintaining the veneer of multilateralism in wrestling the initiative away from the communists in Southeast Asia. To make things more complicated for Johnson, he had to deal with the new British prime minister, Harold Wilson, who had entered Number 10 Downing Street in October 1964 by the narrowest of margins (the Labour Party having secured just a four-seat parliamentary majority in the general election). Wilson, like Johnson, prided himself on being plainspoken and independent-minded. But whereas Johnson saw Britain merely as one of many allies, Wilson and key members of his foreign and defense policy team, such as Michael Stewart and Patrick Gordon Walker, were Atlanticists with a commitment to making strong Anglo-American relations the foundation of British security.[60] Wilson was motivated by a desire to act as an international peace broker, and one of his most significant early decisions regarding Vietnam was to reignite Britain's role as cochair of the Geneva Accords, signed in 1954, which monitored the division between North and South Vietnam after the withdrawal of French colonial power. This was a means of ensuring both a diplomatic solution to the escalating conflict and a way of avoiding committing British troops to the American war effort without seeming detached from events in Southeast Asia. Compounding things further was the way Johnson's rigidly hierarchical manner of dealing with problems (with himself firmly ensconced at the top), clashed with Wilson's desire to bring a greater level of informality to US-UK relations through more frequent one-to-one conversations between president and prime minister as a means of leveraging greater influence in Washington.[61]

It was with this aim in mind that Wilson crossed the Atlantic in December 1964 to meet Johnson in his first American trip as prime minister. The war in Vietnam was to be one of the major talking points. In advance of Wilson's arrival, National Security Adviser McGeorge Bundy felt compelled to temper President Johnson's expectations of just how much support he could expect from the new British leader. Acknowledging the precarious domestic political situation

Wilson was in and the weight of British public opinion, Bundy offered a realistic analysis of the alliance:

> I think you should know that the British will find it very, very difficult indeed to increase their commitment in Vietnam right now. . . . There is no political base whatever in England, in any party, for an increased British commitment in Vietnam now. For 10 years we have accepted a situation in which the British give political support, but avoid any major commitment on the ground. . . . The most Wilson could possibly do at this stage would be a slight enlargement of the Thompson advisory mission. . . . All this he would have to do quietly.[62]

The meeting itself took place on December 8 and saw the British delegation mouth platitudes about offering support, knowing full well that the exact opposite of Bundy's hope of an enlarged BRIAM was being implemented. Foreign Secretary Patrick Gordon Walker assured President Johnson that "the British wanted to help the US in ways that could be publicized—training Vietnamese troops in jungle warfare, providing medics, putting police in Saigon." Yet Walker did go out of his way to caution the Americans against using disproportionate military force, urging "the importance of keeping retaliatory action related to things retaliated against."[63] It would be Wilson's repetition of this theme in 1965 that caused one of the greatest ructions in Anglo-American relations during the entire war.

In advance of another trip to Washington in February 1965, the Foreign Office cautioned Wilson about the potential damage to relations between London and Washington if it was seen that the British were wading into the Vietnam debate with the "cold detachment" of an "outsider." The brief warned the prime minister that until the Johnson administration had undertaken their own strategic review, "we could do grave harm to Anglo-American relations by rushing in with unpalatable proposals."[64] With a large dose of irony, only two days after receiving this memo Wilson made a telephone call to Johnson in the early hours of the morning that would achieve everything the Foreign Office had warned him against.

A Viet Cong attack on the American military barracks at Qui Nhon on February 10 that resulted in the deaths of thirty US service personnel seemed to indicate an escalation of the conflict. In London, Wilson found himself afraid that Johnson would retaliate disproportionately, in breach of the advice he had offered at their meeting back in December. Fraught with worry and unable to sleep, Wilson insisted on phoning Johnson at three o'clock in the morning, London time, on February 11 to convince Johnson to allow him to fly to Washington immediately to calm the situation. The transcript of the phone conversation is worth quoting at length as it tells its own story not only about the personal relationship between the two leaders but also about the American disdain for perceived British interference:

> P.M [*sic*; Prime Minister Wilson]: The feeling is that I should come over as quickly as possible.
>
> Johnson: That would be a serious mistake.... I would not get upset. Keep a normal pulse and I would wait until I was called upon to do something and consider it on the merits.... If one of us jumps across the Atlantic every time there is a critical situation, next week I shall be flying over when Sukarno [President of Indonesia] jumps on you [in Malaysia] and I will be giving you advice.
>
> P.M: We do not want to dash over. We just want to talk.
>
> Johnson: We have telephones!... As far as my problem in Vietnam we have asked everyone to share it with us. *They were willing to share advice but not responsibility*. Let me send you the exact situation as I view it on classified cable....
>
> P.M: I cannot show it to the House of Commons, that is my trouble.
>
> Johnson: You would not want to use me as an instrument to deal with the House of Commons.... I won't tell you how to run Malaysia and you don't tell us how to run Vietnam.... If you want to help us in Vietnam send us some men and send us some folks to deal with these guerrillas....
>
> P.M: All I want to do is to reassure the House of Commons. Do you think I can do this on the basis of a trans-atlantic call in the middle of the night?
>
> Johnson: You were the one who placed the call.
>
> P.M: I have got to be able to tell them.
>
> Johnson: You needn't say it was the middle of the night.[65]

Ultimately, Johnson's obstinacy in the face of Wilson's eagerness meant that the prime minister had to settle for the phone call as reassurance, along with a memorandum outlining the situation to be sent to London along with Ambassador David Bruce the following week. This one conversation encapsulates the utter absence of any feelings of "specialness" toward the British on behalf of Johnson. Wilson later claimed in his memoirs that he felt compelled to make this middle-of-the-night phone call because "I feared his patience might falter and that he would give way to the hawks. . . . I felt that this was a time for a personal discussion with him to remind him of the attitude his friends, and indeed the rest of the world, might take if he were provoked too far."[66] His attempt to depict himself as a dovish, calming influence on Johnson did not go down well in Washington. Walt Rostow phoned John Killick, the head of chancery at the British embassy in Washington, to pass on a vivid account of Johnson's reaction once he had hung up on the call from Wilson: "He said we got enough pollution around here already without Harold coming over with his fly open and his pecker hanging out, peeing all over me."[67]

Johnson took some succor off former President Eisenhower when the two met a week after the phone call. Eisenhower placated Johnson by reminding him that Wilson "has not had much experience with this kind of problem" and dismissed British suggestions that negotiations with the North Vietnamese needed to happen, by adding that his answer to the British would be "Not now boys."[68] Bundy echoed Eisenhower's caution, telling the president that "we can always get to the conference table when we need to, and that there is no great hurry about it right now"—although he did add in parentheses that "Dean Rusk agrees, though he wants to keep the British happy enough to hold them aboard."[69]

Back in London, disillusionment with the direction of the American counterinsurgency effort was intensifying. The new foreign secretary, Michael Stewart, did not take long to inform Wilson of his damning personal perception of the war. He wrote to the prime minister in March 1965, asserting that "the Americans are in a hopeless position in South Vietnam." He described Johnson as a "bear with a sore head" whenever he comes to explain to the British his war aims, leading Stewart to conclude that "the Americans cannot win." Tellingly, Wilson scribbled "Yes, I very much agree" on the top of his copy of the memo.[70] Wilson's despondency carried over into a meeting soon afterward with American ambassador David Bruce, where he informed Bruce that the British could not afford to support an escalation in the American war effort because it would place "their most loyal ally . . . in an intolerable position" of having to be "hearing stories about satellites and the 51st state."[71] Wilson was starting to see the special relationship as a liability to Britain and bear grave concerns about perceptions of slavishness should the United Kingdom offer unconditional support to the Americans in Vietnam. Wilson told Stewart he refused to let Britain be seen as "the tail-end Charlie in an American bomber [over Vietnam]."[72] One way that Wilson intended to put some distance between British and American approaches to the war was to turn the heat up on Washington to enter talks with North Vietnam. This did not go unnoticed in Washington, but Bundy dismissed Wilson's suggestion as the product of "a lot of yammering."[73] With memories still fresh of Wilson's "outrageous phone call," Bundy was unwilling to do anything to ease Wilson's difficulties on the domestic political front that the Vietnam War was causing him. Perhaps hitting on a truism of the special relationship at large, Bundy concluded that "when we fall out with Prime Ministers it's usually painted as our fault."[74]

Johnson's fiery Texan temperament ensured that he did not take well to criticism of his conduct of the war. David Bruce noted in his diary how the president described himself as "get[ting] all hunkered up like a jackass in a hailstorm" when people he thought less well informed on the details sought to offer advice."[75] Wilson had given Johnson plenty of jackass moments. But by mid-1965, the White House's stance on Britain began to shift. Bundy in particular started to soften the president's perception of Britain by pressing on him just how "every experienced observer from David Bruce on down has been astonished by the overall strength and skill of Wilson's defense of our policy in Vietnam. . . . The support of the UK has been of real value internationally—*and perhaps of even more value in limiting the howls of our own Liberals*."[76] Bundy had come to acknowledge how the purported value of the special relationship could be played up to fulfill domestic political purposes. If the left-wing leader of America's closest ally was seen to be supporting the war, then Johnson's problematic liberal flank within his own party would look increasingly isolated. Bundy therefore advised Johnson to hug Wilson closer in order to reap some domestic political benefit, noting that "the only price we have paid for this support is the price of keeping them *reasonably* well informed and fending off one ill-advised plan for travel. . . . [I]t is well worth our while to keep the British on board as long as it can be done simply by keeping them fully informed *and giving them the feeling that they are in the know as we go ahead*."[77] This last line is revealing inasmuch as it demonstrates Bundy's willingness to only foster the illusion of diplomatic intimacy and play on the inevitable British fawning over any inkling of influence.

The summer of 1965 provided a string of British-induced hailstorms to rile the jackass in Johnson. It started in June when Wilson hatched an idea that would see Britain head a four-member Commonwealth mission (consisting also of Ghana, Nigeria, and Trinidad and Tobago) to act as an intermediary between the principle warring factions in Vietnam. Johnson expressed "considerable concern" at this proposal and "said he saw no point" in what would inevitably "achieve little in the interest of peace, and might turn out to be a further embarrassment to the United States foreign policy."[78] The final installment came in July when Wilson initiated another diplomatic intervention, this time spearheaded by the relatively unknown junior minister Harold Davies, who was sent to Hanoi as a "special envoy." Davies had met with North Vietnamese leader Ho Chi Minh eight years previously and had maintained links with his regime ever since. Unlike the Commonwealth mission idea, the Davies mission received American backing for the Foreign Ministry to conduct talks with middle-ranking North Vietnamese officials. But two days of talks, with access to ministers blocked, produced no breakthrough, due to insurmountable differences between North Vietnamese perceptions of intrinsic British pro-Americanism and British perceptions of Hanoi's fundamental ideological intransigence. Frustrated, Davies left Hanoi and returned to Britain to cross-party and media criticism of his failed mission.[79] By the end of the year, Bundy was vowing to "spike his [Wilson's] guns" amid rumors the prime minister had "some new Vietnam gambit up his sleeve" ahead of a trip to Washington in December.[80] The only real ally the British government had in Johnson's inner circle appeared to be Secretary of State Dean Rusk, who championed Wilson to the president, describing the prime minister as "a paragon of courage," especially when compared to other supposed allies who were "doing nothing." Unmoved, Johnson witheringly demolished Rusk's glowing character sketch of Wilson's courage: "He wants a DSC [Distinguished Service Cross] for fending off his enemies in Parliament."[81] For Johnson, real political courage necessitated sending British troops in to Vietnam alongside the Americans.

This was one step Wilson would not take. But it did not stop Johnson from persisting. He wrote to Downing Street in June 1966: "I deeply hope that you will find a way to maintain solidarity with us on Vietnam."[82] Wilson seemed unwilling. Later that month the prime minister disassociated himself from the American decision to bomb gasoline and oil storage depots around Hanoi and Haiphong, causing considerable damage.[83] White House concerns at the lack of overt British support clearly still rankled as the year drew to a close. Johnson conveyed to his new national security adviser, Walt Rostow, that the State Department should take a "tough line on the British and European position with respect to Vietnam." Recalling Wilson's threat to "disassociate" himself from the United States should it escalate the war, Johnson simultaneously lamented and threatened: "It is unfortunate that the concept of disassociation has been introduced to the vocabulary of the Alliance. It is a concept that can cut both ways."[84]

Wilson's attempt to depict Britain as a self-appointed honest broker over Vietnam, especially through efforts to bring the Americans and Soviets together as a way of de-escalating the war, was severely undermined by an admission from Washington in January 1967 that for the past six months the Johnson administration had been using representatives of the Polish government to open back channels with the North Vietnamese government in a set of secret talks codenamed "Marigold."[85] When the Marigold Talks were exposed, Downing Street hauled in the US ambassador David Bruce so that Wilson could express how "disturbed" he was. The prime minister's anger was compounded by the way in which the British had found out about the talks only after "the Foreign Secretary was 'put into bat' in Moscow without a complete knowledge." Wilson went on to tell Bruce that the Marigold episode "raised a major issue of confidence in relations between the Foreign Secretary and himself and the President and Mr Rusk."[86] Wilson drafted a long telegram to Johnson outlining how "seriously concerned" he was at the "equivocal position" the Marigold Talks had put Britain in.[87] Yet Wilson did not send this message, instead opting for a short telegram that encouraged Johnson to talk to Bruce about their recent meeting in order to get a sense of the damage of trust that Wilson felt was "pretty fundamental to our relationship."[88] By way of explanation, Chester Cooper, a senior CIA liaison officer, was sent to London to meet with Wilson to offer the British "the fullest possible briefing on every aspect of the Vietnam situation and United States Government policy toward Vietnam." Cooper explained to the prime minister that one of the reasons why Washington had kept London in the dark with regard to the Marigold Talks was that President Johnson "was in a 'psychotic' state about leaks. . . . [T]his is why there had been a total 'clamp down' on security about the exchanges."[89]

This setback to the state of Anglo-American relations was the background against which Wilson tried to organize a renewed round of diplomatic talks. In contrast to the Marigold Talks, which had seen Britain remain out of the loop, Wilson ensured London would host the next set of talks between the Soviets and the Americans in what would come to be known as the Sunflower Talks. The Soviet premier, Alexei Kosygin, flew to London for a week of talks in February 1967. Chester Cooper remained in London after his attempts to defuse the fallout from the Marigold Talks a few weeks earlier. Discussions focused on persuading the North Vietnamese to pull back their forces and the Americans to instigate a bombing pause. But the Sunflower Talks ultimately failed, hinging around some American tinkering with a draft resolution that choreographed the timing of halts to American bombing with North Vietnamese de-escalation (the so-called Phase A–Phase B sections of the proposal). It became clear that the Americans refused to hold back the bombers until they had seen tangible signs of North Vietnamese military withdrawals. Johnson later admitted that the rewording of the resolution was "a diplomatic mix-up for which we shared a certain amount of responsibility" yet defended the action by arguing that he "refused to risk the safety of our men . . . by stopping air strikes before Ho Chi Minh had acted."[90] The talks therefore ended amid suspicion, resentment, and mistrust between London, Washington, Moscow, and Hanoi. "Kosygin Week" ended with little more than mutual recriminations between Downing Street and the White House.[91] It would act as a fitting epitaph to Anglo-American relations over the Vietnam War during the Johnson presidency. Relations would improve only marginally under Nixon, and that was due only to the return to prominence of Robert Thompson.

Nixon, Thompson, and the End of the Vietnam War

After the disbanding of BRIAM in March 1965, Robert Thompson had found himself frozen out of the White House inner circle. His sense of influence over the Kennedy administration had evaporated under Johnson. But, by 1968, Johnson had danced his last waltz with "that bitch Vietnam." He decided not to run for reelection, and, after Vice President Hubert Humphrey was defeated, the presidency passed from the exhausted Johnson to the mercurial Richard Nixon. Thompson held the new president in high regard. Indeed, it was somewhat of a Mutual Appreciation Society. Nixon had read Thompson's book *No Exit from Vietnam* and asked his aides to set up a meeting with the former BRIAM head in October 1969. In their meeting Thompson found that Nixon's "grasp of practical foreign affairs was impressive. He was always well briefed and a realist." But perhaps his most admirable quality, Thompson approvingly asserted, was that "he was not tempted by the soft option."[92] They shared a similar strategic vision, and the president appreciated his adviser's independent counsel that mainly advocated the need for strategic patience.[93] In this first meeting between the two men, Thompson stuck to his line that nothing less than the future of Western civilization was at stake in the outcome of the Vietnam War. After hearing Thompson voice support for increasing levels of "Vietnamization" (a pet project of Nixon's that would see an increased combat role for the South Vietnamese as a prelude to American withdrawal), the president asked that Thompson return to Vietnam as a personal envoy and compile a situation report. On this trip, Thompson was given the equivalent civilian status of a four-star general, with all the resources of Gen. Creighton Abrams, the US commander, at his disposal.[94] Thompson's eventual report in November 1969 was cautiously optimistic about the progress made by the US military and intrinsic weaknesses of the Viet Cong. He informed Nixon that US victory could be achieved "within two years . . . either in the sense of an accepted negotiated settlement or of having prepared the South Vietnamese to carry out the burden of the fighting on their own."[95]

A change of American president had clearly altered Thompson's outlook on the war. Gone was his creeping pessimism during the later BRIAM years as his outward confidence from the Kennedy years returned in his work for Nixon. This did not go unnoticed by the razor-sharp Henry Kissinger, Nixon's national security adviser. He felt that the upbeat tone of Thompson's 1969 report ran contrary to the view expressed in the Vietnam Special Studies Group within the NSC.[96] But the president had clearly decided what sort of views he wanted to heed regarding the war. Nixon therefore sent Thompson on another mission to Vietnam in 1970, after which he exclaimed that "pacification and Vietnamization as programs were now unassailable."[97] Another fact-finding trip in 1971 saw Thompson head up a small British team to investigate the problems within the South Vietnamese police force. Surrounded by ex-colonial police commissioners, including Bill Carbonell and Richard Catling, Thompson spent two months touring the country, making recommendations for changes to force structure and operating procedures.[98] Nixon and Thompson were becoming kindred spirits. The president asked that Thompson become his personal representative on a tour of Southeast Asian capital cities in July 1972, with Nixon wanting his trusted adviser to gauge the regional temperature of support for a peace initiative in

Vietnam.[99] When Kissinger pushed these peace efforts forward, Thompson detected ulterior motives, admitting later that he "did not realise the extent to which Henry would be prepared to go to satisfy dissent in the run-up to the election."[100] Securing Nixon a second term in the White House took precedence. For this reason, it is perhaps that Thompson's advice never truly shaped the Nixon administration's efforts to wind down the Vietnam War. His "stick the course" approach rubbed against the more impatient desires of Kissinger in particular to change course and seek a voter-friendly "peace with honor."[101] This is perhaps a fitting way to assess the totality of British efforts to influence the direction of American counterinsurgency efforts in Vietnam—lots of talk, but with no one really listening.

Conclusion

The Vietnam War inverted many preconceptions about the dynamic of the special relationship. Although providing an advisory mission, London expended a significant amount of effort, especially under the Wilson government, trying to simultaneously distance itself from greater involvement in Vietnam while offering itself as a conduit for diplomatic discussions. The British were also not averse to providing indirect assistance via the provision of intelligence material on communist activity, mainly via its Government Communications Headquarters (GCHQ) signals intelligence outposts scattered across Southeast Asia.[102] But the squeeze placed on Wilson by economic problems on home, by an incredibly slim parliamentary majority, and by Britain's own interests in Asia meant that Britain could not afford to play up to notions of a special relationship with the United States.[103] This outcome is of particular importance considering how during Britain's own counterinsurgency wars over the previous two decades London had harbored a sense of grievance at American abuse of the special relationship. Now it was the Americans as the counterinsurgents trying to juggle complex civil-military pressures on the ground with national, regional, and international politics, and it was London's turn to start stepping away from notions of specialness.

The work of BRIAM had minimal effect on American policy, even if Thompson's counterinsurgency wisdom was absorbed by key members of the Kennedy administration. This, though, was the extent of British influence over the United States in the Vietnam War.[104] Although there was no serious pressure put on Downing Street to authorize the deployment of British troops to Vietnam, Lyndon Johnson did subsequently admit that "the British government's general approach to the war and to finding a peaceful solution would have been considerably different if a brigade of Her Majesty's forces had been stationed just south of the demilitarized zone in Vietnam."[105] Undoubtedly even Johnson, once his anger had subsided at Britain's lack of troop involvement, would have acknowledged that a brigade of British soldiers could not have pulled victory from the jaws of defeat for the Americans in Vietnam. The problems ran far deeper and wider than the simple presence of more allied forces on the ground. The massive groundswell of opposition to the war within the United States became insurmountable. Thompson's time spent with Nixon had clearly rubbed off by the time Thompson declared in his memoirs that domestic opponents of the war were the ultimate cause of American defeat. The major lesson Thompson took from the Vietnam War thus became "Do not rely on the United States as an ally. It is its own worst enemy."[106] Such words needed heeding over another counterinsurgency war that had flared up at the same time as Vietnam's degeneration into a quagmire. This time it was on British soil.

Notes

Epigraphs: "Secret and Guard: Letter from Gordon Etherington-Smith to J. I. McGlue," July 3, 1961, The National Archives, UK (hereafter TNA), FO 371/160157.

"Secret: Background Brief—Prime Minister's Visit to Washington," February 9, 1965, TNA, FO 371/180539.

1. Steininger, "'Americans Are in Hopeless Position,'" 237–85; and McAllister and Schulte, "Limits of Influence in Vietnam," 22–43.
2. Vickers, "Harold Wilson, the British Labour Party," 41–70.
3. For a comprehensive narrative of the growth of the American presence in Vietnam from the end of French rule to the Kennedy era, see chapters 5, 6, and 7 of Karnow, *Vietnam*.
4. "South Vietnam: Un-numbered Briefing Document," February 14, 1961, TNA, FO 371/159673.
5. "Memorandum of a Conversation, Department of State, Washington," February 21, 1961, document #13, in *Foreign Relations of the United States* (hereafter *FRUS*), *1961–63, Vol. 1*, 36.
6. "Secret Cypher: From Saigon to Foreign Office," February 28, 1961, TNA, FO 371/160108.
7. "Letter from Tunku Abdul Rahman Putra to Duncan Sandys," April 19, 1961, TNA DO 169/109.
8. "Secret Cypher: From Washington to Foreign Office," April 29, 1961, TNA, DO 169/109.
9. "Secret Cypher: From Foreign Office to Washington," May 1, 1961, TNA, DO 169/109.
10. "Secret Cypher: From Washington to Foreign Office," May 2, 1961, TNA, DO 169/109.
11. "Secret Intel: From Foreign Office to Certain of Her Majesty's Representatives," May 15, 1961, TNA, DO 169/109.

12. "Draft Memorandum of the Conversation of the Second Meeting of the Presidential Task Force on Vietnam, the Pentagon," May 4, 1961, document #43, in *FRUS, 1961–63, Vol. 1*, 122.
13. "Telegram from the Chief of the Military Assistance Advisory Group in Vietnam (McGarr) to the Chairman of the Joint Chiefs of Staff (Lemnitzer), Saigon," June 7, 1961, document #66, in *FRUS, 1961–63, Vol. 1*, 166–67.
14. "Secret Cypher: From Saigon to Foreign Office," May 30, 1961, TNA, DO 169/109.
15. "Memorandum of Conversation, Quai d'Orsay, Paris," August 7, 1961, document #115, in *FRUS, 1961–63, Vol. 1*, 268.
16. "Secret Memorandum: United Kingdom Assistance to South Vietnam—Proposals by the Foreign Office," n.d., TNA, DO 169/109.
17. Thompson, *Make for the Hills*, 127.
18. Ibid., 123.
19. Ibid., 124.
20. Varsori, "Britain and US Involvement," 104.
21. Busch, *All the Way with JFK?*, 84.
22. McGeorge Bundy, oral history interview #3, John F. Kennedy Presidential Library Digital Oral History Program, http://archive2.jfklibrary.org/JFKOH/Bundy,%20McGeorge/JFKOH-MGB-03/JFKOH-MGB-03-TR.pdf.
23. Thompson, *Make for the Hills*, 129.
24. A copy of this report is replicated in document #51, "Draft Paper by the Head of the British Advisory Mission in Vietnam (Thompson)," in *FRUS, 1961–63, Vol. 2*, 102–9.
25. Busch, *All the Way with JFK?*, 97–98.
26. "Secret: From Saigon to Foreign Office," November 9, 1961; "Secret: From Foreign Office to Washington," November 9, 1961, TNA, PREM 11/3736.
27. "Secret and Guard: Letter from British Embassy, Saigon, to Lord Home," January 16, 1962, TNA, FO 371/166717.
28. "Telegram from the Embassy in Vietnam to the Department of State, Saigon," November 30, 1961, document #299, in *FRUS, 1961–63, Vol. 1*, 698–99.
29. "Paper Prepared by the Director of the Bureau of Intelligence and Research (Hilsman)," February 2, 1962, document #42, in *FRUS, 1961–63, Vol. 2*, 82n3. Douglas Blaufarb in his book *The Counterinsurgency Era* noted how Hilsman's plan "leaned heavily on the British approach" in Malaya (p. 108). Interestingly, Hilsman served as an Office of Strategic Services guerrilla leader during World War II in Burma where he acted as liaison to the British forces there. That experience certainly shaped his thinking toward the British military. See his memoir, *American Guerrilla*, for further details. I am grateful to Don McKeon for bringing this to my attention.
30. "Memorandum from the Naval Aide to the President's Military Representative (Bagley) to the President's Military Representative (Taylor), Washington," April 5, 1962, document #147, in *FRUS, 1961–63, Vol. 2*, 307–8; and "Memorandum from

Director of the Vietnam Task Force (Cottrell) to the Assistant Secretary of State for Far Eastern Affairs (Harriman)," April 6, 1962, document #149, in *FRUS, 1961–63, Vol. 2*, 310–15.

31. "Minutes of a Staff Meeting, United States Information Service, Saigon," May 2, 1962, document #179, in *FRUS, 1961–63, Vol. 2*, 371.
32. Busch, *All the Way with JFK?*, 126.
33. Thompson, *Make for the Hills*, 129.
34. Ibid., 129–30.
35. Duncanson, *Government and Revolution*, 314; and Blaufarb, *Counterinsurgency Era*, 104–5.
36. "British Advisory Mission in Vietnam: Minute from Foreign Secretary to Chief Secretary to Treasury," February 25, 1963, TNA, FO 371/170100.
37. "Memorandum from the Director of the Vietnam Task Force (Cottrell) to the Assistant Secretary of State for Far Eastern Affairs (Harriman)," April 27, 1962, document #172, in *FRUS, 1961–63, Vol. 2*, 352.
38. "Secret Memorandum: The Situation in South Vietnam," March 11, 1963, TNA, FO 371/170100.
39. Mumford, "Thompson's Lessons for Iraq," 177–94.
40. Thompson, *Make for the Hills*, 132.
41. Ibid., 138.
42. "Memorandum of Conversation, White House, Washington," April 4, 1963, document #77, in *FRUS, 1961–63, Vol. 3*, 198–200.
43. Ibid.
44. Thompson, *Make for the Hills*, 137.
45. "Secret—Guard Cypher: From Washington to Foreign Office," September 18, 1963, TNA, FO 371/170101.
46. "Secret: R. G. K. Thompson to E. H. Peck (Foreign Office)," October 9, 1963, TNA, FO 371/170102.
47. "Secret: Report for President Kennedy by Mr Thompson of BRIAM," October 23, 1963; "Secret: Summary of Differences between Mr R. G. K. Thompson and H. M. Ambassador, Saigon, Concerning the Present Situation in South Vietnam," n.d.; and "Secret and Personal: Letter from E. H. Peck to R. G. K. Thompson," October 24, 1963, TNA, FO 371/170102.
48. For an analysis of the Konfrontasi from the perspective of Anglo-American relations, see Jones, *Conflict and Confrontation in South East Asia*.
49. Busch, *All the Way with JFK?*, 168. The "Buddhist crisis," which occurred from May to November 1963, saw the majority Buddhist population engage in acts of passive resistance in the face of repressive moves by the pro-Catholic regime of Diem (whose assassination brought the crisis to a close).
50. Thompson, *Make for the Hills*, 127.
51. "Memorandum for the United States Secretary of Defence from R. G. K. Thompson," March 9, 1964, TNA, FO 371/175482.

52. "Confidential: Letter from R. G. K. Thompson to E. H. Peck," August 5, 1964, TNA, FO 371/175483.
53. "Memorandum from Michael V. Forrestal of the National Security Council Staff to the Secretary of Defense (McNamara), Washington," February 14, 1964, document #45, in *FRUS, 1964–68, Vol. 1*, 79.
54. "Draft Memorandum for the President, Prepared by the Secretary of State's Special Assistant for Vietnam (Sullivan), Washington," May 24, 1964, document #170, in *FRUS, 1964–68, Vol. 1*, 361.
55. "Confidential: Letter from R. G. K. Thompson to E. H. Peck," August 5, 1964, TNA, FO 371/175483.
56. "Confidential: Foreign Office to R. A. Burrows, Saigon," August 20, 1964, TNA, FO 371/175483.
57. "Memorandum from the Secretary of State's Special Assistant for Vietnam (Sullivan) to the President's Special Assistant for National Security Affairs (Bundy), Washington," June 24, 1964, document #223, in *FRUS, 1964–68, Vol. 1*, 526.
58. Nagl, *Learning to Eat Soup*, 130.
59. "Confidential Cypher: From Saigon to Foreign Office," December 9, 1964, TNA, FO 371/175484.
60. Vickers, "Harold Wilson, the British Labour Party," 46.
61. Dockrill, "Anglo-American Global Defence," 111.
62. "Memorandum from the President's Special Assistant for National Security Affairs (Bundy) to the President, Washington," December 5, 1964, document #438, in *FRUS, 1964–68, Vol. 1*, 981.
63. "Memorandum of a Conversation, White House, Washington," December 8, 1964, document #441, in *FRUS, 1964–68, Vol. 1*, 986.
64. "Secret: Background Brief—Prime Minister's Visit to Washington," February 9, 1965, TNA, FO 371/180539.
65. "Top Secret: Record of a Telephone Conversation between the Prime Minister and President Johnson, on Thursday, February 11 [1965] at 3.15am," TNA, PREM 13/692 (emphasis added). The American transcript can be found in *FRUS, 1964–68, Vol. 2*, document #103, 229–32.
66. Wilson, *Labour Government*, 80.
67. Sir John Killick, interview #69, British Diplomatic Oral History Programme (hereafter BDOHP), Churchill College, Cambridge, https://www.chu.cam.ac.uk/media/uploads/files/Killick.pdf.
68. "Memorandum of Meeting with the President," February 17, 1965, in Barrett, *Lyndon B. Johnson's Vietnam Papers*, 122.
69. "Memorandum to the President from M. Bundy," March 6, 1965, in Barrett, *Lyndon B. Johnson's Vietnam Papers*, 134.
70. "Vietnam: Memo to Prime Minister, 1 March 1965," TNA, PREM 13/693.
71. "Record of a Conversation between the Prime Minister and the United States' Ambassador, Mr David Bruce," March 12, 1965, TNA, PREM 13/693.

72. “Telegram to Washington from the Prime Minister for the Foreign Secretary,” March 23, 1965, TNA, PREM 13/693.
73. “Memorandum from the President’s Special Assistant for National Security Affairs (Bundy) to President Johnson,” March 6, 1965, document #183, in *FRUS, 1964–68, Vol. 2*, 404.
74. “Memorandum from the President’s Special Assistant for National Security Affairs (Bundy) to President Johnson,” March 22, 1965, document #209, in *FRUS, 1964–68, Vol. 2*, 468.
75. “Diary Entry by the Ambassador to the United Kingdom, Washington,” March 23, 1965, document #211, in *FRUS, 1964–68, Vol. 2*, 471.
76. “Memorandum from the President’s Special Assistant for National Security (Bundy) to President Johnson,” June 3, 1965, document #330, in *FRUS, 1964–68, Vol. 2*, 717 (emphasis added).
77. Ibid. (emphasis added).
78. “Memorandum for the Record,” June 23, 1965, document #15, in *FRUS, 1964–68, Vol. 3*, 40.
79. Young, “Wilson Government,” 545–62.
80. “Memorandum from the President’s Assistant for National Security Affairs (Bundy) to President Johnson,” November 27, 1965, document #208, in *FRUS, 1964–68, Vol. 3*, 583.
81. “Notes of a Meeting, Washington,” December 17, 1965, document #231, in *FRUS, 1964–68, Vol. 3*, 644.
82. “Letter to Prime Minister Harold Wilson of Britain, from the President,” June 14, 1966, in Barrett, *Johnson’s Vietnam Papers*, 350–51.
83. Ellis, *Britain, America and the Vietnam War*, 160–79.
84. “Memorandum to Eugene V. Rostow, State Department, from W. Rostow,” November 19, 1966, in Barrett, *Johnson’s Vietnam Papers*, 375.
85. Ellis, *Britain, America and the Vietnam War*, 208. For a thorough discussion of the Marigold Talks, see Hershberg, *Marigold*.
86. “Secret: Record of Conversation between Prime Minister and the United States Ambassador at No.10 Downing Street,” January 10, 1967, TNA, PREM 13/1917.
87. “Secret and Personal: Draft Message to the President from the Prime Minister,” n.d., TNA, PREM 13/1917.
88. “Secret Cypher: Immediate Foreign Office to Washington,” January 12, 1967, TNA, PREM 13/1917.
89. “Top Secret: Record of a Conversation between the Prime Minister and Mr Chester Cooper in the Prime Minister’s Room in the House of Commons,” January 18, 1967, TNA, PREM 13/1917.
90. Johnson, *Vantage Point*, 254.
91. Dumbrell and Ellis, “British Involvement in Vietnam Peace Initiatives,” 129.
92. Thompson, *Make for the Hills*, 158.
93. Fitzgerald, “Thompson, Strategic Patience and Nixon’s War,” 8.

94. Thompson, *Make for the Hills*, 158.
95. Nixon, *Memoirs of Richard Nixon*, 413.
96. Kissinger, *White House Years*, 436.
97. Thompson, *Make for the Hills*, 165.
98. Ibid., 165.
99. Ibid., 175.
100. Ibid., 177.
101. Fitzgerald, "Thompson, Strategic Patience and Nixon's War," 2.
102. Aldrich, *GCHQ*, 277.
103. Young, "Britain and 'LBJ's War,'" 63.
104. Shaw, "Policemen versus Soldiers," 51.
105. Johnson, *Vantage Point*, 255.
106. Thompson, *Make for the Hills*, 185.

8

The Old Country

America and the Northern Irish "Troubles"

> There are few more nauseating sounds than ignorant Irish-American politicians visiting Dublin and grubbing around for votes in the United States by venting their spleen on Britain.
>
> —Robert Adley, Conservative member of Parliament, April 1979

Few issues provoked more grassroots political activism in America in the second half of the twentieth century than the cause of Irish republicanism. Significant immigration from Ireland to America in the preceding decades resulted in powerful political machinery being created in key American cities by Irish Americans with strong views about the ongoing British presence in the "old country." Such political influence percolated through governance at all levels, creating entrenched anti-British feeling in quarters of Congress with large Irish American constituencies. Such sentiments hardened after 1969 with the breakout of the modern "Troubles" in Northern Ireland. Renewed Irish Republican Army (IRA) violence and British military operations across the province provided a stimulus to Irish American political activity in Washington.

At the outbreak of the Troubles, the number of Irish American citizens was five times larger than the population of Ireland itself.[1] With forty-four million Americans claiming to be of Irish descent, this made Irish Americans the second largest ethnic population in the United States,[2] providing a significant base of domestic interest in the Northern Ireland conflict. When taken alongside the Social Democratic and Labour Party (SDLP), Sinn Féin (the IRA's political wing), and the Irish government, the Irish American lobby constituted the fourth element of a broad pronationalist coalition. Rose-tinted views of the old country and traditional Catholicism bonded Irish Americans to the cause. However, as subsequent generations of Irish Americans became more socially and economically mobile after an immigration resurgence at the start of the twentieth century, the base of Irish American nationalism narrowed. Consequently, despite an almost nationwide inclination toward a united Ireland solution, there is no cohesive "shamrock vote" in the United States, despite a high demographic concentration of Irish Americans in the northeastern states.[3] Yet this has not necessarily diminished the presence and electoral power of a large Irish American lobby in Washington. This bloc would prove vitally important in shaping American public and political attitudes toward not just the IRA but, crucially, also toward the British military efforts to quash its campaign.

The story of the modern Troubles in Northern Ireland is steeped in centuries of conflict, repression, and reprisal. The catalyst for violence in the province is one intertwining politics and religion and stretches back to the occupation of Oliver Cromwell's army in the seventeenth century. Enforced union with Britain gave way to home rule in the twentieth century, prompting civil war and eventual independence for the twenty-six southern counties of the Irish Free State in 1921. Under the 1920 Government of Northern Ireland Act, six counties in the north were retained as part of the United Kingdom, with semiautonomous political institutions established at the seat of Northern Irish politics at Stormont Castle. The push for a united Ireland quickly took a violent turn in some quarters. Wolfe Tone's United Irishmen of the eighteenth century had set a precedent for the Fenians of the nineteenth century and the IRA of the twentieth century. Yet it was the actions of the IRA, its early members blooded in the 1916 Easter Rising, that would come to create the bloodiest insurgent opposition against unionist rule in Northern Ireland. Its campaign in the province, and against the British mainland in the 1930s and 1940s, marked a significant increase in the insurgent nature of the conflict. A "border campaign" was conducted from 1956 to 1962, as IRA members attacked targets in the north before fleeing south for refuge in Eire.

This chapter will restrict itself to analyzing the first decade of the modern Troubles, from the eruption of violence in 1969. This period represents the peak of Britain's application of an outright counterinsurgency strategy in the province and allows us to trace nascent American political interaction with the conflict.

The emerging political discourse of civil rights in the 1960s injected a new element to the tensions in Northern Ireland and provided the initial platform of engagement with American political agendas. The civil rights agenda had profoundly altered race relations in the United States and was manifesting itself in Northern Ireland by offering the minority Catholic population a means to express its perceptions of institutionalized prejudice and discrimination in the province's predominantly Protestant workforce and its near monopoly over social housing allocations. The left-leaning appeal of the civil rights movement inclined itself toward elements of the republican faction, which harnessed the civil rights discourse to reinforce its own proclamations of inherent political injustice in the Northern Irish political structure. As a consequence, the civil rights agenda combined a wider social movement for change with a justificatory vehicle for renewed IRA violence—with significant implications on how the Troubles were viewed across the Atlantic.

Two powerful and parallel influences crossed eastward from America during the 1970s in regard to the Troubles. The first affected the paramilitary potency of the IRA—namely, large amounts of money raised by Irish American groups in the United States and sent to Northern Ireland to bolster the cause. The second impacted the political dimension of the conflict due to the proactivity of key congressional figures. This political support that emanated from quarters of Capitol Hill bestowed a certain legitimacy on the republican cause and helped soften broader American perceptions of the nature of the conflict. This chapter will analyze each of these influences in turn. But first it is necessary to understand why this was to be the first British counterinsurgency campaign since the end of the Second World War that the White House went out of its way to avoid getting embroiled in. The administrations of Richard Nixon and then Gerald Ford abstained from involving themselves in Northern Irish politics, resulting in Congress being the most activist branch of American government in regard to this particular counterinsurgency war.

Nixon, Ford, and the Troubles in the White House

When British troops were first deployed to the streets of Northern Ireland in August 1969, the US secretary of state, William Rogers, let it be known that "official intervention on our part in the affairs of Northern Ireland would be objected to in much the same manner as we would object to outside intervention in civil rights problems within the United States."[4] It is noticeable from the analogy drawn by Rogers that the Nixon administration was willing to see the flaring of the Troubles predominantly through the lens of civil rights and not terrorism. Rogers was not the only one to see it this way. Many media commentators equated Northern Irish Catholics with African Americans in their mutual struggle for equal political and social rights. In liberal quarters of American politics, this analogy helped create a more favorable stateside image of the republican cause.[5]

Anglo-American relations during the Richard Nixon–Edward Heath years of the early 1970s, as chronicled in much of the "special relationship" literature of this period, were already strained, given both the cold personal chemistry between the two leaders and Heath's conscientious efforts to align Britain more closely with Europe.[6] There was therefore little capacity for the president and prime minister to discuss the implications of Northern Ireland's descent into violence. After a brief meeting with Heath at the prime minister's country retreat of Chequers in September 1970 (at which terrorism in Northern Ireland was not discussed, according to Henry Kissinger's recollection), Nixon rounded off his European tour with a stopover in Ireland. Again, no serious talks about the IRA were had in Dublin. Instead, as Kissinger later admitted, "the stop was frankly a domestic political one," designed for Nixon to "bring his claim of Irish ancestry to the attention of Irish American voters."[7] At no point was a serious diplomatic initiative launched to bring violence to an end. Dabbling in the troubled politics of Ireland was only an expedient vote-winner for Nixon. Indeed, so keen was the Nixon administration to placate Irish American anger over British actions in Northern Ireland that the president asked Kissinger to phone the powerful mayor of Chicago, Richard J. Daley, whose constituents' demographics caused him to publicly raise concerns. During the call, Daley urged the national security adviser to encourage Britain to remove all troops from Northern Ireland, arguing that "there is only going to be murder as long as they are there."[8]

Even after the dreadful events of "Bloody Sunday," when fourteen protestors on a civil rights march were killed by the British Army in Londonderry/Derry in January 1972, the Nixon administration refused to get embroiled in the Troubles, despite contradicting pressures being placed on Washington by Dublin (to increase levels of diplomatic pressure) and London (to keep interference to a minimum).[9] On February 2, the day an angry mob in Dublin torched the British embassy, Irish foreign minister Patrick Hillery arrived in Washington to implore William Rogers to pressure the British government to temper the actions of its military. Rogers maintained that the Troubles were an "internal affair" and did not warrant American intervention.[10] Appearing before Congress later that month, Rogers's assistant secretary of state for European Affairs, Martin Hillenbrand, stuck to the administration's line that unless acting on the express behest of the British and Irish governments, "US intervention [in Northern Ireland] would be both inappropriate and counter-productive."[11]

In July 1972, the British cabinet secretary, Burke Trend, visited Washington for talks with Kissinger on a wide range of defense matters. During Trend's brief meeting with the president, Nixon brought up the issue of Northern Ireland, which had been the subject of a policy review that summer inside the White House.[12] Trend reported that Nixon was sure that "during the forthcoming Presidential Election campaign the Democrats might try to make political capital out of the situation in Ulster." Conversely, the Democrat speaker of the House, Carl Albert, let it be known to British embassy sources that he felt Nixon would consider greater American intervention in Northern Ireland if it meant shoring up the Irish American vote for his reelection.[13] Yet knowing that Irish Americans were not a core Republican demographic, Nixon, rather piously, promised "to steer clear of the whole business."[14] Keeping the United States out of the Northern Irish Troubles was thus seen as good politics (both domestic and foreign) for the president. In the end, the issue was an academic one for Nixon in the 1972 election, as he swept to victory over his Democratic challenger, George McGovern. In a background note to Heath in advance of his trip in January 1973 to see the president for the first time after his reelection, the Northern Ireland Office assessed that although debates about the Troubles had been absent from the campaign, "had the two candidates been more evenly matched the temptation to make a play for the Irish vote might have been irresistible."[15]

The Nixon administration soon became engulfed with the Watergate scandal, along with plans to extract American troops from Vietnam and engineering détente with the Soviets. This all pushed Northern Ireland even further from minds in the White House. Staging a nonessential intervention in Northern Ireland to please the Irish government amid the welter of other purportedly essential Cold War interventions in Asia was a non sequitur for those conducting American foreign policy, especially the archrealist Kissinger.[16] After Nixon's downfall in 1974, there was little difference in Gerald Ford's approach regarding Northern Ireland. Typifying Ford's stance on the conflict was a restatement of the US position in early 1976: "Longstanding US Government policy is one specifically of avoiding direct involvement since we do not believe this would serve any useful or productive purpose." But efforts were made to skim over the contributions of American groups to IRA coffers, with Ford making a bland reference to efforts to "enforce the laws against such involvement to the best of [our] ability."[17]

Even the government of the Republic of Ireland acknowledged that the US presidency could play a crucial role in stemming the flow of guns and money to republican groups in Northern Ireland. At a White House reception on St. Patrick's Day in America's bicentennial year, even the *taoiseach* (Irish prime minister), Liam Cosgrave, pressed Ford to lend his name to a communiqué urging Irish Americans not to give money to pro-IRA groups, pointing to the way in which this would diminish terrorist violence.[18] But Cosgrave was trying to influence the wrong branch of American government. The Troubles was to stir a flurry of congressional activity that is unrivaled by actions in any other British counterinsurgency campaign.

Congress and the Domestic Politics of the Northern Irish Troubles

Despite the White House paying little or no attention to Belfast, a core of Irish American politicians (all Democrats) within Congress had formed the Friends of Ireland group and became known as the "Four Horsemen": Sen. Edward Kennedy, Speaker Tip O'Neill, Rep. Hugh Carey (beginning in 1975, governor of New York), and Sen. Patrick Moynihan. The moderate nationalist agenda of this group found a sympathetic hearing inside the White House of Jimmy Carter, who defeated Gerald Ford at the polls in November 1976. After the Four Horsemen met with new secretary of state, Cyrus Vance, in the summer of 1977, President Carter made the first moves toward forging a cohesive government policy on Northern Ireland. In a statement on August 30, 1977, Carter condemned the use of violence, lent support for cross-community human rights, and promised American aid should a peace settlement be reached.[19] British fears that nationalist sympathies were entrenched within the American political community were cemented in August 1979 when the State Department suspended arms sales to the Royal Ulster Constabulary (RUC), a move usually reserved for regimes guilty of human rights abuses, in protest at what it felt was heavy-handed policing in Northern Ireland. This alarmed the British government, which was keen to utilize the Irish American lobby to act as a restraint on IRA violence, yet who resented US interference in London's handling of a domestic insurgency.

The Four Horsemen provided a transatlantic mouthpiece for criticism of British actions in Northern Ireland. Events such as the introduction of internment without trial for IRA suspects in 1971, which Kennedy labeled the "nadir of British policy in Ulster,"[20] and Bloody Sunday provoked fierce condemnation as the Troubles ceased to be a set of domestic counterinsurgency operations conducted by the British and became an internationalized conflict via the spread of media coverage and especially via the intercessions of the powerful Irish American lobby.[21]

In October 1971, in the wake of the introduction of internment, Edward Kennedy introduced a resolution on the floor of the Senate that called for the withdrawal of British troops from Northern Ireland and the establishment of all-party talks to work out moves toward a united Ireland. A key way in which Kennedy attempted to build public sympathy in the United States for his stance was by invoking analogies with the ongoing US war effort in Vietnam. Sympathetic journalists started referring to the Troubles as "Britain's Vietnam" as a way of depicting it as a brutal and illegitimate occupation that was merely a waste of money and lives. Prime Minister Heath slapped down Kennedy's resolution as "an ignorant outburst," highlighting the senator's notable silence when it came to condemning IRA violence.[22]

Kennedy's resolution (cosponsored by Democrat Abraham Ribicoff) gained significant traction in the wake of the appalling events of Bloody Sunday (which made headline news across America). Even by the admission of the British embassy in Washington, Bloody Sunday had "changed the picture" of the Troubles in the eyes of the American public to the extent to which "there is a danger of our losing the propaganda battle." The embassy feared that unless the British government "step up [its] propaganda effort, the myth that Northern Ireland is another British Colonial war will get firmly implanted in the American mind."[23] The anti-British backlash in the United States after Bloody Sunday would create, embassy staff feared, "irresistible pressure" on American political leaders to adopt stridently prorepublican policies. Utilizing the analogy of Palestine, the embassy noted that "the damage done to Anglo-American relations . . . could be at least as great as that created by the US support for the Jews in the late 1940s."[24]

Such fears were soon realized. The House of Representatives Foreign Affairs Committee established a subcommittee on Europe, which focused predominantly on events in Northern Ireland. Hearings were held in late February and early March 1972 that called on witnesses to give evidence on the nature of the Troubles and the American role in preventing more violence—predominantly by the British military.[25] Three of the most prominent attendees at the hearings, Representatives Leo Ryan, Herman Badillo, and Bella Abzug, all represented districts with sizeable Irish American populations. Their engagement with the Northern Irish issue after the midterm elections in November 1972 waned significantly after they had been returned to Washington and the furor over Bloody Sunday had died down.[26] Electoral pandering was never far away from congressional stances on Northern Ireland. Indeed, so inured had the British embassy in Washington become to political point-scoring over Northern Ireland that when two New York congressmen submitted identical resolutions to the House of Representatives in June 1974 decrying British military action, diplomats calmly dismissed them as "routine gestures with elections in mind."[27]

But Ryan, Badillo, and Abzug's fading anger toward the action of the British Army after 1972 is symptomatic of a wider pattern of behavior across the American political spectrum, which began to take a more moderate turn. This was in large part due to the growing influence of the nationalist SDLP leader John Hume over key figures such as Edward Kennedy. Hume attempted to establish a prounity, antiviolence credo within Irish American circles, which bore fruit when it was adopted as a core platform from which the Four Horseman made their pronouncements.[28]

One of the most effective Irish American lobby groups pressing for US intervention was the Irish National Caucus, founded in 1974. The caucus, made up of republican hardliners, aimed to highlight the perceived brutality of the British military, the rough-justice policing meted out by the RUC, and the social discrimination of Catholics. The creation of the caucus denoted the growing number of high-profile Irish American lobby groups with militant views on the Troubles that put them at odds with mainstream nationalists. Jimmy Carter's pliancy toward the moderate nationalist agenda (directed in large part by the Four Horsemen) had triggered a broader dip in Irish American support for hardline republicanism. Yet the extreme fringe of American IRA supporters refused to give in. Turning their backs on the Four Horsemen, whom they now considered as traitors for (belatedly) denouncing IRA violence, American republicans sought new avenues to influence Capitol Hill. Using Democratic congressman Mario Biaggi as a front man, they successfully established an Ad Hoc Congressional Committee for Irish Affairs in September 1977, whose membership grew to 130 members of Congress. But the British embassy in Washington was deeply unimpressed with the establishment of Biaggi's committee. Diplomats noted that the congressman had a "cavalier attitude to facts" and that the members who had signed up to Biaggi's cause were "unwitting Congressmen who knew little about Northern Ireland."[29] Indeed, so frustrated were members of the Irish government with support in some congressional quarters for groups like the Irish National Caucus that Taoiseach Jack Lynch wrote to Biaggi personally in February 1978, stating his displeasure at noticing Biaggi's "public identification . . . with supporters of violence" and warned members of his committee to stop "seriously misrepresent[ing]" the position of the Irish government to Congress in regard to the withdrawal of British troops from Northern Ireland.[30] Lynch need not have worried. The committee met infrequently and achieved little beyond achieving publicity for Biaggi personally.[31]

By the end of the first decade of the Troubles, American political opinion had swung firmly behind the moderate nationalist agenda and support for continuing political initiatives to bring peace. This in part was the product of determined efforts by the Northern Ireland Office in London, the British embassy in Washington, and the British Information Services in New York to push positive stories in the American media about the "normality" of the situation in the province after the process of "Ulsterization" was initiated in 1976, leaving the RUC in charge of the security situation and giving the British Army a back seat.[32] The perceptible dip in loud denunciations of British action and fervent espousals of "Brits out" by congressional figures was noticed by the Northern Ireland Office, which in January 1978 had noted that "there has been a diminution of political interest from those [American politicians] who had initiated it earlier."[33]

Yet the most influential Americans on the direction of the Troubles were not leading political figures. The effectiveness of republican paramilitary violence in the early 1970s was significantly boosted by assistance from private Irish American organizations. For the first time since the swell of support offered to the Zionists fighting the British in Palestine by Jewish sympathizers, the actions of well-organized private groups in America helped alter the dynamic of a British counterinsurgency campaign.

Americans, Guns, and Money: Supplying the IRA from the United States

As a community, Irish Americans were largely repelled by the use of terrorist means to achieve a united Ireland. As the British consul general in Boston observed at the height of IRA violence in the early 1970s, the Irish American community harbored "an underlying sense of shame . . . that it should be their people, rather than the Blacks, or long-haired campus radicals, or the Chicanos, whose violence should be dominating the TV screens and press headlines."[34] But a sizeable number of Irish Americans still remained committed to aiding the violent overthrow of British rule in Northern Ireland. They were to prove critical in maintaining IRA potency for much of the early insurgency.

American interest in the Northern Ireland issue was reawakened by the civil rights marches that swept the province in 1968 and 1969. This represented the most attention paid by the United States to Northern Ireland since the end of the Irish Civil War in the 1920s. As the civil rights marches grew in size, a Friends of the Northern Ireland Civil Rights Association was set up, with branches established in cities across America, attracting fund-raising tours from figures such as activist, and later Nationalist member of Parliament, Bernadette Devlin. Other groups emerged, notably the American Committee for Ulster Justice, which aimed to lobby for American intervention in Northern Ireland in favor of a united Ireland solution. Yet such civil rights–oriented groups were counterbalanced by organizations that favored a more direct approach. Irish Republican Clubs were established across the US in 1971 to help aid the Official IRA (the predominantly Marxist faction) after the republican movement had split the year before.[35] But the most prominent group—the Irish Northern Aid Committee (NORAID)—favored the Provisional IRA (PIRA), which had come to dominate the republican movement given its violent commitment to a united Ireland that avoided the political pretenses of the Official IRA.[36]

NORAID was established by Michael Flannery in April 1970, over forty years after he had immigrated to the United States from Ireland, having fought in the Irish War for Independence.[37] NORAID appealed to many émigré "old warriors" and their families who came to perceive the group as a means of extending their participation in the struggle. NORAID information leaflets relied heavily on romanticizing the Irish struggle for an American audience, as well as playing up stories of British Army brutality and acts of loyalist terrorism against Catholics. Similar lines were taken in stories in NORAID's newspaper, *The Irish People*, which became the leading pro-IRA publication in the US.[38] This romanticized view of the struggle relied heavily on tapping into a traditional form of nationalism that was felt by large numbers of Irish Americans. This meant focusing their rhetoric on the narrow issue of "Brits out" and avoiding broader political issues such as civil rights. Indeed, when leading Northern Irish republicans made trips to the US, they were briefed by NORAID to drop any reference to socialism and to avoid criticizing the Catholic Church, in deference to the conservative disposition of the Irish diaspora in America.[39] Given the heavy mythologizing that Irish Americans were prone to when interpreting the Troubles, there were those within the British embassy in Washington who sought ways to muddy the rose-tinted view of the conflict in the US. They fell back on a tried-and-tested method: Raise the specter of communism. David Walker, the head of chancery at the embassy, argued to London in March 1974 that "if the IRA can be firmly linked in the American public mind with the Soviet Union or Arab extremism I am pretty sure that American funds for the IRA would begin to diminish."[40] But even this tactic did not dry up the flow of money back to the old country.

NORAID facilitated an extensive fund-raising schedule across America that included hosting testimonial dinners and organizing collections in Irish pubs. NORAID insisted that all money raised went to support the families of republican prisoners as a humanitarian gesture. Yet the British and Irish governments strongly suspected that NORAID's funds were being channeled into weapon purchases for the PIRA. This perspective was fueled by the presence in the United States of Joe Cahill, a founding member of the PIRA and treasurer of Sinn Féin. Initially deported from the US in 1971, he continued to make fund-raising trips there, traveling on false passports.[41] Cahill was a middleman for NORAID and the PIRA, and his very presence in the US must be seen as an active attempt by the group to secure American funds.

Indeed, this had been going on for a long time. Three months after the riots in the Bogside area of Londonderry/Derry that had sparked the outbreak of violence in 1969, Sean Keenan, a leading IRA member, was sent to the United States, where he publicly appealed for money and privately attempted to cultivate a weapon supply network. Keenan's visit bore fruit in August 1970 when the first IRA arms shipment arrived in Ireland from Philadelphia, including several hundred Armalite rifles, dramatically modernizing the IRA's cache of aging weapons.[42] The IRA's initial phase of American arms purchasing was small-scale in an attempt to avoid arousing the suspicion of the authorities. IRA agents would travel to gun fairs across the Midwest and then transport weapons to East Coast sea- and airports, where they were taken to Ireland in collusion with sympathetic dockworkers and airplane crews. However, such routes were shut down in October 1971 when the Irish police found six unclaimed suitcases full of guns and ammunition at terminals in Dublin. There is little doubt that such arms-trading activities could not have taken place without the cooperation of prorepublican elements within the longshoremen's union and US Customs.[43]

From its creation, NORAID was suspected of being the IRA's American wing, used not only for fund-raising but also for organizing the purchase and transportation of arms. Such an opinion was hardened when it emerged that two of the five Americans who put together the Philadelphia arms shipment were officers in NORAID. It was thus little surprise that the Federal Bureau of Investigation (FBI) infiltrated NORAID, as well as the equally radical Irish National Caucus, to uncover illicit weapon smuggling. The IRA relied on arms purchased by criminal gangs and professional arms dealers. One such dealer, George de Meo, a Corsican American with Mafia connections based in New York, helped supply the IRA with shipments of M-60 machine guns stolen from a US National Guard armory in August 1976. De Meo would organize biannual shipments of unlicensed arms until his arrest in 1980. While in custody he struck a deal with the FBI: In return for leniency, he would expose the names behind the IRA arms-buying networks in America. It was during the subsequent FBI investigation that the FBI, while shadowing Brooklyn security guard George Harrison (the IRA's main arms supplier, who the FBI estimated had shipped over twenty-five hundred weapons to Ireland[44]), taped a conversation between Harrison and NORAID chief Michael Flannery in which Harrison requested nearly $17,000 from NORAID for which to buy ammunition for an Ireland-bound M-79 grenade launcher and 20mm cannon. Both men and four other NORAID members were then arrested; however, they were acquitted when the jury accepted the defense's argument that their actions had received the blessing of the Central Intelligence Agency (CIA), as the purchase prevented the IRA from seeking arms from the Soviets instead.[45] In spite of this verdict, the explicit NORAID-IRA connection was made at another arms-smuggling trial in 1983 when a former arms procurer for the IRA testified that a slice of the money sent to Ireland by NORAID was then returned by courier to the United States to be spent on arms.[46]

As far back as the early 1970s, the British government was seeking an American commitment to crack down on NORAID fund-raising, although all the US consul general to London, Grover Penberthy, could tell Northern Ireland Office officials in November 1973 was that it was "difficult to prove and prosecute unless one had specific supplementary intelligence that the funds were being used for other than innocent purposes."[47] Two months earlier the Irish government had stepped up its efforts to crack down on IRA fund-raising in America, with explicit requests to the US authorities to deny visas to known IRA members.[48] The State Department refused to place all IRA members on a visa "stop list" but did confirm it would treat cases on an individual basis.[49] This Anglo-Irish pressure on the State Department paid off in 1974 when the new Ireland desk officer in Foggy Bottom, Steve Dawkins, brought with him to his new job a commitment to cracking down on NORAID. In July that year, Dawkins requested from Secretary of State Henry Kissinger what he called a "hunting license" to go after IRA fund-raising groups in the United States.[50] By October, Kissinger had granted it to Dawkins by directing his department to scrutinize more closely the IRA's money sources in America. Back in London, the Foreign Office took this directive (which was passed on in confidence to the British embassy) as an "encouraging indication" that "the United States authorities are taking a much more robust line in relation to the IRA."[51] This relief stemmed from new assessments relating to the effectiveness of American weaponry in the IRA's arsenal. In 1975, British intelligence estimates indicated that up to 85 percent of all IRA weapons bought since the beginning of the Troubles were thought to have been shipped from America.[52] This built on a US naval intelligence report concluding that, from 1971 to 1974, nearly seven thousand weapons and over one million rounds of ammunition had been stolen from US military facilities for the purpose of being shipped to the IRA.[53] By 1979, a leaked British Army intelligence report had estimated that of the IRA's £950,000 annual income, some £120,000 came from overseas, with NORAID accounting for half of that sum alone. The report concluded that the United States had become the "IRA's main weapon source."[54]

The American connection to IRA violence had been noted with anger by Downing Street. In a speech to the Association of American Correspondents in London in December 1975, Prime Minister Harold Wilson lambasted "the financing of IRA terror, brutality and murder by misguided Irish-American sympathisers," warning American backers that they were "playing the role of vicarious merchants of death."[55] Even the chief of staff of the Official IRA, Cathal Goulding, was ready to admit before his group disbanded that there was a link between the perpetuation of republican violence in Northern Ireland and American money: "They [supporters in America] couldn't support us financially unless there was some form of revolutionary activity. . . . [T]hey would only support those that were using force alone."[56] Such an admission, together with the intelligence picture built up by agencies on both sides of the Atlantic, generated a depiction of American funding as the most influential element of the external support dynamic propagating republican paramilitary activities in the first decade of the Troubles.

The American law-enforcement community was slow to react to the potency of the American arms market and its ability to foster violence on the streets of Northern Ireland. From 1969 to 1976, only twenty-seven people (including both Irish and American citizens) were prosecuted in the United States on gunrunning charges.[57] But certain high-profile cases, such as that of the "Philadelphia Five," did increase the levels of cooperation between the British and American authorities in curtailing the flow of American-sourced weapons to the IRA.[58] In the wake of the guilty verdict on two of the defendants in the Philadelphia Five case, the Department of Justice started legal proceedings against NORAID in February 1977 on the grounds that the organization had violated the Foreign Agents Registration Act and failed to properly account for overseas donations.[59] But the real turning point did not come until August 1979 with the assassination of a cousin of Queen Elizabeth II, Lord Mountbatten, and, on the same day, the killing of eighteen British soldiers at Warrenpoint by the IRA. The targeting of high-profile figures and the deaths of large numbers of troops in a supposed "domestic" conflict in an industrialized Western democracy forced the American intelligence community to wake up to the role of IRA arms procured in the United States. This can be proven by the decision of the FBI in May 1980 to establish its own "PIRA Squad" in New York, under Agent Lou Stephens, to smash weapon-smuggling networks out of the East Coast ports. At its peak, the PIRA Squad was tapping the phones of half a dozen IRA arms smugglers in an operation code-named "Hit and Win." This operation was successful in thwarting the attempted purchase of surface-to-air missiles to be used against British Army helicopters.[60] In September 1984, an FBI tip-off to the Irish authorities led to the interception of seven tons of guns and ammunition worth £1.5 million on a ship from Boston.[61]

By the early 1980s, the British had shifted their strategic focus away from counterinsurgency at the same time as President Ronald Reagan was scaling back American involvement in the Northern Ireland issue. Ongoing IRA violence had discredited the republican cause in the eyes of the mainstream Irish American majority, and support for NORAID waned as a result. This dip in transatlantic support had been building for some time. As part of its 1973 intensification of bombings against targets on the British mainland, the IRA also sent a parcel bomb to the British embassy in Washington on August 27, severely injuring a secretary.[62] This attack caused a huge backlash against the republican movement in the American media. Opprobrium within the wider American public grew only as the IRA took to bombing civilian targets such as pubs and shopping centers across England in 1974. The insurgency, thanks to tactical hubris, came to alienate an integral support base.

Conclusion

In the early years of the Troubles, the United States tried to distance itself from Northern Ireland in an attempt not to embarrass the United Kingdom. The inclination to intervene was always stronger in the legislative branch than in the executive, arguably up until Jimmy Carter's election, when the White House became more interventionist in line with the administration's new policy priority of human rights promotion.

The assertion of American political leverage over the first decade of the Troubles remains the single most important external element of the conflict—an element that remained strongly in place over the subsequent decades, culminating in President Bill Clinton's efforts to shepherd the peace process toward its climax with the 1998 Good Friday Agreement. In the absence of a potent prounionist American lobby group, the only countervailing force to prorepublican opinion in Washington was the perceived value of the US-UK special relationship (which the British authorities in America were at pains to conjure up). This may have been a consideration during the Nixon and Ford years, with the White House vowing to distance itself from the conflict in deference to London's desire to handle its own domestic insurgency. However, Carter's censure of British security force activity and even Clinton's later willingness to make concessions to Sinn Féin (such as granting Sinn Féin leader Gerry Adams a visa without a renunciation of IRA violence) led to a dramatic deterioration in the special relationship over Northern Ireland, so much so that by the early stages of the Clinton presidency no special privileges were being granted to Britain.[63]

The British military presence in Northern Ireland during the first decade of Operation Banner (the official name given to the deployment lasting from 1969 to 2007 in Northern Ireland) was a standard target for American politicians hoping to cultivate Irish American opinion. But the campaign caused the US diplomatic and national security apparatus very little concern—with one notable exception. In February 1974, Harold Wilson and the Labour Party formed a minority government in Britain. Before the election, key figures on the Labour benches had been making noises about the full and immediate withdrawal of British troops from Northern Ireland. Two months after the election, the American embassy in Dublin passed on to the UK Foreign Office intelligence from "a well-placed source in the Irish government" (thought to be Foreign Minister Garrett FitzGerald) that the Irish "are more worried about the situation in the North than their public statements indicate." What startled the Americans about Dublin's concerns was its perceptions regarding the possibility of Britain deciding to "cut their losses and withdraw troops from Northern Ireland altogether, leaving the Protestants and Catholics to fight it out amongst themselves."[64] Fearful that this would inevitably lead to the deployment of a UN peacekeeping force that would require American backing, the US embassy in Dublin (acting on behalf of the State Department) sought reassurances on British plans for any troop withdrawals. This flurry of worry from Washington was wryly observed by the Foreign Office as being "the first time we have heard that the Americans are getting worried about Northern Ireland and are beginning to give serious thought to contingencies there."[65] It appeared that Washington really woke up to the violence in the province at the point at which it appeared it may have to support a large-scale UN intervention amid a religiously motivated civil war. This scenario was given high-level consideration. The Ireland desk officer at the State Department, Steve Dawkins, revealed to the British embassy in Washington that "analysts in the CIA, Pentagon and State Department were all busy looking for 'straws' on British withdrawal." This was the result, Dawkins explained to David Walker, the head of chancery at the embassy, of there being "some feeling [in Washington] that the British were carefully weighing things and some thought that the Labour Government was seriously considering pulling out of Northern Ireland." Dawkins was used as a conduit to relay back to the State Department that this was not truly being discussed by ministers as an option.[66] Wilson's victory in the second general election of 1974, in October that year, returned Labour with a workable if razor-thin parliamentary majority of three. No legislation on full withdrawal was introduced, but given the origin of the initial rumor, this entire episode says more about Eire's concerns at being left with a full-blown civil war on its northern border than it does about American indifference to the day-to-day work of Operation Banner. What is more, the episode also demonstrates how Washington was yet again opposed to British troop withdrawal from another counterinsurgency war—a trend already observable in the more overtly colonial wars chronicled in the earlier chapters of this book. The British Army, yet again, was a bulwark against unpalatable alternatives (in this case almost certain civil war) in the eyes of Washington.

The lobbying power of Irish Americans, when combined with the external support directly offered to the IRA by American sympathizers, had a tangible impact on the Troubles on both a political and paramilitary level. The official report by the Ministry of Defence evaluating the end of Operation Banner vastly underestimated the impact of such international influence: "The rest of the world was, by and large, little more than an audience to the drama in Northern Ireland."[67] Irish Americans were not merely the audience. When we account for the large role they played inside and outside Congress, we can see that they were actually part of the cast.

Notes

Epigraph: Quoted in Wilson, *Irish America and the Ulster Conflict*, 156.

1. Bishop and Mallie, *Provisional IRA*, 233.
2. Tonge, *Northern Ireland*, 151.
3. John Dumbrell, "Hope and History: The US and Peace in Northern Ireland," in Cox et al., *Farewell to Arms?*, 219.
4. Quoted in Cronin, *Washington's Irish Policy*, 301.
5. Sanders, *Inside the IRA*, 98.
6. For a discussion of this period, see Spelling, "Heath and Anglo-American Relations," 638–58.
7. Kissinger, *White House Years*, 935.
8. "Telephone Conversation between Henry Kissinger and Mayor Daley," August 24, 1971, Digital National Security Archive (hereafter DNSA), www.nsarchive.chadwyck.com/nsa/documents/KA/06340/all.pdf.
9. MacLeod, *International Politics and Northern Ireland*, 40.
10. Wilson, *Irish America and the Ulster Conflict*, 64.
11. "Statement on the Northern Ireland Situation by Martin J. Hillenbrand," February 29, 1972, The National Archives, UK (hereafter TNA), FCO 87/102.
12. MacLeod, *International Politics and Northern Ireland*, 82.
13. Ibid., 50.
14. "Discussions with Dr Kissinger at Washington," July 28, 1972, DNSA, www.nsarchive.chadwyck.com/nsa/documents/KA/00533/all.pdf.
15. "Prime Minister's Meeting with President Nixon—Background Note on Item No.12: Northern Ireland," January 17, 1973, TNA, FCO 87/237.
16. Williamson, "Taking the Troubles," 188–89.
17. "White House Announcement of Cosgrave Visit," February 5, 1976, Gerald R. Ford Presidential Library Digital Collections (hereafter GFPL DC), www.fordlibrarymuseum.gov/library/document/0204/1511967.pdf.

18. "Memorandum of Conversation," March 17, 1976, GFPL DC, https://www.fordlibrarymuseum.gov/library/document/0314/1553398.pdf.
19. "Northern Ireland Statement on US Policy," August 30, 1977, Public Papers of the President, http://www.presidency.ucsb.edu/ws/index.php?pid=8014&st=&st1.
20. Kennedy, "Ulster Is an International Issue," 60.
21. For a picture of the international, and in particular the American, response to the introduction of internment, see "Foreign Reactions towards Internment in Northern Ireland," TNA, FCO 33/1471.
22. Wilson, *Irish America and the Ulster Conflict*, 58–60.
23. "Confidential: From D. C. Tebbit, British Embassy, Washington, to G. F. N. Reddaway, Foreign Office, 16 February 1972," TNA, FCO 26/944.
24. Ibid.
25. For a bound copy of the transcript of the entire oral testimony and written evidence presented at the hearings, see TNA, FCO 87/106.
26. Sanders, *Inside the IRA*, 106.
27. "From D. C. Walker (British Embassy, Washington) to B. J. Donnelly (Foreign Office), 16 July 1974," TNA, FCO 87/368.
28. Sanders, *Inside the IRA*, 108.
29. "Ad Hoc Congressional Committee on Ireland," February 3, 1978, TNA, CJ 4/2661.
30. "Letter from Taoiseach Jack Lynch to Mario Biaggi," February 17, 1978, TNA, CJ 4/2661.
31. Wilson, *Irish America and the Ulster Conflict*, 139–42.
32. For documents detailing these propaganda efforts, see TNA, CJ 4/2661.
33. "United States Involvement in Northern Ireland," TNA, CJ 4/2127.
34. "Memo from British Consulate-General in Boston," August 30, 1971, TNA, FCO 33/1472.
35. Sanders, *Inside the IRA*, 100.
36. The Official IRA declared a permanent cease-fire in 1972. Therefore, any subsequent references in this book to the IRA will be an automatic inference to the Provisionals.
37. Ibid., 99.
38. Ibid., 101–2.
39. Wilson, *Irish America and the Ulster Conflict*, 45.
40. "Confidential: from D. C. Walker (British Embassy, Washington) to J. B. Simeon (Foreign Office)," March 28, 1974, TNA, FCO 87/368.
41. Guelke, *Northern Ireland*, 135.
42. Bishop and Mallie, *Provisional IRA*, 233.
43. Ibid., 234.
44. Taylor, *Provos*, 1.
45. Bishop and Mallie, *Provisional IRA*, 235–36.
46. Guelke, *Northern Ireland*, 133.

47. "Record of Conversation between the Minister of State for Northern Ireland, Mr van Straubenzee and the US Consul-General, Mr Grover Penberthy," November 27, 1973, TNA, FCO 87/236.
48. "Secret: Fundraising for the IRA," September 25, 1973, TNA, FCO 87/236.
49. "Flash Cypher from Dublin," October 2, 1973, TNA, FCO 87/236.
50. "From D. C. Walker (British Embassy, Washington) to B. J. Donnelly (Foreign Office)," July 24, 1974, TNA, FCO 87/366.
51. "Letter from Linwood Holton, Assistant Secretary for Congressional Relations (State Department) to Senator J. W. Fulbright," TNA, FCO 87/367.
52. Wilson, *Irish America and the Ulster Conflict*, 90.
53. Ibid., 88.
54. Guelke, *Northern Ireland*, 133.
55. Wilson, *Final Term*, 205–6. See also TNA, CJ 4/1411, for text of full speech.
56. Goulding, "New Strategy of the IRA," 58.
57. "Assistance Provided by the US Authorities to Counter Fund-Raising and Gun-Running—Northern Ireland Briefing Note," TNA, CJ 4/1830.
58. "Trial of the 'Philadelphia 5,'" January 15, 1976, TNA, FCO 87/589.
59. "Outline of Complaint: Attorney General v. Irish Northern Aid Committee, 14 February 1977," TNA, CJ 4/2316.
60. Taylor, *Provos*, 2–5.
61. Urban, *Big Boys' Rules*, 129.
62. Wilson, *Irish America and the Ulster Conflict*, 82.
63. O'Grady, "Irish Policy Born in the USA," 6.
64. "Confidential: From G. W. Harding to Sir G. Arthur," April 18, 1974, TNA, FCO 87/368.
65. "Confidential and Personal: From Geoffrey Arthur," April 19, 1974, TNA, FCO 87/368.
66. "American Views on Northern Ireland," May 20, 1974, TNA, FCO 87/368.
67. "Operation Banner: An Analysis of Military Operations in Northern Ireland," report prepared under the direction of the chief of General Staff (Army Code 71842), Ministry of Defence (July 2006), para. 317.

9

"Shoulder to Shoulder"

The War in Iraq

> Despite our so-called "special relationship," I reckon we were treated no differently to the Portuguese.
>
> —Col. J. K. Tanner, former chief of staff for the British mission in Basra

From its identification by President George W. Bush as a member of an "Axis of Evil" operating in the world after the 9/11 attacks on America, the Iraqi regime of Saddam Hussein was a target for overthrow. The unprecedented publication of intelligence material pertaining to Saddam's possession of weapons of mass destruction was marshaled behind claims of neoconservative hawks within the Bush administration who aligned Pentagon planning toward a ground war that would finish business that the 1990–91 Gulf War had started. The war drums in Washington got louder during 2002 and into the spring of 2003, most notably with the forging of an international "coalition of the willing" that indicated a willingness to forcibly remove the Ba'athist regime in Baghdad.

In March 2003, militaries from twenty-seven countries provided troops for this coalition that invaded Iraq. Yet the distribution of the burden of removing Saddam would not be as even as the size of the coalition would seemingly imply. The British were to be the second-biggest contributors to the invasion and would be the only other nation involved in any way in prewar planning. The United States would supply 91 percent of all combat troops for Multi-National Force–Iraq (MNF-I) during the initial invasion, with a total of 424,000.[1] The second-largest military grouping was the 41,000 British troops sent into battle by Tony Blair—one-third of the non-US coalition force.[2]

"Victory" would take less than two months, from the first "shock and awe" air strikes on Baghdad on March 20 to President Bush declaring "mission accomplished" on May 1. Yet the war had only just begun. The bête noire of Washington's neoconservatives, Saddam (who fulfilled a role akin to Gamal Abdel Nasser for the Tory "Aden Group" in the 1960s), may have been deposed, but his overthrow marked the beginning of a welter of ethnic, religious, and nationalist insurgent violence. A successful initial invasion quickly became eclipsed by poor postwar planning and underwhelming operational performance as the demands of a counterinsurgency war were ramped up. The story of Anglo-American adaptation to these new necessities makes for two different outcomes.

However, the primary interest of this chapter is not how George W. Bush and Tony Blair justified the decision to go to war (the focus of much "special relationship" literature[3]) but rather with the British and American political and military management of the ensuing counterinsurgency campaign (unenvisaged though it was at the time of the original invasion). The analysis will triangulate the relationship between British and American soldiers on the ground in Iraq, between diplomats in Baghdad and the capitals of the two leading nations in the coalition, and between the leaders in London and Washington themselves. An evaluation of this management is heightened in importance, given that, when combined with parallel operations in Afghanistan, it was the first time British troops had been junior partners in a counterinsurgency coalition and had deployed alongside their American allies in this form of war.[4]

The coalition's military control of Iraq saw the country split into six main areas of responsibility (AORs), with the British providing the leadership in Multi-National Division (South East), or MND-SE, which comprised the four provinces of Basra, Maysan, Dhi Qar, and Muthanna. The initial postconflict stage was a relatively quiet period in southern Iraq as operations focused on securing the oil fields and the long stretch of border with Iran. However, in late 2005, the security situation in and around Basra deteriorated significantly as a result of local competition among rival militant groups for political and economic control. Attacks on British troops increased, as did violence between rival Shi'a factions. Sectarian violence in Basra reached a bloody crescendo in May 2006, forcing the Iraqi prime minister, Nouri al-Maliki, to declare a month-long state of emergency, testing the efficacy of contemporary British counterinsurgency conduct. A controversial withdrawal to an "overwatch" role at the Basra airport in September 2007 created a security vacuum in the city that was filled by the militias and was arguably not plugged until the joint Iraqi-American operation Charge of the Knights, which largely bypassed British involvement in 2008. All this shaped a negative perception within the American military of the British legacy in this particular counterinsurgency war. This was in large part due to the significant intellectual upheaval that had occurred inside the US Army in the face of the counterinsurgency "turn" in the war.

The Americans faced a very different conflict environment in Baghdad and the infamous "Sunni Triangle" in central Iraq than what faced the British in southern Iraq, particularly in relation to the quantity of foreign jihadists belonging to such groups as al-Qaeda in Iraq. Incessant insurgent attacks and a stifled response to the rapidly shifting nature of the conflict from within the Pentagon set in motion an intellectual revolution within strands of the US Army and Marine Corps that resulted in the redrafting of the military's entire doctrine for counterinsurgency warfare.[5] The rise to prominence and influence of the counterinsurgency wunderkind Gen. David Petraeus and other intellectually curious officers from the junior and middle ranks of the army resulted in the inculcation of counterinsurgency learning at many levels of the American military. This sea change in counterinsurgency competencies meant that the British were no longer seen as exemplars of counterinsurgency conduct.

Political Tensions within the Counterinsurgency Coalition

The British decision to join the American-led invasion of Iraq affected international depictions of Britain's role in the world, especially given characterizations of Blair as "Bush's poodle."[6] In the wake of his crucial meeting with Bush at the president's Texas ranch in April 2002, it became clear that Blair harbored a belief that standing "shoulder to shoulder" with the Americans buttressed a crucial alliance and strengthened the "forces for good" in the world.[7] It also led to a large domestic backlash toward Blair, his government, and an increasingly unpopular war. In his memoirs, Bush warmly described Blair as his "closest partner and best friend on the world stage." Bush felt that they were "kindred spirits in our faith in the transformative power of liberty."[8]

The closeness of the Bush-Blair relationship was initially reflected down the military chains of command, with British commanders being co-opted into the planning for war. Maj. Gen. Tim Cross was tasked in late 2002 with liaising with the American military high command. He noted how at that point the Americans allowed "no one else in the room but Brits."[9] Yet what remains significant is that the Americans did not need the physical presence of British troops (or indeed any other coalition troops) to achieve the goal of toppling Saddam (US troops outnumbered UK troops by nearly ten to one), but British involvement provided political symbolism that denoted international consensus and moral legitimacy, not military dependency.[10]

The interdependence of Bush and Blair's personal relationship was arguably the only way in which US and UK intimacy during the Iraq War remained immune to mutual disgruntlement. Despite the early keenness for (limited) British input (as Cross's inclusion in planning meetings attests), once the Iraq War degenerated into a prolonged counterinsurgency campaign, diplomatic and military tensions were barely concealed.

In 2005, the House of Commons Defence Select Committee lambasted what it euphemistically labeled "the Coalition's strategists" for presiding over "key planning misjudgements" relating to the post-Saddam rise of the insurgency, presumably to avoid directly irking the tight-knit cabal in the Pentagon that controlled the entire planning process.[11] When, in the immediate aftermath of Saddam's downfall, Cross was appointed as one of retired US general Jay Garner's three deputies within the Office for Reconstruction and Humanitarian Assistance (ORHA), he became the highest-ranking British soldier embedded within the American leadership structure in Baghdad. He saw for himself how US Central Command (CENTCOM) and Pentagon planners had "not been interested" in postwar reconstruction issues when he had worked alongside key figures in the Bush administration in spring 2003. With little concern emanating from Washington, and Whitehall showing signs that it wanted to minimize the cost of British participation, Cross admitted that during his spell as ORHA's lead figure with responsibility for international engagement, he was "making it up as [he] went along." US-UK differences regarding the very nature of ORHA during its month-long life span still arose. Cross pushed for ORHA staff to be unarmed in order to project an image of overtly civilian power. Garner disagreed, worried that Cross's idea would come across as weak.[12]

The suspension of ORHA and its replacement by the Coalition Provisional Authority (CPA) in May 2003 revealed to Tim Cross the "failure" of US-UK political cooperation at the strategic level. The inability of any British political figure to influence the Bush administration's handling of the postinvasion situation ("Phase IV" in military parlance) was compounded by Whitehall's "lack of confidence" in outlining Britain's role in the world, especially in relation to the United States, resulting in a "junior partner complex" in the Iraq coalition that saw key British civilian leaders on the ground in Iraq and back in London kowtow to American decisions regarding the political future of Iraq.[13]

The main British contribution to the new CPA was the thirty-odd civil-military staff of the CPA (South), headed by a regional coordinator in Basra. Working with the military commanders in the region, the CPA (South) was tasked with four main goals: security, reconstruction and economic development, democratic governance, and improving Iraqi perceptions of the other three goals.[14] Sir Hilary Synnott, the British coordinator in the south from July 2003 to January 2004, soon became highly critical of CPA chief Paul Bremer's management of the authority's political efforts to achieve these goals, citing the organization's highly centralized structure and the Americans' unabashed focus on Baghdad as the priority for security and reconstruction operations: "CPA Headquarters tended to expect the British to sort out the problem for themselves. . . . [This] put the south in danger of being starved of resources."[15] Importantly, the resources that did eventually reach the British-administered southern provinces, from money to pay Iraqi civil service wages to food aid, came from the American government and not the British, forcing British administrators in Basra to pay police and civil servants wages with confiscated Ba'athist funds to circumvent the poor flow of finances in the immediate postinvasion period.[16] The one hindrance greater than the American obsession with Baghdad to the effective functioning of the British presence in southern Iraq seemed to be the ability of the British government to adequately fund the mission from the outset.

Paul Bremer had a fractious working relationship with the first British commander of Multi-National Division (South-East), Maj. Gen. Andrew Stewart. When Stewart decided to forgo an overtly kinetic approach and instead pursued a policy of creating a dialogue with the main decision makers in the southeast in order to dissuade them from supporting the main Shi'a militia, the Mahdi Army, he found himself at loggerheads with the CPA chief. Bremer accused him of "not killing enough people" and personally requested that Stewart ("a chicken-livered Brit") be removed. Although experiencing up close the neoconservative American political approach to counterinsurgency, Stewart was undeterred and cleverly used Bremer's annoyance to his own advantage by telling local sheikhs that he was under pressure to "turn their town into Fallujah" as a means of securing cooperation for his more noncoercive methods.[17]

Sir Jeremy Greenstock, the former British ambassador to the United Nations (UN) who had reluctantly helped build support for the coalition invasion during 2002, was appointed the UK special representative to Baghdad in 2003. He found the American-led authorities on the ground distinctly unresponsive to advice from their supposed closest allies:

> The Americans are quite a closed group when they're working on an operation, and they are supplying 95% of the power and the resources. This was an American operation. They were generous in allowing us into their office and into their discussions, but they weren't spontaneous in asking for advice. American advice is more valuable to an American than any other kind, and so you had to work through that.... [W]hen I asked one or two questions about his political programme I was told very firmly by Bremer to shut up. So I realised I had to work rather more subtly in expressing a different view.[18]

But this did not put Greenstock off maintaining his good links with contacts in the State Department. He kept them updated with his increasingly pessimistic views about the situation in the Iraqi capital. Influential personnel in Foggy Bottom shared Greenstock's frustration at Bremer's single-mindedness. When Scott Carpenter, one of Bremer's deputies, visited Washington in mid-2003, Assistant Secretary of State Richard Armitage pointedly told Carpenter that "the only reporting the entire administration is getting on Iraq is Jeremy

Greenstock's, and it doesn't sound too good."[19] When this quip made it back to Bremer, the CPA chief decided that his British colleague was briefing against him and responded by beginning to leave Greenstock off the invitation list for important CPA meetings. But it was not just the State Department that was angered by Bremer's reluctance to offer substantive situation reports back to Washington. So frustrated was National Security Adviser Condoleezza Rice at the lack of information she was being passed by the CPA in Baghdad that she resorted to reading cables passed on by British diplomats to the embassy in Washington in order to get a picture of events on the ground.[20]

As the security situation quickly deteriorated after the downfall of Saddam in the spring of 2003, British criticisms started to emerge of the American handling of the situation. In May 2003, Tony Blair appointed John Sawers, the British ambassador to Egypt, as London's envoy in Baghdad. Soon after arriving in the Iraqi capital amid the beginning of the insurgency, Sawers cabled to Whitehall a damning report on the nationwide civil-military counterinsurgency effort, accusing the US military of "not providing the security framework needed."[21] Another memo by Sawers back to London one month later revealed his concerns over the "thin . . . veneer of security in many parts of Iraq," given the prevalence of insurgent violence against the Iraqi infrastructure and the increasing radicalization of young Shi'ites in the south by burgeoning extremist religious movements.[22] The magnitude of Sawers's downbeat assessment of the effectiveness of American political control over Iraq is underlined by his role as the leading British diplomat in the country at the outbreak of the insurgency, especially through his selection by CPA chief Bremer to help jointly construct the membership of the Iraqi Governing Council in the summer of 2003.[23] Once full diplomatic relations with Iraq had been reestablished by the United Kingdom, even British ambassadors to Iraq had difficulty in presenting a positive political picture. In his final diplomatic telegram in mid-2006, which was leaked to the press, William Patey offered a devastating assessment to the prime minister and UK military commanders of the Iraqi situation, three years after Sawers's initial aspersions: "Civil war and a de facto division of Iraq is probably more likely at this stage than a successful and substantial transition to a stable democracy."[24] Depictions of the political failure of the American-led campaign were ubiquitous, in terms of the financial provision for functioning governance and the political will to commit to an increasingly protracted counterinsurgency war.

Military Tensions within the Counterinsurgency Coalition

The war in Iraq offered a complex strategic environment for the American and British military in counterinsurgency terms. It was the first postcolonial and nondomestic counterinsurgency war the British army had faced, given that Afghanistan had not at that point descended into an outright counterinsurgency campaign. It was also essentially the first post-Maoist, perhaps even first post-modern, insurgency the American military had confronted, inasmuch as the disparate groupings were not strategically cogent or territorially defined, rejecting the traditional population-based "center of gravity," in addition to abandoning ideological dogma in favor of a blanket rejection of Western "modernity." Despite close Anglo-American political solidarity in the run-up to the invasion, military adaptability to the emergent insurgent environment would place a heavy strain on the "special relationship," as it would call into question the efficacy of British capabilities in irregular war environments and force a wholesale shift in American approaches to this form of war.

Growing animosity at the political level between British and American officials on the ground in Iraq and within respective diplomatic institutions in London and Washington was driven by British frustration at the overall American approach to the war and American dismay at the British military performance in the south of Iraq. This "rising querulousness" between diplomats soon spread to the military sphere to the extent that British and American officers developed a working relationship akin to "scorpions in a bottle."[25]

Symptomatic of this querulousness were American efforts to stamp uniformity across all coalition military action at the expense of British military independence. In one such example, the chief of staff of the UK Seventh Armoured Brigade, Maj. Chris Parker, pressed the 188 officers and cadets of Basra's naval academy in to a self-styled River Force to patrol the city's waterways and streets in an effort to enforce security in Basra in the immediate aftermath of the invasion. Pleased with his pragmatic approach, Parker was incredulous when he was informed by his divisional headquarters to disperse his ad hoc security force. Parker's River Force breached Bremer's first order as CPA chief, which was to disband the Iraqi military. Since Parker had transferred serving members of Saddam's armed forces into the new unit, Washington pressed the British to shut the River Force down immediately. Parker was given no option but to follow orders.[26] Looting in Basra continued, while CPA Order #1 extended its purge of Ba'athist elements in an effort to build an entirely new military. There was to be little room for British innovation in the face of a deteriorating security situation and stringent American political management of the occupation.

But more often than not, the greatest obstacle to British action in Iraq was other Brits. Civil-military relations within the British contingent in Iraq in the first few years after the invasion were so poor that the former British CPA administrator in Maysan Province, Rory Stewart, observed that "most of the soldiers did not even know there had once been a civilian presence in the province."[27] Indeed, all civil-military efforts to kick-start reconstruction projects, via the $127 million Emergency Infrastructure Programme set up by the British government, were effectively curtailed by early 2004 as the security situation in and around Basra significantly degenerated.[28] From 2003 to 2006, Whitehall earmarked £544 million for postwar reconstruction in Iraq,[29] despite the absence of a coherent structural program for the delivery of reconstruction and relief work for much of this period. It was not until 2006, three years after the invasion of Iraq, that the Foreign and Commonwealth Office, the Ministry of Defence (MoD), and the Department for International Development jointly established the Post Conflict Reconstruction Unit (soon to be renamed the Stabilisation Unit) to coordinate the delivery of British reconstruction plans. This three-year gap represented a crucial window of time during which the Iraqi people were most in need of coalition-provided security, economic provision, and the maintenance of national infrastructure. In the absence of this, support for the militias in southern Iraq multiplied.

This did not go unnoticed by the Americans. Commanders on the ground and officials visiting from Washington observed inertia in British-led reformation of the security sector in particular. Journalist and author Bob Woodward retells a story of how on a visit to Basra in March 2004 by US National Security Council representative Frank Miller, his British military escorts set up a meeting with a local police chief, having already given Miller "a happy-face briefing about their great success teaching the local Iraqi police how to patrol":

> "Tell me," Miller asked an overweight, elderly Iraqi police brigadier. "What do your men do when they come to work in the morning?" The Iraqi said, "Well, they come in and they have a coffee and they sit here until I tell them to go out and arrest somebody." Miller shot a glance at the British two-star and lieutenant colonel. "Hey guys, this is what Saddam did," he said. "You give me all this bullshit about how you've reformed the police. You haven't done a goddamn thing."[30]

Although acknowledging the strong bonds that exist, especially at the senior level, between the British and American militaries, even General Cross—the only two-star British general to play a part in preinvasion discussions in Washington—admitted to the existence of "creative tensions" over how to best adapt to the new insurgent environment that gripped Iraq soon after Saddam's removal from power. Discussions were had within the highest military circles in London in the early summer of 2003 about the possibility of sending a brigade of British troops from Basra to Baghdad to help the Americans adapt to what was being seen by key British commanders as an imminent operational turn toward counterinsurgency.[31] The following year, the Americans requested that the British command a second Multi-National Division, as well as demanded that a British battle group be sent to assist American troops retake the city of Fallujah in 2004. A politically wary Downing Street, a Treasury with tight purse strings, and an overstretched military hierarchy agreed to refuse these requests.[32] A perception within the British military in the early phases of the Iraq War that HM Armed Forces were still the preeminent purveyors of finely accumulated counterinsurgency theory and practice was fundamentally destroyed by such logistical and financial restrictions.

This mind-set helped turn US-UK relations sour on the ground. By August 2003, just three months after capturing Basra, Bremer was accusing the British military of going "weak in the knees" by showing reluctance to take action against the increasing influence of radical cleric Muqtada al-Sadr and his Mahdi Army militia.[33] But there were many in Washington who were blind to Bremer's interpretation of the emergent insurgency. Ali Allawi, the Iraqi finance minister in the Transitional National Government, credited the British for being first to appreciate the development of a nascent insurgency in the country; however, "the situation had not yet deteriorated to the point where they could challenge the entrenched American thinking" that postinvasion violence was orchestrated by what Defense Secretary Donald Rumsfeld referred to as "regime dead-enders."[34]

An early warning to the British of the levels of nascent lawlessness came in June 2003 when six Royal Military Police officers were killed by a mob in Majar al-Kabir in Maysan Province.[35] Yet such incidents were seen as isolated against the backdrop of British troops patrolling Basra in their regimental berets, shunning helmets and sunglasses as part of a "hearts and minds" approach, as progress was made in ingratiating the military with the local population. Arguably this perception of a relatively secure south lasted up until 2005, when the situation "deteriorated significantly" due to a rise in attacks on British and Iraqi troops and a rise in inter-Shi'a militia violence,[36] primarily between the rival factions of al-Sadr's Mahdi Army and the Badr Organization, the paramilitary wing of the Supreme Council of the Islamic Republic of Iraq, the largest Shi'a political party in the south. The intensity of the insurgency facing the British in and around Basra was far short of that facing the Americans in Baghdad or the infamous "Sunni Triangle" in central Iraq, yet the swift corrosion of British control over the south was exposing British adaptability to counterinsurgency as inadequate.

In the face of this evident breakdown in the British ability to implement sustainable reconstruction and ensure effective security, the Iraqi prime minister, Nouri al-Maliki, declared a state of emergency in Basra in May 2006 and promised to crush the insurgents and criminal gangs.[37] The visible manifestation of an "iron fist" approach was Operation Sinbad, launched in late September 2006. This was to be a joint British-Iraqi mission designed to curtail the power of militia death squads and shore up the political power of Basra's civil leaders. Taking areas of the city systematically, around a thousand British troops and twenty-three hundred Iraqi soldiers cordoned off and searched districts for militia members and provided security for reconstruction work to be carried out. Planned to last five months, activities for Sinbad "virtually came to a halt after one wave of raids" in the face of militia opposition, ensuring that the operation was characterized as "a last attempt to be seen to be doing something" before security responsibilities were transferred to the Iraqis.[38] The timing of the operation was questionable, given it occurred just a few months before the US "surge" was enacted, placing the British out of step with shifts in American strategy. Furthermore, the operation lacked sufficient support from Whitehall, heavily compromising its chances of success. Operation Sinbad became symptomatic of the overall British malaise in Iraq. Overstretched and operationally inert, the military was caught between the rock of vicious and multiple insurgencies and the hard place of political mismanagement and financial constraint. An additional constraint was identified by Brig. Justin Maciejewski, who commanded the British battle group during Operation Sinbad. He ruefully observed how perceptions of the special relationship shaped the entire war effort: "The first and over-riding factor shaping the British campaign in Iraq was that its purpose had nothing to do with Iraq. It was instead about the British political and institutional obsession with British-US security relations."[39] The subservience shown by Downing Street to the concept of a special relationship placed a strategic straightjacket on the British military in Iraq from which it was never able to escape.

By the end of 2007, Basra was gripped by gangland warfare driven by efforts to control oil exports.[40] Government institutions in the city had been infiltrated by rival extremist factions, fueling a cycle of politically motivated assassinations, intimidation, and vigilante law enforcement. This all occurred in a security vacuum because the British military had in early September withdrawn to their contingency operating base at the Basra airport on the outskirts of the city, leaving all inner-city patrolling to their fresh Iraqi trainees.

The withdrawal to an "overwatch" position was achieved peacefully despite the regularity of attacks that British troops had been facing. However, it soon emerged that this unmolested departure was the product of a deal struck between the British military and the Mahdi Army. An MoD spokesperson reluctantly justified the dialogue in pragmatic terms but denied a negotiated settlement as a precursor to withdrawal: "We talk to the Mahdi Army and other military groups in our area of operations as part of the strategy of political engagement. . . . [A]n outright refusal to engage in dialogue with them would not be in Iraq's or Basra's best interests."[41] However, a Mahdi Army leader claimed that the British had initiated talks with the militia group as their resilience had been broken: "They [the British] wanted us to stop attacking their compounds and troops. . . . It was obvious they had suffered enough attacks and could not deal with more."[42] The Mahdi Army claimed they had agreed a deal not to harass the British withdrawal on two conditions: that the withdrawal take all British troops out of the city and that detained Mahdi Army members be released. The fulfillment of both of these provisos understandably led to claims that the British ceded to insurgent demands, even if the result was a reduction in violence against British troops. Col. Peter Mansoor, Petraeus's executive officer at the time, confirmed that the British passed on to the American commander a request to release Mahdi Army prisoners. Petraeus resignedly acquiesced, appreciating that "there was really no option, given the prevailing sentiment in London" to get British troops out of Basra as quickly as possible.[43] The subsequent increase in Sadrist violence was widely perceived as a result of al-Sadr's desire to claim the credit for forcing the British out. Although the Americans had started to cut deals with Sunni insurgents as the "Awakening Movement" took hold in Anbar Province, including cash incentives not to attack US forces, the consequences of the British deal with Shi'a militias were far greater—essentially surrendering control of a city to the insurgency.

Key British generals tried to place a positive spin on the Basra withdrawal. The chief of the Defence Staff, Air Chief Marshal Sir Jock Stirrup, dismissed "the nonsense about the British having failed in Basra,"[44] while even the newly installed head of CENTCOM, Petraeus, felt compelled to argue that "the significance of the United Kingdom's contribution should not be underestimated. Its military activities . . . have been instrumental in successful capacity building and the progress that we have made in various endeavours."[45] However, this interpretation is overly benevolent and out of step with views held across the American civil-military spectrum. After the British withdrawal from Basra, a senior US official in Baghdad told the *Washington Post* that "it's hard now to paint Basra as a success story." A top intelligence agent weighed in too with the assessment that "the British have basically been defeated in the south."[46] Again speaking anonymously, a US general bitterly observed that "the British withdrawal was a rebuke to the whole US surge strategy."[47]

The repercussions for the British military became evident in 2008 when a furious Prime Minister al-Maliki deliberately did not include British commanders in the planning of Operation Charge of the Knights—what was to become a massive US-Iraqi military operation to rid Basra of the influence of the militias, including the Mahdi Army, in April 2008.[48] Iraqi government anger at the reluctance of the British military to reduce the power of the Mahdi Army in 2007–8 marked a distinct low point not only in UK-Iraqi relations, but also in terms of the perceived efficacy of the British military counterinsurgency effort in the country. As a consequence the Americans felt the need to step up their presence in the areas under nominal British control. Several senior commanders were sent to augment the fight against Shi'a militias in the south. Rear Adm. Edward Winters was sent to act as al-Maliki's personal coalition force liaison officer in Basra, while the US Marine Corps established a forward command post in the city to aid the British.[49]

The message was clear: The Americans had lost faith in the ability of the British to keep up their end of the counterinsurgency fight in Iraq. Having started the war as the second-largest coalition partner, the British soon became unable and uninterested in tackling the insurgency head-on. In large part this was due to the lack of political will in London for a protracted war, which played havoc with morale within the ranks on the ground and frustrated American commanders to the point of despair.[50] Col. Richard Iron, formerly a British adviser to key Iraqi generals in the south of the country, labeled the entire Basra campaign "an 'economy of effort' mission" by the British military.[51] Peter Mansoor concurred with this assessment, blaming senior British military personnel for assuming that militia-facilitated crime in Basra was not connected to the insurgency, as well as underestimating the Iranian influence on Muqtada al-Sadr and failing to adequately train the new Iraqi security forces. The result, Mansoor felt, was a withdrawal from Basra that represented an abdication of responsibility for the city by the British.[52] Mansoor was not the only senior US commander who felt pessimistic about the British war effort. US corps commander Lt. Gen. Pete Chiarelli told the British battle group commander, Brig. Justin Maciejewski, he thought that the British approach in Basra was "all about you and not about the mission."[53]

This opinion was reinforced across much of the American military by the relative success of the US-Iraqi Operation Charge of the Knights in tackling the violence of the Mahdi Army in Basra. US general Jack Keane, one of the architects of President Bush's troop surge strategy, criticized the British military performance in Basra, stating he was "frustrated" by the "disengagement" of British troops.[54] This represented a fundamental shift in perception with regard to the British, who in the early phase of the campaign perhaps felt rather superior to the Americans when it came to counterinsurgency. Epitomizing the initial British condescension toward the Americans when it came to counterinsurgency war-fighting were the comments of one British sergeant serving in Basra who told American journalist George Packer he thought that "the Americans don't think. They react."[55] But by 2007, the British had been outshone by the Americans since the Petraeus-implemented surge had radically reformed the situation in the American-occupied provinces.[56] But it is worth bearing in mind that the British had been cut out of any decision making that led to the surge. Upon assuming command of the British-controlled MND-SE at the same time as the surge was announced by President Bush in January 2007, Maj. Gen. Jonathan Shaw quickly discovered that the new American strategy has been formulated "with no apparent prior consultation with the UK," given how his brief to reduce British troop levels stood in stark contrast to the arrival of twenty-thousand additional US troops.[57] The allies had clearly begun to pull in different strategic directions.

At the heart of this Anglo-American friction lay the weight of the British historical experience in counterinsurgency wars. Hilary Synnott, the leading British political coordinator in Iraq during the early phases of the war, had warned that "extol[ling] the merits of the British approach" to countering insurgents in southern Iraq "implied that the British could manage such challenges better than the United States." Synnott also noted that praise for the British counterinsurgency effort in 2003–4 was an irritant to American military commanders, who "proved remarkably sensitive on this point."[58] The lessons from Northern Ireland in particular were initially interpreted by the British as having great utility for Iraq, but this soon began to grate on American commanders. When asked in 2008 by Mohan al-Furayji, the Iraqi general in charge of Basra, to devise a security plan for the city, Richard Iron admitted that he modeled it on "the security framework for Belfast in the 1970s and 1980s." This would involve placing company and battalion bases in the midst of insurgent strongholds to break "no-go areas."[59] This drew criticism from American commanders, including Colonel Mansoor, who lamented that "the British Army remained locked in a mindset that treated southern Iraq as if it were Northern Ireland."[60] The Americans were increasingly coming to see the British military as victims of its own history, trapped in analogies with previous counterinsurgency campaigns that were neither appropriate nor transferable.

Benign constructions of a discernable "British way" of counterinsurgency not only certainly shaped expectations of what the British military would achieve in Iraq but also formed malignant perceptions of American military culture in the realm of irregular warfare.[61] Such intra-alliance division between the British and the Americans over counterinsurgency in Iraq arguably sourced its roots to the nature and balance of the coalition.[62] Junior-coalition-partner status had become a strategic norm for Britain in the post–Cold War world, as demonstrated in the Gulf War and again in Kosovo and Afghanistan under a NATO rubric. Yet Iraq presented an unprecedented strategic scenario for the British military inasmuch as it represented the first time it had to operate as a junior partner in a counterinsurgency coalition. This placed the British in a strategic bind through which any discernable "British approach" to counterinsurgency was mitigated by overarching American coalition leadership. A strand of thought emerged within the British military that perceived significant barriers to the application of a distinctly British way stemming from the American suzerainty over the whole of Iraq, thus restricting the independent ability of the British to forge separate civil-military solutions in southern Iraq. As a consequence of this coalition structure, one British colonel noted, British military policy "became confused and suffered as it sought to serve the Americans."[63] All of this would gravely undermine the decades-old faith in British competence at counterinsurgency.

Similar tensions played out within the realm of intelligence-sharing. The nerve center of British intelligence in Iraq during Operation Telic (the operational code name given to the British deployment to Iraq from 2003 to 2011) was based in Baghdad, at Station House, inside the fortified "Green Zone." This intelligence headquarters, containing MI6, Special Air Service, and Special Reconnaissance Regiment officers, doubled as the US intelligence headquarters. Being housed under the same roof was designed to stimulate interagency intelligence cooperation.[64] However, hopes for enhanced intelligence-sharing with the Americans were dashed by a series of bureaucratic barriers. Anglo-American intelligence-sharing became a critical problem at a very early stage in the counterinsurgency campaign. American intelligence protocol classified all intelligence data in Iraq as "NOFORN"—no foreign access. This created the situation whereby British intelligence in Iraq, assembled by Station House, that was passed to the central US intelligence fusion center for collation into an all-source intelligence picture was automatically marked "NOFORN," barring the British from access to their own intelligence material. This became a major issue for British military commanders, who passed their frustration back to Whitehall. Eventually, Tony Blair took this issue up directly with George W. Bush in 2004, who signed a directive allowing British (and Australian, but no other coalition countries) access to intelligence material for the planning and training phases of counterinsurgency operations, although Pentagon foot-dragging ensured this initiative was not properly implemented.[65]

One area that stands out (for bucking the trend) as proof of solid British contribution to American strategic objectives was that of reconciliation with Sunni tribal leaders and "turning" insurgent leaders. In the early phases of the surge in 2007, Petraeus established the Force Strategic Engagement Cell (FSEC), a thirty-member team that was always commanded by a British officer, including Maj. Gen. Paul Newton and then Maj. Gen. Roddy Porter. The purpose of FSEC was to reach out to those elements of the insurgency deemed reconcilable and negotiate terms that would see them lay down their weapons. Petraeus's British deputy, Lt. Gen. Graeme Lamb, was widely credited with the foresight to create FSEC and emphasize the need for reconciliation.[66] FSEC started to change the language used by American commanders, with the blanket label "insurgent" being bifurcated into the more subtle "reconcilable" and "irreconcilable."[67] Porter, who commanded FSEC in 2008–9, felt that "without a shadow of a doubt" the Brits were given control of FSEC because the Americans thought they were strong at undertaking nonkinetic "nuanced operations."[68] Such residual perceptions of old-fashioned British strengths at persuasion over coercion in counterinsurgency were clearly hard to beat in some quarters of the US command structure.

Reflecting on Iraq

The struggle to contain the violence in southern Iraq points to an increasingly inescapable conclusion that the British are not as good at counterinsurgency as was previously assumed. Political posturing resulted in a reluctance to admit to failings, which only served to stifle the implementation of an effective and properly resourced campaign. The bruising experience in Iraq has demonstrated that the British political establishment has no stomach for protracted irregular wars. The result was a severe strain on UK civil-military relations and increased tension between London and Washington, not to mention heightened friction between US and UK forces on the ground. As Maj. Gen. Mungo Melvin, the former director (for land warfare) of the British Army, realistically concluded: "The US and the UK got in together, acted individually and left separately."[69]

Despite the input into preinvasion planning by the United Kingdom (the only coalition nation to have that privilege) and despite providing the second-highest number of troops during the conflict, the House of Commons Defence Select Committee admitted as early as March 2004 in its *Lessons of Iraq* report that, despite over one hundred UK officers being embedded within CENTCOM in the run-up to the invasion, it was not able to discern "the areas in which the British made specific contribution to what was essentially an American campaign plan," aside from offering "niche capabilities such as special forces operations." The report went on to recommend that the MoD apply better adaptability measures to the "highest levels of British command structures" so that they could "operate more closely in parallel with their American counterparts, when UK and US forces are operating together."[70] But as later reports emerging from Baghdad and Basra testifed, the levels of British adaptability counted for little given perpetual American unresponsiveness to the need to cooperate closely with British allies on the ground. Maj. Gen. Andrew Stewart, a key member of the British strategic planning team working with the Americans in the run-up to the war, felt that the timing of the invasion was "driven by the local politics of the timing of the US election," resulting in a premature war that stifled any chance to undertake more in-depth strategic planning or secure more legal legitimacy for regime change.[71] It was certainly not the first time a British general has felt compromised by the whims of American domestic politics, as earlier chapters in this book attest.

But perhaps the most important military legacy of the Iraq War was the effect it had on American and British perceptions of counterinsurgency warfare. It was generally accepted that as the "War on Terror" morphed into a protracted counterinsurgency campaign, the volume of British irregular warfare experience, from Palestine through to Northern Ireland, equated to competence in counterinsurgency operations. British brigadier Nigel Aylwin-Foster's (in)famous *Military Review* article in 2005 that admonished American thinking and performance in Iraq came to encapsulate the entrenched British mind-set of superiority when it came to counterinsurgency.[72] However, the underwhelming British response to the complexities of the multiple and networked insurgencies that arose in the wake of the invasion of Iraq pulled the scales away from American eyes about the competency of their main coalition ally at irregular warfare. The decision by Prime Minister al-Maliki to co-opt the American military and remove British troops from the planning and execution of Operation Charge of the Knights in April 2008 to rid Basra of the growing influence of the Mahdi Army epitomized the degeneration of faith in British counterinsurgency competency.

The involvement of the British military in the initial invasion of Iraq provided a fig leaf of international consensus for a neoconservative administration in

Washington that was intent on removing a dictator but was incapable of forging a rapid response to Iraq's descent into sectarian insurgency. The British may have been the second-largest coalition force, and there may have been special privileges granted to British commanders in terms of intelligence-sharing, but British performance during counterinsurgency operations failed to convince the Americans that the British were of fundamental utility to the attainment of their ultimate goals. Based on his experiences as one of the British deputy commanders of MNF-I, Gen. Sir John McColl observed in 2006 that American forces are "extraordinarily open to involvement and access, but there is no special relationship. Our influence as a junior partner depends upon what we do."[73] The popular American perception that, in the end, the British did not do much cost the United Kingdom a significant amount of influence and reduced the level of transatlantic respect for Britain's purported counterinsurgency prowess.

The final words on this should go to Sir John Chilcot, the man tasked by then prime minister Gordon Brown in 2009 to head up the Iraq Inquiry, which assessed Britain's involvement in the planning, execution, and aftermath of the invasion. Taking seven years to publish and covering twelve volumes containing six thousand pages and 2.5 million words, the Chilcot Report (as it became known) was in no doubt that "the UK's relationship with the US was a determining factor in the Government's decisions over Iraq."[74] When finally released in the summer of 2016, the report concluded in no uncertain terms that the Blair government had deferred to the Bush administration on most prewar planning issues for two reasons: that US-UK relations would be damaged if Britain did not go along with the war plans and that cooperating so closely with the Americans would actually buy greater influence on the direction of the war.[75] The very fact that the United Kingdom failed to achieve either objective is a sign that an unquestioning adherence to the notion that a special relationship existed merely conjured a grand delusion in London that Britain could use it as leverage. Rarely has such an aggrandized interpretation of a diplomatic alliance led to such foreign policy folly. As Chilcot drily concluded, "the US and UK are close allies, but the relationship between the two is unequal."[76] The joint deployment in Afghanistan during the war in Iraq would only compound this problem and enhance American frustration at contemporary British efforts to quell insurgent violence effectively.

Notes

Epigraph: Quoted in "Iraq War: We Have to Face the Truth and Admit We Failed," *Daily Telegraph*, March 9, 2013, http://www.telegraph.co.uk/news/worldnews/middleeast/iraq/9919666/Iraq-War-we-have-to-face-the-truth-and-admit-we-failed.html.

1. Garden, "Iraq," 703.

2. Keegan, *Iraq War*, 66.
3. In particular, see Shawcross, *Allies*.
4 *Stability Operations in Iraq: An Analysis from a Land Perspective*, report prepared under the direction of the Chief of General Staff, 17, http://www.operationtelic.co.uk/documents/uk-stbility-operations-in-iraq-2006.pdf.
5. *FM 3-24: US Army and Marine Corps, Counterinsurgency Field Manual.*
6. For example, see Wither, "British Bulldog or Bush's Poodle?," 67–82.
7. Danchev, "Tony Blair's Vietnam," 189–203.
8. Bush, *Decision Points*, 231.
9. Interview with Maj. Gen. Tim Cross (Ret.), Nottingham, March 5, 2013.
10. Kennedy-Pipe and Vickers, "'Blowback' for Britain?," 208.
11. House of Commons Defence Select Committee, *Iraq: An Initial Assessment of Post-Conflict Operations*," 15.
12. Interview with Maj. Gen. Tim Cross (Ret.), Nottingham, March 5, 2013.
13. Ibid.
14. Synnott, "Statebuilding in Southern Iraq," 43.
15. Ibid., 40.
16. Gordon and Trainor, *Cobra II*, 472.
17. Andrew Stewart, "Southern Iraq 2003–2004," in Bailey et al., *British Generals in Blair's Wars*, 85.
18. Greenstock, British Diplomatic Oral History Programme, interview #99, http://www.chu.cam.ac.uk/archives/collections/BDOHP/Greenstock.pdf.
19. Quoted in Fairweather, *War of Choice*, 79.
20. Ricks, *Fiasco*, 255.
21. Gordon and Trainor, *Cobra II*, 471–73.
22. Ibid., 488–89.
23. Bremer, *My Year in Iraq*, 93.
24. "Iraq Civil War Warning for Blair," BBC News, August 3, 2006, http://news.bbc.co.uk/go/pr/fr/-/1/hi/uk/5240808.stm.
25. Donnelly, "Cousins' Counter-Insurgency Wars," 4.
26. Fairweather, *War of Choice*, 44–45.
27. Ibid., 420.
28. Synnott, "Statebuilding in Southern Iraq," 47.
29. House of Commons Defence Committee, *UK Operations in Iraq*, evidence #22.
30. Woodward, *State of Denial*, 292.
31. Interview with Maj. Gen. Tim Cross (Ret.), Nottingham, March 5, 2013.
32. Elliott, *High Command*, 112–13.
33. Bremer, *My Year in Iraq*, 135.
34. Allawi, *Occupation of Iraq*, 241.
35. For a vivid insight into the British military counterinsurgency approach in Maysan Province, see Holmes, *Dusty Warriors*.
36. House of Commons Defence Committee, *UK Operations in Iraq*, 6.

37. "Iraq Imposes Emergency in Basra," BBC News, May 31, 2006, http://news.bbc.co.uk/go/pr/fr/-/1/hi/world/middle_east/5032294.stm.
38. "Operation Sinbad: Mission Failure Casts Doubt on Entire British Presence in Iraq," *Independent*, October 7, 2006, http://www.independent.co.uk/news/world/middle-east/operation-sinbad-mission-failure-casts-doubt-on-entire-british-presence-in-iraq-419173.html.
39. Justin Maciejewski, "'Best Effort': Operation Sinbad and the Iraq Campaign," in Bailey et al., *British Generals in Blair's Wars*, 157.
40. Ricks, *Gamble*, 242.
41. "US Tells Generals to 'Lay Off' Britain as Mahdi Army Claims It Forced Basra Truce," *Sunday Times* (London), September 9, 2007, http://www.thesundaytimes.co.uk/sto/news/world_news/article71203.ece.
42. Ibid.
43. Mansoor, *Surge*, 237.
44. "Government 'Gave Public False Hopes' on Achieving Iraq Goals," *Times* (London), October 8, 2007, http://www.thetimes.co.uk/tto/news/politics/article2023988.ece.
45. UK Forces Media Operations, "US Commander Thanks UK for Contribution to Iraq and Afghanistan," February 6, 2009, https://helmandblog.blogspot.co.uk/2009/02/us-commander-thanks-uk-for-contribution.html?m=0.
46. Quoted in "As British Leave, Basra Deteriorates," *Washington Post*, August 7, 2007, http://www.washingtonpost.com/wp-dyn/content/article/2007/08/06/AR2007080601401.html.
47. Quoted in Fairweather, *War of Choice*, 316.
48. "Iraq Snubbed Britain and Calls US into Basra Battle," *Times* (London), April 10, 2008, http://www.thetimes.co.uk/tto/news/world/middleeast/iraq/article1991651.ece; and "Secret Deal Kept Army out of Battle for Basra," *Times* (London), August 5, 2008, http://www.thetimes.co.uk/tto/news/world/middleeast/iraq/article1992350.ece.
49. Mansoor, *Surge*, 242.
50. Ucko, "Lessons from Basra," 153.
51. Iron, "Charge of the Knights," 55.
52. Mansoor, *Surge*, 246–47.
53. Maciejewski, "'Best Effort'," 162.
54. "US 'Frustrated' with UK in Basra," BBC News, August 22, 2007, http://news.bbc.co.uk/go/pr/fr/-/1/hi/world/middle_east/6958395.stm.
55. Packer, *Assassins' Gate*, 426.
56. Ricks, *Gamble*, 277.
57. Jonathan Shaw, "Basra 2007," in Bailey et al., *British Generals in Blair's Wars*, 175–76.
58. Synnott, "Statebuilding in Southern Iraq," 40–41.
59. Iron, "Charge of the Knights," 56.
60. Mansoor, *Surge*, 235.

61. In particular, see Garfield, *Succeeding in Phase IV*, Foreign Policy Research Institute report, September 2006, http://www.fpri.org/docs/Garfield.SucceedinginPhaseIV.pdf, and Wither, "Basra's Not Belfast," 611–35.
62. Even the General Staff's report of British stability operations in Iraq felt compelled to document US-UK friction over the utility of Britain's previous counterinsurgency experience. See *Stability Operations in Iraq*, Army Code 71844, 8, http://www.operationtelic.co.uk/documents/uk-stbility-operations-in-iraq-2006.pdf.
63. Alistair Campbell, "Assessing Britain's Legacy: The UK Withdrawal from Iraq," RUSI, https://rusi.org/commentary/assessing-britain%E2%80%99s-legacy-uk-withdrawal-iraq.
64. "Secret War of the SAS," *Sunday Times* (London), September 16, 2007, http://www.thesundaytimes.co.uk/sto/news/uk_news/article71653.ece.
65. Woodward, *State of Denial*, 318–19.
66. Mansoor, *Surge*, 85–86.
67. Urban, *Task Force Black*, 186.
68. Interview with Maj. Gen. Roddy Porter (Ret.), London, April 21, 2015.
69. Quoted in Elliott, *High Command*, 122.
70. House of Commons Defence Select Committee, *Lessons of Iraq*, 5–7.
71. Stewart, "Southern Iraq 2003–2004," in Bailey et al., *British Generals in Blair's Wars*, 79.
72. Aylwin-Foster, "Changing the Army," 2–15.
73. John McColl, "Modern Campaigning: From a Practitioner's Perspective," in Bailey et al., *British Generals in Blair's Wars*, 116.
74. Executive Summary, Report of the Iraq Inquiry, www.iraqinquiry.org.uk, 51.
75. Ibid., 52.
76. Ibid., 130.

10

Into the Hornet's Nest

The "Special Relationship" in Afghanistan

We and Karzai agree the British are not up to the task of securing Helmand.
—Bill Wood, US ambassador to Afghanistan

After the withdrawal from Basra, the British reputation for counterinsurgency competency lay in tatters. The withdrawal of UK forces from Iraq in 2009 meant that Helmand Province in Afghanistan became the arena in which the British contingent of the International Security Assistance Force (ISAF) could restore some of its faded kudos in the realm of counterinsurgency warfare. The Helmand campaign needed to vindicate the ignominious outcome of Operation Telic in Iraq. Yet many of the same mistakes and problems were repeated on the second front of the American-led "War on Terror," leading to similar levels of strategic dysfunction. As John Nagl has put it, "if Iraq was the midterm, Afghanistan is the final exam" for Anglo-American counterinsurgents.[1] The final exam grade certainly offers both militaries room for improvement.

The war in Afghanistan has covered neither Britain nor the United States in counterinsurgency glory. But the travails of the war in Iraq increased the need for Washington and London to salvage the raison d'être of the War on Terror and, more crucially for the British, rebuild damaged bridges with the Americans after the imbroglio in Basra. Even Lt. Gen. Robert Fry, the former senior British military representative and deputy commanding general of the Multi-National Force in Iraq, argued that the Iraq campaign "infected operations in Afghanistan" as the negativity surrounding operations in Basra was transferred to Helmand.[2] The commitment to securing strategically important parts of Afghanistan—namely, the major poppy-producing province of Helmand—was the British government's attempt to remain both close and relevant to American grand strategy. The outcome of the numerous iterations of Operation Herrick in Afghanistan has arguably failed to achieve that goal of restoring American faith in British counterinsurgency proficiency. The "special relationship" is therefore the "elephant in the room" when assessing America's longest military operation,[3] which is an important event to consider when taking stock of contemporary US-UK relations.

Of course, operations in Afghanistan both predated and outlasted the war in Iraq, but the shadow cast over what the Americans codenamed Operation Enduring Freedom was long and ultimately inescapable. It diverted resources and attention at a time when the West had been lulled into believing the war against the Taliban and al-Qaeda in Afghanistan was an accomplished mission—a view that came to be shared by senior military figures.[4] The creation of a two-front War on Terror placed a vastly increased amount of resource pressure on the militaries of the United States and the United Kingdom. But while the American military expanded to meet the need, its British counterparts were unable to follow suit because, according to the then director (for land warfare) for the British Army, Maj. Gen. Mungo Melvin, it was either unable or unwilling to do so.[5]

Even a cursory understanding of Afghan history would reveal an inherent societal suspicion of outsiders that has woven a pattern in the nation's past, stacking the odds heavily against external interference. As far back as the fourth century BCE, Alexander the Great barely made it out of the Konar Valley alive as he faced vicious indigenous opposition to his army's presence. Subsequently, the armies of kings, empires, and superpowers have all launched operations across the great plains and mountains of Afghanistan. All have failed to achieve lasting results in the face of massive resistance. To know your Afghan history, as the former CIA station chief in Kabul in the 1980s, Milton Bearden, put it, is to acknowledge that the country is "the graveyard of empires."[6] When the British military deployed to Afghanistan in 2001 is was the fourth time in 170 years that British forces had trod Afghan soil in an attempt to alter the shape of its body politic.[7] Tales of British intervention in Afghanistan during the "Great Game" of Anglo-Russian competition in the nineteenth century may have receded from historical memory in the United Kingdom, but stories of the nefarious British had been passed down by generations of Afghans ever since. The past did not augur well for contemporary success.

ISAF's strategy in Afghanistan, shaped by America's post-9/11 priorities, contained three broad goals: preventing the return of the Taliban, eradicating al-Qaeda's presence there, and building state political and infrastructural capacity. But the confluence of means and ends proved to be elusive as strategic confusion, resource constriction, and political distraction beset leaders in London and Washington and trickled down to military commanders. The situation on the ground in Helmand Province, which came to be the crucible in which contemporary Anglo-American counterinsurgency theory and practice played out, exacerbated these problems significantly. Helmand's complex conflict dynamic, including fierce tribal rivalries locked in competition for influence and resources, was intensified by the presence of foreign fighters (predominantly Pakistanis of the Quetta Shura Taliban) and the centrality of narcotics production to the local economy. Ultimately, British and American strategy in Afghanistan did not adapt to, or adequately reflect, the societal schisms that divide the country.[8] Indeed, the ISAF allies' perception of the conflict was at odds with how many Afghans viewed the war. As the United States and United Kingdom talked of state-building at the national level, Afghanistan's tribal society came to perceive the conflict predominantly through a civil war lens, based on a struggle for tribal supremacy.[9] The expeditionary counterinsurgency powers became a pawn in a bigger game of intertribal chess over which Washington and London could exert little control.

The Early Years: Victory and Reconstruction, 2001–6

It did not take long for the finger of responsibility for the 9/11 terrorist attacks on the United States to point at the Afghanistan-based group al-Qaeda, led by Osama bin Laden. War planning was kicked into immediate high gear in the Pentagon as the nascent War on Terror got under way. British solidarity with America in the wake of the attacks stretched much further than the playing of the "Star Spangled Banner" outside Buckingham Palace on the night of the attacks. As Sir Anthony Brenton, then minister at the British embassy in Washington, recalls: "Washington was in lock down for more or less three months, while we were coordinating a war with the Americans in Afghanistan. . . . There must be few examples of two governments working as closely together as we did with the Americans over that period."[10]

The shared sense of grief and shock at the 9/11 attacks propelled London and Washington to commit to overthrowing the Taliban regime in Afghanistan as retribution for its sheltering of bin Laden. Al-Qaeda was to be dislodged from the country and the organization smashed. Transatlantic solidarity for these goals led many within British diplomatic circles to acknowledge, as former ambassador to Afghanistan Sir Sherard Cowper-Coles did, that the Blair government "took it upon itself to act as principal cheerleader for the American-led effort in Afghanistan."[11] The invoking of NATO's Article 5 collective security clause symbolized Western solidarity and paved the way for the multinational ISAF force to come into being.

The toppling of the Taliban was a cathartic achievement for the American military. As al-Qaeda fighters scattered, the strategic objective for the next few years turned away from kinetic war-fighting in the absence of a cohesive enemy and toward reconstruction and peacekeeping. One of the key innovations during these early years of the Afghan war was the creation of provisional reconstruction teams (PRTs) to help fulfill the goal of rebuilding the war-torn and poverty-stricken nation. PRTs were the brain-child of the then colonel Nick Carter in 2002 while he was chief planner at the US military headquarters at Bagram Airbase. PRTs, Carter felt, were the solution to providing provincial-level peacekeeping while avoiding an increase in troop numbers. This was arguably the greatest contribution by a British officer to American strategy in Afghanistan, given the way in which the civil-military PRTs pulled the focus away from operations to mop up remnants of the Taliban and pushed it toward providing enhanced reconstruction efforts and the promotion of good governance. The PRTs enhanced the nascent work of American civil affairs teams deployed across the country working in the Quick Impact Projects (QIP) program, doing such things as building schools or digging wells.[12]

Such projects operated in a relatively benign security environment up until 2006. This lulled US and UK political leaders into assuming that Afghanistan was a mission accomplished. Instead, the Taliban had bided their time in regrouping, retraining, and planning a renewed offensive to take back lost territory. The emergence of a "neo-Taliban" insurgency in 2006 marked a new, bloody phase in the conflict in which Anglo-American counterinsurgency effectiveness would be severely tested.

The Helmand Hornet's Nest: 2006–9

As ISAF's strategy unfolded into the fifth year of the conflict, the coalition prioritized a push southward to firmly secure provinces with a residual Taliban presence. For the 3,600-strong British military contingent, this meant deployment to Helmand province—the epicenter of Afghanistan's still burgeoning poppy harvest. Although taking command of operations in Helmand in May 2006 and increasing troop numbers to 5,500, the British still had a physical presence in only a relatively small part of a province roughly the size of Wales.[13]

The predeployment "Joint UK Plan for Helmand" espoused clear notions of the importance of the politically oriented nature of all military operations, the axiomatic nature of all development programs, and the essential collaboration with Afghan National Security Forces. Its aim was to ensure the British deployment fostered "an effective, representative government in Afghanistan, with security forces capable of providing an environment in which sustainable economic and social development can occur, without substantial security support from the international community."[14] However, this idealized set of counterinsurgency goals failed to materialize in practice, given endemic corruption at all levels of Afghan governance, a questionable level of loyalty and proficiency within the new Afghan military, and the continuing reliance on large amounts of foreign aid money.

Indeed, the very policy process that led to the British taking command of Helmand has been the subject of subsequent debate. Matt Cavanagh, a former special adviser to the then UK defense secretary Des Browne, has since argued that there were "serious failings in ministers' decision-making" in the run-up to the Helmand deployment. He cites an absence of strategic clarity within Whitehall, which was the product of "generalised, almost abstract," discussions between key political players—the most culpable of whom was Prime Minister Tony Blair, who was determined to announce the Helmand mission in advance of the London conference on Afghanistan in January 2006 so he could portray himself as a strong, decisive leader.[15] The deployment can also be seen as a move to strengthen the British role as ISAF lead on counternarcotics strategy, which had been decided back at the Bonn Summit in December 2001. Helmand produced nearly half of Afghanistan's entire poppy harvest. Considering that the country virtually monopolizes global opium production, with 92 percent of the worldwide total, it appeared to make political sense to Blair for Britain to take a bigger role.[16] But as each British task force that went to Helmand came to understand, pursuing a stringent counternarcotics policy in a province whose predominant source of local employment and wealth is the poppy harvest became antithetical to the pursuit of a counterinsurgency strategy that required winning over the loyalties of local tribes. This was the perpetual paradox at the heart of the British military mission to Helmand.

What met the British in 2006 was an anarchic situation that was the result of an internecine struggle between a myriad of tribal groups. British commanders had difficulty delineating between tribal leaders who were nominally pro-Taliban or progovernment. In one instance, when UK troops first moved on the strategically important town of Sangin, the "government" tribes immediately offered information on the whereabouts of the "Taliban" tribes. A savvy Afghan National Army (ANA) commander working alongside the British quickly interceded, warning his UK counterparts that such "intelligence" was merely a ruse to settle an intertribal feud.[17] Such was the vicious local politics of Helmand, with the British unsure of whom to trust. The failure to overcome the ferocity of local opposition to outside interference and master the complexities of tribal politics remained the single greatest barrier to the instigation of reconstruction programs in the earliest phase of the Helmand mission.[18]

The first few years of the Helmand mission were beset by a series of other problems affecting the security situation. Eventual tactical successes were compromised by the absence of strategic momentum. The goals established in the joint plan never really lent the mission a driving purpose, which weakened the overarching political narrative of the British role in the war. The military were hamstrung by a murky intelligence picture and an ongoing deficiency in troop numbers.[19] Collectively, these factors made the province-wide delivery of key strategic goals very difficult indeed.

Taking command of the British task force in May 2006, 16 Air Assault Brigade was initially charged with applying "clear-and-hold" operations across the key towns in Helmand, including Musa Qaleh, Sangin, Now Zad, and Lashkar Gah the latter the location of their main base at Camp Bastion. These towns were to become the focal points of a Malaya-style "ink spot strategy," whereby forces were concentrated in these specific locations with the purpose of then percolating strength outward. However, the key weakness of what became known as the "platoon house" strategy of creating a series of small fortified bases throughout Helmand was the way in which it required the thin dispersal of the relatively undermanned battle group—a perennial problem through the numerous iterations of Operation Herrick.[20]

Symptomatic of the weakness of the platoon house strategy was the negotiated withdrawal from Musa Qaleh in October 2006. Having pushed the Taliban out of the town, the task force commander, Brig. Ed Butler, authorized a pullout of British forces with the proviso that local tribal leaders not allow the Taliban to return. Within four months, Musa Qaleh was back under Taliban control and all gains nullified.[21] The Taliban spun this as a humiliating defeat for the British, while UK commanders depicted it as tribal double-crossing that had undone a perfectly pragmatic policy toward handing responsibility for local security over to Afghans themselves. Either way, the entire Musa Qaleh deal had been done without the knowledge or approval of any American commanders. The outcome did not endear British ingenuity to their American allies.[22] Even the British general David Richards, who had become overall ISAF commander six months before the Musa Qaleh deal, distanced himself from the entire platoon house strategy, but neither did he encourage a wholesale rethink of it.[23]

The platoon house strategy did not impress American commanders, as it tied down the vast majority of Britain's available troops in the province. As a result the British were able to contribute only a very small number to Operation Medusa in September 2006, one of the largest joint ISAF efforts to take on the Taliban in southern Afghanistan. American irritation at the inability of British forces to participate in the operation was compounded by an obfuscated chain of command, which meant that despite his desire to do so, the American commander of Task Force 76, Maj. Gen. Ben Freakley, could not compel the British commander of Regional Command South (RC-S), Brig. Ed Butler, to move his forces despite RC-S falling under his technical, but not practical, command. Journalist James Fergusson reported that Butler's apparent refusal to agree to Freakley's request for more British troops to be sent as part of the Medusa force "came close to causing a diplomatic incident" after Freakley angrily complained to ISAFs combined forces commander, Gen. Karl Eikenberry, about Butler's behavior, furiously asserting that "I nearly knocked that Limey's lamps out."[24] So bad were relations between the British and American commanders that journalist Jack Fairweather observed how the "British military leadership live[d] in perpetual fear of American reprimands" for the slow operational progress they were making.[25]

Anglo-American relations on the battlefield were not helped by the launching of Operation Mountain Thrust in the spring of 2006. The objective of the multinational eleven-thousand-strong force was to hunt and capture Osama bin Laden and destroy remnants of al-Qaeda in the Helmand area. The main problem was the prominent role played by US special operations units that roamed through the province pursuing their own agenda without liaising with their allies. Furthermore, the British commander in the town of Now Zad was given no prior warning of US air attacks, mainly by Spectre gunships, in the British area of operations. This "caused bad blood between the allies," and there was grumbling by the British that the American special operations units were relying far too heavily on air power to assist them. A senior British officer in Sangin got so disgruntled with the US special operations forces in his district that he reportedly requested their immediate withdrawal because of concerns he had over their effect on "hearts and minds" efforts.[26]

The behavior of local Afghan leaders in Helmand exacerbated these intracoalition tensions. British commanders repeatedly felt outplayed in a three-way politico-military game with their American and Afghan counterparts. During Operation Herrick IV (May–November 2006), the then governor of Helmand, Mohammed Daoud, used his personal friendship with Afghan president Hamid Karzai to go over the head of ISAF's British commander in the province, Brig. Ed Butler, and get the Americans to coerce the British into taking his own orders. As Butler recalled, "Daoud would ring him [Karzai] and say, 'The British, Ed and the boys, are not supporting me.' Karzai would then talk to the Americans—General Eikenberry at that stage. . . . So then there was a GOA [Government of Afghanistan]-American alliance against the Brits, who were not doing what they were told."[27] The British, initially so keen to play junior coalition ally, soon found that they were losing the game of battlefield politics with the Americans.

Having taken over as the lead formation of the British Army in Afghanistan from 16 Air Assault Brigade in November 2006, 3 Commando Brigade adopted a more kinetic approach to operations and sought out Taliban units. It introduced the concept of mobile operations groups—units of 250 men in forty armored vehicles—as a means of taking the fight to the insurgents. The result was a fourfold increase in enemy engagements compared to the six-month tour of its predecessors.[28] More large-scale, clear-and-hold operations were undertaken by their successor unit, 12 Mechanised Brigade, six months later, but there were significant questions raised over the longevity of the British "hold" over towns, as the Taliban were soon returning to areas the British had departed after declaring them cleared.[29] It was not until the construction of the strategic plan known as the "Helmand road map" in spring 2008 that a substantial reassessment of the British campaign in Afghanistan came about, with responsibility for its execution falling to 52 Infantry Brigade. Population-centric operations took a greater prevalence, which were to be guided by a new Tactical Conflict Assessment Framework, which used quantitative data to measure the "success" of operations. Kinetic operations were to be downsized to focus on achievements within specific Afghan Development Zones,[30] while the platoon house strategy gave way to a more consolidated system of forward operating bases (FOBs) that aimed to embed soldiers in local communities to build links and trust. This, however, was still vulnerable to Taliban exploitation, as the isolated FOBs proved unable to suppress long-term insurgent activity.[31]

In order to coordinate the training of their ANA partners, the British Army participated in NATO-run operational mentoring and liaison teams (OMLTs). These were an important device to aid an eventual exit strategy from Afghanistan as a means of allowing the Afghans to "step up" as ISAF "stood down" from security roles. But funding resources for OMLTs were small and slow, while equipment shortages within the British Army meant that the ANA was left without basic communication devices and vehicles.[32]

Funding shortages also beset the broader development goals of the Afghan war. Quick Impact Projects were designed to gain favorable local opinion by freeing up resources swiftly to initiate small-scale development schemes that could have an immediate effect.[33] But the inability to readily get a large number of QIPs off the ground, combined with increasing Helmandi anger at the number of civilian casualties stemming from coalition air strikes, resulted in a lack of popular support for the overall presence of the British in the province.[34]

This did not go unnoticed by their American allies. In 2007, the American commander of ISAF, Gen. Dan McNeill, was quoted as saying that the British had "made a mess of things in Helmand."[35] This dim view was not just confined to the military. In 2008, the US ambassador to Afghanistan, Bill Wood, sent a memo to Defense Secretary Robert Gates disparaging their biggest ISAF ally: "We and Karzai agree the British are not up to the task of securing Helmand."[36] Wood's candor was a blow to British diplomatic efforts in Kabul. His British counterpart, Sir Sherard Cowper-Coles, later recalled that at one of his first briefings upon arriving in post in 2007, Cowper-Coles told his intelligence liaison officer that his main goal would be to build trust with Karzai: "'Oh no it won't,' he retorted.... 'Your key relationship will be with the American Ambassador. He matters most to us.'"[37]

Wood's successor in Kabul, retired general Karl Eikenberry, was of a similar mind. He sent a memo to Secretary of State Hillary Clinton in January 2010 arguing that instead of trying to persuade the British to stay in Helmand in a show of alliance solidarity, they should instead push for American troops to gradually take over control of the province instead.[38] A discernible shift in Anglo-American working relations in Afghanistan took place soon after Eikenberry sent his memo, and it made for a discernibly strained special relationship.

Here Come the Marines: US and UK Forces in Helmand, 2009–14

The trigger for this marked decline in cordiality was the replacement of the Dutch military contingent in Helmand by the US Marine Corps in mid-2009. Although a battalion of US Marines had been in northern Helmand since 2008, this brigade-sized deployment was a consequence of President Barack Obama's Afghan "surge" strategy that saw nearly a quarter of the entire twenty thousand additional troops reach Helmand Province in time to launch Operation Strike of the Sword in July.[39]

By the time the president had announced his new Afghanistan strategy, the British military had come to a realization that it could not hold large areas of Helmand alone and needed to cede command of large parts of the province to the Americans. As a result of this desire, the UK commander, Lt. Gen. Nick Parker, lobbied Downing Street to have the town of Sangin—the location of the highest number of British casualties—transferred to American control. To his dismay, this request was denied, with Gordon Brown's government having one eye on the upcoming general election and the other on managing the already damaged reputation of the British military. This would look like another Basra, feared the prime minister, especially to the Americans. Lt. Gen. Larry Nicholson, the commander of the US Marine Corps deployment in Helmand, questioned the long-term commitment of the British to the Afghan war effort, leading to American wariness of the reliability of their British allies.[40]

When Sangin was eventually handed over in the autumn of 2010, the US Marines discounted many of the patrolling techniques that the British military had built up over four years of deployment there. This included mine sweeps conducted on foot, with cleared paths then being marked and strictly followed by subsequent patrols. The US Marines preferred not to dismount from their armored vehicles, leading to a lapse in the observation of improvised explosive devices. As a result, the US Marines in Helmand took some of the highest casualty levels since the beginning of the entire war, with 25 dead and 140 injured in the first two months alone. This was a heavy price to pay for deviating from, or ignoring, British tactics.[41]

At the time that Obama was conducting his strategic review into Afghan war strategy soon after coming to office, there were seventeen British military personnel embedded inside US Central Command. Cooperation at the senior levels of military command was augmented later by the appointment of a British three-star general as deputy commander of ISAF and the selection of Mark Sedwill, the then British ambassador in Kabul, to become NATO's senior civilian representative, the highest nonmilitary Western role in the country in January 2010.[42] But such close working relations existed only at the senior military and diplomatic level. On the ground in Helmand, the newly deployed US Marines had a fractious rapport with their British civilian advisers.[43] By the autumn of 2010, the US Marine commander in Musa Qaleh, Lt. Col. Michael Manning, decided that based on what he had seen the British do, their mantra must have been "Promise Everything, Deliver Nothing."[44]

So visible was the discord that the *Washington Post* ran a story observing that "disagreement among the supposed allies are almost as frequent as firefights with insurgents."[45] The root of this disharmony is one that has come to encapsulate modern Anglo-American perceptions of each other's approach to counterinsurgency: American frustration at perceived British timidity and complacency and British anger at perceived American overaggression and bluster. Even the leading COINinista, John Nagl, previously so forceful in his admiration of British counterinsurgency in the "classical era," concluded after seeing the US "Afghan surge" take place that "the sad truth is that only American soldiers were consistently effective enough in an offensive role to clear the Taliban from their sanctuaries."[46] This is hardly a ringing endorsement of coalition counterinsurgency war-fighting with British allies.

So evident were rifts between the allies that even local tribes sought to exploit them. Mike Martin recounted from interviews with tribal leaders in areas where the US Marines had taken control: "Helmandi leaders would often insult the British to the Americans while emphasising how grateful they were that the Americans had taken their place, yet the same leaders would then tell the British that is was terrible that the Americans had come and that they would much prefer to carry on working with the British. Unfortunately, many British and American officers fell for these ploys."[47]

Such manipulation by tribes, mixed with ignorance of local politics and simmering Anglo-American tensions, led to a potent mix that contributed to the inability to fulfill key strategic objectives in Helmand. But the British were keen to dispel notions that the US Marines had been deployed to Helmand to bail out a stalled campaign. As one British officer quipped, "We don't want this to look like another Basra."[48] The result was a series of large British operations designed to secure swaths of Taliban-controlled land. The first was Operation Panther's Claw, launched in June 2009 and focused on retaking the area between Lashkar Gah and Gereshk. But lasting operational success proved illusive. The inability to permanently clear the area of insurgents in the run-up to the August 2009 presidential elections compromised the security backdrop to this milestone political event in which Hamid Karzai eventually won reelection.[49]

The next major British attempt to rejuvenate their flagging counterinsurgency campaign came in the spring of 2010 with Operation Moshtarak II. Constituting part of the new "population-centric" vision of new ISAF commander Gen. Stanley

McChrystal, British forces were tasked with leading the offensive against insurgent elements in the district of Nad-e-Ali. Gains were made in pushing insurgents out of the area, but the biggest challenge remained making a lasting impact on the loyalties of the local people.[50]

But small operational gains were overshadowed by the now obvious fractiousness between the Brits and Americans on the ground. Senior military figures, as has already been noted, were happy to establish liaison and create an image of a close alliance, but their junior officers and noncommissioned officers in Helmand were increasingly frustrated by each other's contending approaches to counterinsurgency. In evidence to the House of Commons Defence Select Committee, the former ISAF commander and then chief of the Defence Staff Gen. Sir David Richards admitted that "at the lower, tactical level" the working relationship between the US Marines and British forces in Helmand left him "worried." Yet he argued that "at the very highest level, relations could not be closer" between the American and British military.[51] But Richards's spin on elite-level relations has been undermined by revelations of testy personal relationships between key US and UK commanders. Lt. Gen. Daniel Bolger, the US Army commander of the NATO Training Mission in Afghanistan from 2011 to 2014, waited until his retirement to launch a broadside at his British counterpart Gen. Nick Carter. As head of NATO's Regional Command South from 2009 to 2010, Carter had pushed the policy of "courageous restraint" to minimize civilian casualties. Bolger interpreted Carter's leadership as "risk averse," accusing the British general of costing American service personnel their lives through his refusal to authorize air and artillery support for US Marines in Helmand. Bolger labeled Carter a "digital chateau general" who avoided frontline visits and obsessed about PowerPoint briefings.[52] This is not evidence of a working relationship that "could not be closer," as Richards depicts.

These insurmountable clashes at the very top blunted the efficacy of the alliance's counterinsurgency campaign. As Rajiv Chandrasekaran, who covered the war extensively for the *Washington Post*, concluded, "the two closest allies in Afghanistan failed to understand each other. . . . The result [of better understanding] almost certainly would have been fewer body bags draped with the Union Jack or the Stars and Stripes."[53] The utter absence of a special relationship at work on the ground in Afghanistan would be one of the most distinguishing legacies of the joint deployment to Helmand.

Afghanistan and Transatlantic Counterinsurgency Legacies

In March 2011, the ISAF commander, Gen. David Petraeus, built into his schedule a two-day visit to London on his way back to Kabul from Washington after giving testimony to congressional hearings on progress in Afghanistan. Aside from formal briefings to the prime minister, the chief of the Defence Staff, and the defense and foreign secretaries, Petraeus also visited Buckingham Palace to informally update Queen Elizabeth II on developments in the conflict. He was surprised by her preexisting levels of knowledge on the war. "She is one well-informed lady," Petraeus exclaimed as he left the palace.[54]

Knowledge exchange was not necessarily the main problem stifling US-UK relations over the Afghan war. The British never managed to stamp any real influence on the grand strategy of the conflict. London was preoccupied in the immediate post-9/11 moment with standing in absolute solidarity with Washington over the need to remove terrorist havens in Afghanistan. This morphed into the British taking the role of acquiescent junior partner in the war, which severely limited Britain's ability to forge a distinct civil-military approach. The need to present a united front to new Afghan partners in democracy prevailed. Former UK ambassador Sir Sherard Cowper-Coles revealed how, during his tenure in Kabul, once a week a self-styled "war cabinet" would meet with President Karzai, including key Afghan ministers, senior ISAF commanders, and the US and UK ambassadors. Cowper-Coles's description of these meetings is interesting largely for what they reveal about the balance and nature of the special relationship at work on the ground in Afghanistan: "With the President and the American Ambassador seated in the armchairs on either side of the fireplace, the foreigners and the Afghans ranged themselves on two sofas facing each other. . . . Among the foreigners the American would speak most, with me intervening, usually in support: we tried never to disagree in front of Karzai."[55]

What we see here is an implicit acknowledgement that the British were not there necessarily to shape events but to provide nodding agreement for American efforts to do so. The Americans were not so willing to return the support when the British began to encounter difficulties prosecuting counterinsurgency operations in Helmand Province. In Afghanistan the British came to realize that junior partner status provided a one-way route of critique.

The Afghan campaign brought to a head contrasting cultural and psychological differences in the Anglo-American approach to learning about counterinsurgency, differences in the perceived role of utilizing past campaign histories in order to shape contemporary strategy, and differences in the willingness and flexibility to learn and adapt in theater. Maj. Chris Bell, commander of the First Battalion of the Scots Guards during Operation Snakebite to retake the Helmand town of Musa Qaleh in 2007, noted, "While the half-educated Brit recalled the false lessons from a Malayan and Northern Irish history he only half-understood, his American counterpart was asking, 'What have I got wrong?' and 'What do I need to do it right?' The British were well ahead in 2003—but five years later the Americans were streets ahead and moving away."[56] Lt. Patrick Bury, a platoon commander with the First Battalion of the Royal Irish Regiment, found himself reflecting on the comparative nature of US and UK adaptation to counterinsurgency war-fighting when deployed alongside a company of US Marines in Sangin:

"These guys got it, they understood the environment and they knew how to operate in it. And they had the resources behind them to do it properly." Long gone were the days of the early years of the Afghan war, Bury ruminated, when American generals would make fawning references to Britain's imperial counterinsurgency record that "just confirmed what the vastly superior British army thought of itself anyway."[57] The tables had turned, the British legacy debunked by the troublesome and laborious campaigns in Afghanistan and Iraq.

But there was a determination back in London to burnish some sort of counterinsurgency legacy in Afghanistan. In July 2011, Prime Minister David Cameron alongside Afghan president Hamid Karzai announced the establishment of a military officer training academy in Kabul. Dubbed "Sandhurst in the sand," the academy would be run by several hundred UK military personnel who would oversee the training of 1,350 officer cadets each year after the full ISAF combat troop withdrawal occurred in 2014.[58] The ultimate legacy in the security realm clearly lies with the ability of the ANA to keep the Taliban at bay. By the time of Cameron's announcement, there were 159,000 troops in the ANA and 125,000 officers in the ranks of the Afghan National Police.[59] Yet there remain large question marks over retention rates, corruption levels, and the extent of Taliban infiltration throughout the Afghan National Security Forces. The ultimate legacy hangs in the balance and may not be fully evident for some time after the 2014 pullout of all ISAF combat troops.

Other legacies are, however, open to contemporary scrutiny. Foremost among these is the counternarcotics strategy that Blair was so eager to pursue back in 2006. A report by the United Nations Office for Drugs and Crime concluded in November 2013 that Afghan opium production had reached its highest recorded level, witnessing a 36 percent increase from the year before. With over 200,000 hectares of land now sown with poppy, the potential yield was put at 5,500 tons. Most of this poppy, and indeed the scene of the largest increase in harvesting, was Helmand Province.[60] Such news seriously undermines the push to reduce Afghan opium production.

Ultimately even the American political and military hierarchy lost all appetite for protracting an already sapping war in Afghanistan. War is a results-orientated activity, and the conflict in Afghanistan was not producing any readily apparent successes. Carter Malkesian, who spent two years as a State Department political officer in the Garmser district of Helmand Province, concluded that after more than a decade of war, "Afghanistan had become prolonged and morally messy, exactly the kind of conflict Americans preferred to avoid. Good governance did not materialize as expected. Violence persisted. The whole intervention looked like a great misadventure."[61] Such perceptions crept into the conscience of policymakers, but there was an unwillingness to face up to the difficulties of prosecuting a complex counterinsurgency war in a country that had never been successfully occupied by outside forces. As journalist Stephen Grey concluded after time embedded with British forces in Afghanistan in 2009, "the story of Helmand was more often of commanders who pushed soldiers into harm's way, sent back endlessly optimistic reports, and extended the conflict beyond the resources and political will back home."[62] Senior British officers were chastened by the House of Commons Defence Select Committee in July 2011 for "moderating the demands of commanders in the field" when briefing ministers on the Afghan war. This led to a situation whereby the unwarranted optimism of the highest ranks "denied the necessary support to carry out the mission from the outset."[63]

The lack of a consistent campaign narrative and chronic equipment shortages were also factors cited by the committee as failings of the British war effort. Both of these factors were in large part the result of the demands placed on the military by the parallel campaign in Iraq, especially at the height of insurgent violence in both war zones in 2007 and 2008. This stood in contrast to an earlier problem, namely that the lull in violence in Afghanistan in the years after the fall of the Taliban emboldened the sense of accomplishment that the British military felt by defeating the Iraqi Army with ease in 2003. Such hubris, conjured up by Tony Blair's zeal to give Britain a new global mission after 9/11 and by senior British commanders' complacency at the military's ability to fulfill such a mission, resulted in dangerous levels of overstretch that imperiled the lives of British soldiers and demolished American conceptions of British effectiveness in counterinsurgency environments.

But these failings of Whitehall and military top brass could not account for some endemic problems within the Afghan body politic. The broader counterinsurgency effort, with all its emphasis on building links with local leaders and the wider population, was chronically stymied by the inherent role of corruption across all levels of governance in the country. As a consequence, the ability of ISAF nations to effectively fund development projects in Afghanistan was heavily compromised.

British combat operations in Afghanistan officially ended on October 26, 2014, as Camp Bastion, the last British military base in the country, was handed over to Afghan forces.[64] It was fittingly symbolic that only an American general spoke at the flag-lowering ceremony. No British voice was heard.

Notes

Epigraph: Quoted in Chandrasekaran, *Little America*, 206.

1. Nagl, *Knife Fights*, 3.
2. Fry and Bowen, "UK National Security Strategy," 69.
3. Ledwidge, *Investment in Blood*, 205.
4. Petraeus, "Reflections on the Counterinsurgency Era," 84.
5. Melvin, "Learning the Strategic Lessons," 59.

6. Bearden, "Afghanistan, Graveyard of Empires."
7. Ledwidge, *Losing Small Wars*, 67.
8. Malkesian, *War Comes to Garmser*, 270.
9. Martin, *Intimate War*, 3–4.
10. Anthony Brenton, interview #127, British Diplomatic Oral History Programme (hereafter BDOHP), http://www.chu.cam.ac.uk/archives/collections/BDOHP/Brenton.pdf.
11. Cowper-Coles, *Cables from Kabul*, 238.
12. Fairweather, *Good War*, 127–28.
13. Fergusson, *Million Bullets*, 74.
14. Hansard Parliamentary Debates, House of Lords, January 22, 2007, http://www.publications.parliament.uk/pa/ld200607/ldhansrd/text/70122w0001.htm#07012211000025.
15. Cavanagh, "Ministerial Decision-Making," 48–54.
16. Fergusson, *Million Bullets*, 77.
17. Martin, *Intimate War*, 163.
18. Chin, "British Counter-Insurgency," 212.
19. Egnell, "Lessons from Helmand," 297.
20. King, "Understanding the Helmand Campaign," 321.
21. Farrell and Gordon, "COIN Machine," 20.
22. Fergusson, *Million Bullets*, 354.
23. Ibid., 353.
24. Fergusson, *Million Bullets*, 222–23.
25. Fairweather, *Good War*, 198.
26. Ibid., 167–69.
27. Ibid., 215.
28. Farrell, "Improving in War," 576–77.
29. Egnell, "Lessons from Helmand," 305.
30. Ibid., 307.
31. King, "Understanding the Helmand Campaign," 316.
32. Fergusson, *Million Bullets*, 112.
33. Pritchard and Smith, "Thompson in Helmand," 77.
34. Martin, *Intimate War*, 163.
35. Quoted in Chandrasekaran, *Little America*, 206.
36. Quoted ibid., 207.
37. Cowper-Coles, *Cables from Kabul*, 18.
38 Chandrasekaran, *Little America*, 214.
39. "Marines Launch Mission in Afghanistan's South Focused on Security and Governance," *Washington Post*, July 2, 2009, http://www.washingtonpost.com/wp-dyn/content/article/2009/07/01/AR2009070103202.html?hpid=topnews&sid=ST2009070103271.
40. Fairweather, *Good War*, 353–55.
41. Ibid., 383.
42. House of Commons Foreign Affairs Committee, *Global Security: US-UK Relations*, 24.

43. Chandrasekaran, *Little America*, 205.
44. "A Twofold Conflict in Helmand," *Washington Post*, September 4, 2010, http://www.washingtonpost.com/wp-dyn/content/article/2010/09/03/AR2010090305996.html.
45. Ibid.
46. Nagl, *Knife Fights*, 198.
47. Martin, *Intimate War*, 192.
48. "Twofold Conflict in Helmand."
49. Egnell, "Lessons from Helmand," 308–9.
50. For a comprehensive, and ultimately optimistic, assessment of the operation, see Farrell, "Appraising Moshtarak," https://www.rusi.org/downloads/assets/Appraising_Moshtarak.pdf.
51. House of Commons Defence Select Committee, *Operations in Afghanistan*, 37.
52. "British Army Chief 'Cost Lives,'" *Sunday Times* (London), November 16, 2014.
53. Chandrasekaran, *Little America*, 215–16.
54. Broadwell, *All In*, 220–21.
55. Cowper-Coles, *Cables from Kabul*, 90.
56. Grey, *Operation Snakebite*, 146.
57. Bury, *Callsign Hades*, 139.
58. House of Commons Defence Select Committee, *Operations in Afghanistan*, 46.
59. Ibid., 46.
60. United Nations Office for Drugs and Crime, *Afghanistan Opium Survey 2013*, November 2013, http://www.unodc.org/documents/crop-monitoring/Afghanistan/Afghan_report_Summary_Findings_2013.pdf.
61. Malkesian, *War Comes to Garmser*, xviii–xix.
62. "Cracking on in Helmand," *Prospect*, September 2009, 50–51.
63. House of Commons Defence Select Committee, *Operations in Afghanistan*, 6.
64. "UK Ends Afghan Combat Operations," BBC News, October 26, 2014, www.bbc.co.uk/news/uk-29776544.

Conclusion

The Asymmetrical Alliance: Anglo-American Relations Then and Now

> The term "Special Relationship" . . . is not used within the Foreign Office or the Diplomatic Service abroad except with heavy inverted commas. . . . [W]e are constantly reminded of the reality that, in almost every instance, we are small beer compared with the volume and power of the United States. The extent of our influence is constrained and it never does us any good to forget it.
>
> —Sir Jeremy Greenstock, former British ambassador to the United Nations

Casting the Anglo-American dynamic in Nietzschean terms, Alex Danchev once argued that the "special relationship" is "a shimmering illusion lost in a never-never land, marooned somewhere between the monumentalised past and a mythical fiction." More intrinsically, Danchev added, it is "a community of belief, whose celebrants dwell in high places."[1] Yet this community has an asymmetry in terms of adherents, with those on the eastern side of the Atlantic demonstrating a verve not always seen in its western Atlantic coreligionists. The British have had to place enormous faith in the creed of the special relationship in order to maintain some semblance of power and relevance to post-1945 international relations. For the Americans, on the other hand, it became an occasional fillip to foreign policy goals in corners of the world where the rising tide of the Cold War met the fading glory of the British Empire. It was an expedience to the United States, perhaps an occasional embarrassment; however, to the United Kingdom the special relationship remained a necessity that permanently required the assurance of reciprocity, yet has in reality received the tepid granting not of "specialness" but of equity within a league of other allies around the globe.

In the introduction to this book, three fundamental research questions were identified as guiding it. These were about the nature of transatlantic relations over the last seventy years that would guide the analysis of counterinsurgency war-fighting since 1945. The answers to these questions have underpinned the narrative of each case-study chapter, but it would help to draw out the collective response to each question in turn. Each question is repeated as a subheading below.

Why did America compromise its anticolonial tradition by helping Britain maintain its empire in the face of rebel insurgents?

Although clearly uncomfortable with pandering to notions of a "special" relationship with Britain, it was clear that successive administrations in Washington were keen to harness any political capital they could out of Britain's position as an imperial power (albeit a fading one) in the latter half of the twentieth century. The omnipresence of anticommunism in the formulation of US foreign policy after the end of the Second World War ensured an unlikely alliance between American Cold War–fighting and Britain's attempt to quash insurgent challenges to imperial control in Asia and the Middle East. Washington came to perceive some of Britain's "small wars" of decolonization as tacit contributions to the anticommunist battle, given the way in which Britain tried to stage-manage the retreat from empire by fighting insurgent rebellions with implicit or explicit communist support at the same time as forging postcolonial constitutional settlements that were to London's liking.

The attainment of Washington's acquiescence toward numerous colonial counterinsurgency campaigns was helped along the way by less than subtle nudges from London about the possibility for Soviet or Chinese exploitation of any political vacuum that may arise should British counterinsurgency efforts fail. In Palestine, Malaya, Cyprus, and South Arabia, British officials manipulated American diplomatic approaches to military operations by overhyping either the support insurgents were receiving from communist sources or by playing up the prospects for communist expansionism if the British campaign were to be unsuccessful. Although such moves by Downing Street and the Foreign Office may appear to be acts of flagrant political opportunism, they were pushing at an open door. The White House and State Department under successive administrations from Harry Truman's onward had become so singularly obsessed with the goal of stifling the spread of communism that America's Cold War policy of containment made a de facto ally out of Britain's small wars of decolonization. Counterinsurgency wars against communist enemies (both real and imagined, thanks to British exaggeration) were seen as a bulwark against communist enlargement. Some US officials, such as Dean Acheson, were more welcoming of the British imperial presence in Asia and the Middle East than other skeptics. But Cold War realpolitik ensured that the remnants of British colonialism were certainly the lesser of two evils when faced with the alternative of a Soviet or Chinese takeover. The creation of an informal empire through a postwar Pax Americana required Washington to carefully assist in the dismantling of the Pax Britannica first, which frequently required the United States to benignly view a string of British counterinsurgency campaigns that were to play an effective part in preventing Dwight Eisenhower's fear of a "domino theory" manifesting itself across the third world.

How did successive American administrations pander to domestic electoral blocs in a way that undermined British conduct of counterinsurgency wars against certain ethnic groups?

During the Palestine campaign, Dean Acheson confided to the British ambassador, Lord Inverchapel, that he felt President Truman was "the unhappy prisoner of the domestic politics" when it came to formulating policy toward that particular British counterinsurgency campaign.[2] Every subsequent occupant of the White House has been similarly imprisoned by the demands of electoral mathematics and vocal lobby groups whose objectives often stood in stark contrast to the requests of their supposedly special British ally. Although the overarching imperatives of Cold War geopolitics resulted in American acceptance of the overall conduct of British counterinsurgency campaigns, it is evident that the intrigues of the American domestic political scene did not stop America playing what British deputy prime minister Herbert Morrison labeled as far back as 1945 "the part of irresponsible critic."[3]

American policymaking in relation to British counterinsurgency wars has seen a reflection of Kenneth Waltz's "second image" of causal attributes in war dominate repeatedly. Domestic political concerns infuse the construction of foreign policy, and we can see how a "two-level game" of foreign policy construction based on domestic political pressures, as enunciated by Robert Putnam, played out in regard to American attitudes toward British counterinsurgency wars. Electoral success trumped alliance solidarity time after time from 1945 onward. We have seen this through Truman's cynical delivery of major policy statements regarding Palestine at opportune moments in the electoral cycle to appease vocal Jewish lobby groups, through Eisenhower's obstinacy during the Cyprus Emergency in large part due to frustration that controversial British action over Suez coincided with his reelection campaign, through Lyndon Johnson's desire to solicit a British military deployment to Vietnam to quell liberal disquiet at ongoing unilateral operations, and most notably through Jimmy Carter's pacification of muscular congressional representation of the Irish American diaspora, which took a pronationalist stance after the modern "Troubles" flared in Northern Ireland. American conduct in regard to British counterinsurgency campaigns has given weight to the credence that all politics (let alone charity) begins at home.

What level of specialness was at work in counterinsurgency wars?

No doubt, close Anglo-American working relationships were forged at points during counterinsurgency wars between respective country desk officers at the State Department and Foreign Office and between individual military commanders deployed together to the two battlefields of the "War on Terror." But these examples of interpersonal cooperation between allies are not demonstrable proof of a special relationship at a political or strategic level. Individual friendships forged in these wars belie more complex frictions that existed as a result of often competing political priorities, mutual frustration at respective operating procedures, and frequent incomprehension of each other's working practices, military culture, and political machinations. As a phrase and as an idea, the US-UK special relationship is a mythological Churchillian construct. Its manifestation during counterinsurgency wars from Palestine to Afghanistan has shown it to be far more contentious and fragile than platitudes stemming from conventional spheres of defense and security would have us believe. By analyzing not just working relationships between American and British diplomats, political leaders, and generals during these wars, but also the private and public exchange of views about their respective decisions in counterinsurgency conflicts, this book has offered a holistic assessment of a diplomatic relationship consistently strained by the demands placed on it by frequent counterinsurgency wars. The regularity of such types of conflict, combined with their conduct in areas of strategic sensitivity to both the Cold War and the War on Terror, means that counterinsurgency warfare is a useful vehicle to explore the special relationship at large as it becomes a yardstick by which to measure levels of influence and solidarity.

The historical record reveals low levels of Anglo-American solidarity in counterinsurgency wars, low levels of British influence over American actions, and therefore low levels of specialness in the relationship. Each campaign that this book has explored has revealed friction, faction, and frustration between British and American leaders, diplomats, and soldiers. This was as true in Afghanistan in recent years as it was in Palestine over seventy years ago. Indeed, if we go back to 1945, we can see how the Palestine campaign becomes formative for our understanding of the lineage of US-UK relations in counterinsurgency war. It demonstrated for the first time just how influential domestic political pressures in the US would be on the management of British counterinsurgency campaigns. It also witnessed what would be an oft-used British response to unwelcome American interference: the raising of fears about communist expansionism in the eventuality of a British defeat.

Subsequent campaigns also reveal crucial trends in the special relationship at large. The Malayan Emergency is important in this sense because the United States came to see a British counterinsurgency campaign explicitly through a Cold War lens for the first time. Policy calculations in Washington were made off the back of perceptions about how the outcome of an irregular war conducted by the British would affect the spread of communism regionally.

Despite an increasing alignment with American geopolitical priorities and Britain's careful disentanglement from empire, mistrust between London and Washington was palpable during subsequent small wars of British decolonization. The Foreign Office shut down the flow of diplomatic information to American officials during the Cyprus Emergency over fears that the United States was briefing Greece behind British backs. American interference in this conflict riled British diplomats to the extent that they, in the words of the British ambassador to the United Nations Sir Pierson Dixon, "[made] our flesh creep."[4] Similar wariness was seen in the South Arabia campaign, with a pantomime of British denials and American awareness of secret weapon shipments to royalist fighters being played out in the Oval Office. The Vietnam War offered British counterinsurgency theorists such as Robert Thompson the first chance to observe American counterinsurgency practice up close. The result was British despondency at American tactics and the American sidelining of British advice. Over Vietnam the special relationship was caught in the middle of mutual misapprehension: Washington wanted help from London to demonstrate the presence of a multilateral war effort but resented any sign of interference from Downing Street, whereas the British wanted to create an impression of influence over an increasingly belligerent Johnson administration without actually committing sizeable enough resources to warrant a significant say over the direction of US strategy. The Troubles, which broke out at the height of the Vietnam War, again demonstrated in a mode similar to the Palestine campaign the effect that well-organized lobby groups can have on American political opinion in regard to a British counterinsurgency war, as well as the active role played by some

American citizens in promulgating fund-raising and gun-smuggling activities for insurgent groups to fight the British.

The Asymmetrical Alliance: Counterinsurgency and the Special Relationship Today

Despite talk of being "shoulder to shoulder" in the War on Terror, the poor British military performance in Iraq and Afghanistan has resulted in a fundamental loss of American faith in this alliance. The bruising experience in Iraq has demonstrated that the British political establishment has no stomach for protracted irregular wars. The desire to undertake such missions in the future with others, let alone on a unilateral basis, has been further diminished by global financial crisis–induced reductions to the Ministry of Defence budget since the withdrawals from Iraq and Afghanistan. Single-state counterinsurgency campaigns are now much less likely. Junior coalition partner status had become a strategic norm for Britain in the post–Cold War world, as demonstrated in the Gulf War and again in Kosovo and Afghanistan. Yet Afghanistan and Iraq presented the British military with difficult strategic scenarios inasmuch as they had to adapt in order to operate as a junior partner in a counterinsurgency coalition. Coalition-based campaigns are likely to be the norm for the foreseeable future, given the spatial and temporal freedom cleaved by the self-proclaimed caliphate of the Islamic State of Iraq and Syria (ISIS). But the current Western proclivity to deal with ISIS using a combination of air strikes and the arming of chosen proxies reveals just how Washington and London have retreated from the appeal of large-scale ground wars involving protracted counterinsurgency operations in favor of indirect initiatives that minimize the military's exposure to risk.

Even before the rise of ISIS, all the signs were pointing toward multinational efforts to tackle jihadism. In his introduction to the February 2010 Ministry of Defence green paper, the then defense secretary Bob Ainsworth openly stated the need for the British military to plan for long-term coalition commitments: "Increasing globalisation ties our security to that of our allies. . . . Therefore we must increase cooperation with our international partners to deliver defense more efficiently and effectively."[5] For "international partners" read "the United States." Therefore, the real challenge to effective coalition functioning, especially in any future counterinsurgency war against ISIS, is Britain proving it can still bring military capabilities to the American table. The legacy of British warfighting in Iraq and Afghanistan may have irreparably damaged this reputation.

One of the biggest impediments to British effectiveness that was evident in Iraq and Afghanistan, and would be a significant barrier to future deployments, is the micromanagement of campaigns by London. This was a predilection for which Tony Blair showed an acute weakness, to the extent that American commanders in Iraq felt British command-and-control lines were irreparably blurred. Maj. Gen. Roddy Porter, the former British commander of the Forces Strategic Engagement Cell in Iraq, observed, "Commanding from a distance is a British disease.... The Americans hated it."[6] But the US military has had difficulty in adapting to the demands of counterinsurgency, not just in the vicious crucible of Iraq but in a protracted way in Afghanistan too. Despite reaping the benefits of the fortunately timed synchronicity of the "surge" and the Anbar Awakening in Iraq, there had been a failure to transfer many of the hard-earned lessons from Iraq to Afghanistan. Chief among these were the failure to swiftly establish an intellectual "COIN Academy" for commanders in Kabul and an insufficient level of training and briefing for newly arrived officers about to begin their tour of duty.[7]

British thinking in the run-up to the campaigns in Afghanistan and Iraq was arguably shaped by the formative experiences in Northern Ireland. It had molded the military's thinking on irregular warfare, had versed a generation of officers in the nuances of urban population pacification. The ability during Operation Banner to seek and maintain an "acceptable level of violence," combined with the hyperbolized colonial successes, especially in Malaya, ensured that British thinking on the issue of countering insurgencies earned respect within foreign militaries and was exported as a rare example of how a state army can subdue a substate enemy without compromising strategic goals. However, the British performance in Helmand Province in Afghanistan since the resurgence of the Taliban by 2006–7 has done much to warrant an overhaul of such a benevolent perspective. Indeed, the picture that emerged from Helmand was arguably one of a struggling and stretched military, searching for a level of strategic clarity and operational potency. Afghanistan was the primary testing ground of newfound American confidence in the realm of counterinsurgency, and Helmand was the crucible in which the British military could salvage their reputation after the pullout from southern Iraq. Yet thirteen years of Operation Herrick produced further evidence of a slow lesson-learning process (especially pertaining to the lessons emanating from Iraq regarding sufficient military resources and reconstruction efforts) and certainly a slow-burning strategy, given the protracted inability to reduce the strength of the Taliban or sufficiently reduce their latent avenues of support and finance (namely the Afghan poppy harvest and heroin trade).

The Iraq War–era "COINdinistas" certainly drew influence from what they saw as the lessons stemming from Britain's colonial small wars. But has the noticeable "British accent" in the recent reworking of American counterinsurgency doctrine been fundamentally misguided? As the British experience has demonstrated, even regular counterinsurgency deployments are no guarantor of practitioner effectiveness or shifts in institutional readiness. But much of the post-Iraq debate within the US military and defense circles about counterinsurgency, which has been infused with positive references to the historical British experience, has involved a lot of heated argument between people talking past each other, largely because both sides have been posing fundamentally different questions. The procounterinsurgency camp has been eager to explore *how* best to adapt the military to counterinsurgency, discussing tactical innovations and operational nuance that could be rendered if levels of historical awareness of previous counterinsurgency "best practices," including from British campaigns such as Malaya, could be increased by reorienting the curriculum at professional military education establishments. Yet the anticounterinsurgency camp has been primarily asking *why* counterinsurgency is even a form of war that the United States should be involved in, questioning its underlying strategic value.[8] This latter position is based on a fundamental premise that the post-9/11 emphasis on counterinsurgency is a fad and brings undue focus on low-intensity and peace-support operations because it undermines the ability to conduct potential future conventional wars.[9] But despite these concerns, there is a discernable need to adapt in the face of these seemingly polar-opposite strategic options. Preparing for counterinsurgency operations can still be achieved with a degree of flexibility that does not ignore high-intensity, regular-warfare training. As David Ucko and Robert Egnell have convincingly argued, "Rather than treat counter-insurgency as a dead end on the basis of operations gone awry, a better approach would be to deepen our study of this topic and of war writ large so as to make better decisions in the future."[10] It is hoped that this book will have both deepened the study of counterinsurgency by placing it in the comparative context of its two most frequent exponents across a large time frame. As to the future decisions that Ucko and Egnell encourage, this book will give pause to decision makers who take Anglo-American political cooperation during times of war for granted.

Rereading the final paragraph of Douglas Blaufarb's 1977 assessment of post-Vietnam irregular warfare, *The Counterinsurgency Era*, one is struck by the prescience of his conclusions as to the relevance and meaning of counterinsurgency for the American military and political system after Iraq and Afghanistan:

> The fundamental lesson to draw from our misadventures of the counterinsurgency era is the one already emphasized by many—the lesson of the limits of American power. Too many have fallen back on the easy excuse that we failed in Indochina because our firepower was constrained and leashed that [*sic*] more bombs, more destruction, more firepower was the answer. . . . [But] the failure was one of understanding: an inability to perceive the underlying realities of both our own system and that of those countries into which we thrust our raw strength. . . . If, in addition, some turn of the wheel should once again bring us to the brink of such

> involvement, the lessons which are our only return for all the blood and fortune that was spent will stand us in good stead, provided only that we finally have understood and digested them.[11]

The American military system, as Blaufarb indicates, inherently turns inward to soul-search on its own experiences after each traumatic campaign. It will be because of intramilitary tussles over the direction of the "American way of war" that will lead to the maintenance or dropping of counterinsurgency training and doctrine after Afghanistan, not because it adopted generations-old British mantras about how to fight irregular war. In any case, the experience of the British in recent wars in which they have deployed alongside US forces has largely eroded any goodwill within the American military intelligentsia regarding the value of British counterinsurgency theory and practice.

After the withdrawal of combat forces from Afghanistan, the Anglo-American practice of counterinsurgency conduct stands at a crossroads. The underwhelming performance by the British Army in Basra and Helmand coincided with the Americans attaining a distinct new level of counterinsurgency strategic vision and tactical ability, given the rise to prominence and influence of a counterinsurgency-savvy officer corps that revolved around the new military intelligentsia of David Petraeus, H. R. McMaster, John Nagl, and others; the inculcation of counterinsurgency learning at all levels of the American military; and the ubiquity of counterinsurgency discussion in the United States across the academic-military divide. But the institutionalization of such newfound competencies has been the subject of vicious intramilitary debate in the US, with post-Vietnam trends being repeated that see counterinsurgency warfare being reduced to a temporary phenomenon unworthy of consistent intellectual investment or high-priority defense planning. All this has contributed to a distinct shifting of the sands in irregular warfare terms—all of which has had an impact on the way in which Britain and America, as two of counterinsurgency's foremost practitioners, view each other's competencies as allies in such wars. But this could have severe knock-on implications in regard to the effect that such negative American perceptions of British performance in counterinsurgency wars could have on other forms of war-fighting. Preventing the percolation of such antipathy throughout the American military is now an important task for British military leaders, who will have to demonstrate the veracity of other British strengths outside the remit of "peace-support operations" to which counterinsurgency belongs, such as special forces covert operations or Royal Air Force precision air-strike capabilities. Iraq and Afghanistan left the impression that when at war, the British political management of such conflicts lacks long-term commitment, coherent planning, a convincing strategic narrative, and a fundamental willingness to financially support the war effort to a sufficient level. There is a real danger that not only will this be the lasting testament of the political management of modern British counterinsurgency war-fighting, but also of British approaches to war in general. Cuts to the size and funding to HM Armed Forces since the 2008 global financial crisis have done little to stem this slide. In short, the British military is currently losing the perception battle about its own capabilities.

As far as counterinsurgency is still concerned, the American military no longer needs to look to Malaya or Northern Ireland as exemplars of counterinsurgency conduct—misguided though that endeavor was from the start. It can now look at Anbar Province and the surge as new case studies in counterinsurgency textbooks. The Americans have learned the hard way, and, like for the British before them, it has been a slow and painful process. However, the combination of British difficulties in Basra and eventual American cogency in central and western Iraq snuffed out residual opinion relating to British competence at counterinsurgency. The volume of criticism directed at the British over Iraq has swept away long-standing perceptions that counterinsurgency is the British army's default mode. This has created significant military tensions that contribute further to the dispelling of notions of a special relationship existing between the United States and the United Kingdom. There may have been liaison and discussion regarding the execution of counterinsurgency operations in Iraq and Afghanistan, but the different approaches to this type of warfare and the exasperated perceptions of the way in which each other goes about such operations simply reinforces Harold Wilson's view from 1964 that was discussed in the introduction: Britain and America share a close relationship, but it is not special. Recent counterinsurgency operations have done much to reveal the relative ordinariness of relations, characterized as they were by Anglo-American frustrations, resentment, and recrimination. The wars in Afghanistan and Iraq have not just cast a shadow over the future operability and desirability of counterinsurgency warfare by Western nations—they have also put a strain on Anglo-American diplomatic and military relations. The stories of counterinsurgency and US-UK fraternity are thus intertwined, and both remain asymmetrical at heart.

Notes

Epigraph: Greenstock, *Iraq*, 99.

1. Danchev, "Tony Blair's Vietnam," 190.
2. "Telegram from Washington to Foreign Office, 9 August 1946," The National Archives, UK (hereafter TNA), FO 371/52551.
3. "Cabinet: Palestine—A Report by the Lord President of the Council," October 10, 1945, TNA, CAB 129/3/16.
4. "Confidential: From New York to Foreign Office," February 12, 1957, TNA, FO 371/130099.

5. Defence Secretary's introduction, "Adaptability and Partnership: Issues for the Strategic Defence Review," Cm 7794 (London: Stationery Office, February 2010), 6.
6. Interview with Maj. Gen. Roddy Porter (Ret.), London, April 21, 2015.
7. Nagl, *Knife Fights*, 187.
8. Biddle, "Afghanistan's Legacy," 74.
9. Gentile, "Freeing the Army," 121–22.
10. Ucko and Egnell, *Counterinsurgency in Crisis*, 12.
11. Blaufarb, *Counterinsurgency Era*, 310–11.

Bibliography

Primary Sources

Archival Material

The UK National Archives (TNA), Kew, London

Cabinet Office files: CAB 128/29; 129/3/16; 129/23, 7; 133/85; 159/3; 537/7136.
Colonial Office files: CO 537/5698, 6006; 1022/187; 1035/139 CO.
Dominions Office files: DO 169/109.
Foreign and Commonwealth Office files: FCO 26/944; 33/1471, 1472; 87/102, 106, 236, 237, 366, 367, 368, 589.
Foreign Office files: FO 371/ 52551; 61762; 75337; 75814; 76386; 92067; 103515; 112855; 117621; 117647; 123894; 123900; 123901; 123928; 123929; 130099; 130102; 130128; 159673; 160108; 160157; 166717; 168656; 170100; 170101; 170102; 174628; 175482; 175483; 175484; 180539.
Ministry of Defence files: DEFE 13/398, 569, 570; 55/418.
Northern Ireland Office files: CJ 4/1411, 1830, 2127, 2316, 2661.
Prime Ministerial files: PREM 8/627/1, 2, 3, 5; 11/1105, 1176, 3736, 4356, 4928; 13/692, 693, 1917.
War Office: WO 32/10260.

US National Archive and Records Administration (NARA), College Park, Maryland

Record Group (RG) 43: 250/10/16/4.
RG 59: 747C.00; 797.00; 867.00; 867N.01; POL 16 Yemen; POL 27 Yemen.

Digital Archival Material

British Diplomatic Oral History Programme, https://www.chu.cam.ac.uk/archives/collections/bdohp/.

Declassified Documents Reference System (DDRS), http://gdc.gale.com/products/declassified-documents-reference-system/.

Digital National Security Archive, www.nsarchive.chadwyck.com.

Freedom of Information Act Electronic Reading Room, www.foia.cia.gov.

Gerald R. Ford Presidential Library Digital Collections, www.fordlibrarymuseum.gov.

Harry S. Truman Presidential Library Digital Archive Collection, www.trumanlibrary.org.

John F. Kennedy Presidential Library Digital Archive Collection, www.jfklibrary.org.

Papers of the Presidents, American Presidency Project, www.presidency.ucsb.edu.

Government Publications

House of Commons Defence Select Committee Reports

Iraq: An Initial Assessment of Post-Conflict Operations. Vol. 1 (HC65-1), sixth report of session 2004–5. London: Stationery Office, March 24, 2005.

Lessons of Iraq. Vol. 1 (HC57-1), third report of session 2003–4. London: Stationery Office, March 16, 2004.

Operations in Afghanistan. HC 554, fourth report of session 2010–12. London: Stationery Office, July 17, 2011.

UK Operations in Iraq. HC 1241, thirteenth report of session 2005–6. London: Stationery Office, August 10, 2006.

House of Commons Foreign Affairs Select Committee Reports

British-US Relations. HC 327, second report of session 2001–2. London: Stationery Office, December 18, 2001.

Global Security: UK-US Relations. HC 114, sixth report of session 2009–10. London: Stationery Office, March 28, 2010.

Government Foreign Policy towards the United States. HC 695, eighth report of session 2013–14. London: Stationery Office, April 3, 2014.

UK Ministry of Defence Reports

Adaptability and Partnership: Issues for the Strategic Defence Review, Cm 7794. London: Stationery Office, February 2010.

British Army Field Manual: Volume 1 Part 10; "Countering Insurgency," army code 71876. October 2009.

Operation Banner: An Analysis of Military Operations in Northern Ireland. Report prepared under the direction of the Chief of General Staff, army code 71842. July 2006.

Stability Operations in Iraq: An Analysis from a Land Perspective. Report prepared under the direction of the Chief of General Staff, army code 71844. Undated.

United Nations Report

United Nations Office for Drugs and Crime (UNODC), *Afghanistan Opium Survey 2013.* November 2013. http://www.unodc.org/documents/crop-monitoring/Afghanistan/Afghan_report_Summary_Findings_2013.pdf.

US Department of Defense Publications

FM 3-24: US Army and Marine Corps Counterinsurgency Field Manual. Chicago: University of Chicago Press, 2007.

Quadrennial Defense Review. Washington, DC: US Department of Defense, February 6, 2006.

US Department of State Publications

Bulletin 30, no. 758-783, January 4–June 28, 1954.

Foreign Relations of the United States (*FRUS*)

1945, Vol. 8: The Near East and Africa.
1946, Vol. 7: The Near East and Africa.
1947, Vol. 5: The Near East and Africa.
1948, Vol. 5 (Part II): The New East, South Asia and Africa.
1951, Vol. 6 (Part I): Asia and the Pacific.
1952–54, Vol. 3: United Nations Affairs.
1952–54, Vol. 12 (Part I): East Asia and Pacific.
1955–57, Vol. 22: Southeast Asia.
1955–57, Vol. 24: Soviet Union; Eastern Mediterranean.
1958–60, Vol. 10 (Part I): Eastern Europe Region; Soviet Union; Cyprus.
1961–63, Vol. 1: Vietnam 1961.
1961–63, Vol. 2: Vietnam 1962.
1961–63, Vol. 3: Vietnam, January–August 1963.
1961–63, Vol. 18: Near East, 1962–1963.
1964–68, Vol. 1: Vietnam 1964.
1964–68, Vol. 2: Vietnam, January–June 1965.
1964–68, Vol. 3: Vietnam, June–December 1965.
1964–68, Vol. 10: Near East Region; Arabian Peninsula.
1964–68, Vol. 12: Western Europe.
1964–68, Vol. 21: Near East Region; Arabian Peninsula.

Document Collections

Documents on British Policy Overseas (DBPO)

Series II, vol. 2, *The London Conferences: Anglo-American Relations and Cold War Strategy, January–June 1950*. London: HMSO, 1987.

Hansard, House of Commons Debates

February 25, 1947, vol. 433.
May 14, 1964, vol. 695.

Hansard, House of Lords Debates

January 22, 2007, WA197.

Secondary Sources

Books

Aldous, Richard. *Thatcher and Reagan: A Difficult Relationship*. London: Hutchinson, 2012.

———. *The Hidden Hand: Britain, America and Cold War Secret Intelligence*. Woodstock, NY: Overlook, 2002.

Aldrich, Richard J. *GCHQ: The Uncensored History of Britain's Most Secret Intelligence Agency*. London: HarperPress, 2010.

Aldrich, Richard J., and Michael F. Hopkins, eds. *Intelligence, Defence and Diplomacy: British Policy in the Post-War World*. London: Frank Cass, 1994.

Allawi, Ali A. *The Occupation of Iraq: Winning the War, Losing the Peace*. New Haven, CT, and London: Yale University Press, 2007.

Anderson, David. *Histories of the Hanged: Britain's Dirty War in Kenya and the End of Empire*. London: Orion, 2006.

Aron, Raymond. *The Imperial Republic: The United States and the World, 1945–1973*. Englewood Cliffs, NJ: Prentice Hall, 1974.

Bacevich, Andrew. *American Empire: The Realities and Consequences of US Diplomacy*. Cambridge, MA: Harvard University Press, 2002.

Bailey, Jonathan, Richard Iron, and Hew Strachan, eds. *British Generals in Blair's Wars*. Farnham: Ashgate, 2013.

Balfour-Paul, Glen. *The End of Empire in the Middle East: Britain's Relinquishment of Power in Her Last Three Arab Dependencies*. Cambridge: Cambridge University Press, 1991.

Barber, Noel. *The War of the Running Dogs: Malaya, 1948–1960*. London: Fontana Books 1972.

Barrett, David M., ed. *Lyndon B. Johnson's Vietnam Papers: A Documentary Collection.* College Station, TX: Texas A&M University Press.

Bennett, Huw. *Fighting the Mau Mau: The British Army and Counter-Insurgency in the Kenya Emergency.* Cambridge: Cambridge University Press, 2012.

Bishop, Patrick, and Eammon Mallie. *The Provisional IRA.* London: Heinemann, 1987.

Blaufarb, Douglas. *The Counterinsurgency Era: US Doctrine and Performance, 1950 to the Present.* New York: Free Press, 1977.

Boot, Max. *The Savage Wars of Peace: Small Wars and the Rise of American Power.* New York: Basic Books, 2003.

Branch, Daniel. *Defeating Mau Mau, Creating Kenya: Counter-Insurgency, Civil War, and Decolonisation.* Cambridge: Cambridge University Press, 2009.

Bremer, L. Paul. *My Year in Iraq: The Struggle to Build a Future of Hope.* New York: Simon & Schuster, 2006.

Broadwell, Paula (with Vernon Loeb). *All In: The Education of General David Petraeus.* New York: Penguin, 2012.

Brown, Craig. *One on One.* London: 4th Estate, 2011.

Bullock, Alan. *Ernest Bevin: A Biography.* London: Politico's, 2002.

Burk, Kathleen. *Old World, New World: The Story of Britain and America.* London: Abacus, 2007.

Burleigh, Michael. *Small Wars, Far Away Places: The Genesis of the Modern World, 1945–1965.* London: Macmillan, 2013.

Bury, Patrick. *Callsign Hades.* London: Simon & Schuster, 2010.

Busch, Peter. *All the Way with JFK? Britain, the US and the Vietnam War.* Oxford: Oxford University Press, 2003.

Bush, George W. *Decision Points.* London: Virgin Books, 2010.

Byford-Jones, W. *Grivas and the Story of EOKA.* London: Robert Hale, 1959.

Carruthers, Susan L. *Winning Hearts and Minds: British Governments, the Media and Colonial Counter-Insurgency, 1944–1960.* London: Leicester University Press, 1995.

Cesarani, David. *Major Farran's Hat: Murder, Scandal and Britain's War against Jewish Terrorism, 1945–1948.* London: William Heinemann, 2009.

Chandrasekaran, Rajiv. *Little America: The War within the War for Afghanistan.* London: Bloomsbury, 2012.

Clutterbuck, Richard. *The Long, Long War: The Emergency in Malaya, 1948–1960.* London: Cassell, 1967.

Cohen, Michael J. *Palestine and the Great Powers, 1945–1948.* Princeton, NJ: Princeton University Press, 1982.

Cormac, Rory. *Confronting the Colonies: British Intelligence and Counterinsurgency.* London: Hurst, 2013.

Cowper-Coles, Sherard. *Cables from Kabul: The Inside Story of the West's Campaign in Afghanistan.* London: HarperPress, 2011.

Cox, Michael, Adrian Guelke, and Fiona Stephen, eds. *A Farewell to Arms? From Long War to Long Peace in Northern Ireland.* Manchester: Manchester University Press, 2000.

Cronin, Sean. *Washington's Irish Policy, 1916–1986.* Dublin: Anvil Books, 1987.

Dallek, Robert. *Nixon and Kissinger: Partners in Power.* London: Penguin Books, 2008.

Danchev, Alex. *On Specialness: Essays in Anglo-American Relations.* Basingstoke, UK: Macmillan, 1998.

Darby, Philip. *British Defence Policy East of Suez, 1947–68.* London: Oxford University Press, 1973.

Davidson, Lawrence. *America's Palestine: Popular and Official Perceptions from Balfour to Israeli Statehood.* Gainesville: University Press of Florida, 2001.

Dickie, John. *"Special" No More: Anglo-American Relations; Rhetoric and Reality.* London: Weidenfeld & Nicholson, 1994.

Dobson, Alan P., and Steve Marsh, eds. *Anglo-American Relations: Contemporary Perspectives.* Abingdon, UK: Routledge, 2013.

Dorril, Stephen. *MI6: Inside the Covert World of Her Majesty's Secret Intelligence Service.* New York: Free Press, 2000.

Doyle, Michael W. *Empires.* Ithaca, NY: Cornell University Press, 1986.

Dumbrell, John. *A Special Relationship: Anglo-American Relations from the Cold War to Iraq.* 2nd ed. Basingstoke, UK: Palgrave, 2006.

Duncanson, Dennis J. *Government and Revolution in Vietnam.* London: Oxford University Press, 1968.

Durrell, Lawrence. *The Bitter Lemons of Cyprus.* London: Faber & Faber, 2000. First published 1959.

Eden, Anthony. *Full Circle: The Memoirs of Sir Anthony Eden.* London: Cassell, 1960.

Edwards, Aaron. *Defending the Realm? The Politics of Britain's Small Wars since 1945.* Manchester: Manchester University Press, 2012.

Eisenhower, Dwight D. *The White House Years: Waging Peace, 1956–1961.* New York: Doubleday, 1965.

Elkins, Caroline. *Britain's Gulag: The Brutal End of Empire in Kenya.* London: Jonathan Cape, 2005.

Elliott, Christopher L. *High Command: British Leadership in the Iraq and Afghanistan Wars.* London: Hurst, 2015.

Ellis, Sylvia. *Britain, America and the Vietnam War.* Westport, CT: Praeger, 2004.

Fairweather, Jack. *The Good War: Why We Couldn't Win the War or the Peace in Afghanistan.* London: Jonathan Cape, 2014.

———. *A War of Choice: Honour, Hubris and Sacrifice; The British in Iraq.* London: Vintage, 2012.

Ferguson, Niall. *Colossus: The Rise and Fall of the American Empire.* London: Penguin Books, 2005.

Fergusson, James. *A Million Bullets: The Real Story of the British Army in Afghanistan.* London: Corgi, 2009.

Fitzgerald, David. *Learning to Forget: US Army Counterinsurgency Doctrine and Practice from Vietnam to Iraq.* Stanford, CA: Stanford University Press, 2013.

Foot, Hugh. *A Start in Freedom.* London: Hodder & Stoughton, 1964.

French, David. *The British Way of Counter-Insurgency, 1945–1967*. Oxford: Oxford University Press, 2011.

Galula, David. *Counterinsurgency Warfare: Theory and Practice*. Westport, CT: Praeger Security International, 2006. First published 1964.

Gentile, Gian. *Wrong Turn: America's Deadly Embrace of Counterinsurgency*. New York: New Press, 2013.

Gilbert, Martin. *Israel: A History*. London: Black Swan, 1999.

Gordon, Michael, and Bernard Trainor. *Cobra II: The Inside Story of the Invasion and Occupation of Iraq*. London: Atlantic Books, 2006.

Greenstock, Jeremy. *Iraq: The Cost of War*. London: William Heinemann, 2016.

Grey, Stephen. *Operation Snakebite: The Explosive True Story of an Afghan Desert Siege*. London: Viking, 2009.

Grob-Fitzgibbon, Benjamin. *Imperial Endgame: Britain's Dirty Wars and the End of Empire*. Basingstoke, UK: Palgrave Macmillan, 2011.

Guelke, Adrian. *Northern Ireland: The International Perspective*. Dublin: Gill & Macmillan, 1988.

Hale, Christopher. *Massacre in Malaya: Exposing Britain's My Lai*. Stroud, UK: History Press, 2013.

Halliday, Fred. *Arabia without Sultans*. Harmondsworth, UK: Penguin, 1974.

Healey, Denis. *The Time of My Life*. London: Penguin, 1990.

Heinlein, Frank. *British Government Policy and Decolonisation, 1945–1963: Scrutinising the Official Mind*. London: Frank Cass, 2002.

Hershberg, James G. *Marigold: The Lost Chance for Peace in Vietnam*. Washington, DC: Woodrow Wilson Center Press, 2012.

Hilsman, Roger. *American Guerrilla: My War behind Japanese Lines*. Washington, DC: Brassey's (US), 1990.

Hinchcliffe, Peter, John T. Ducker, and Maria Holt. *Without Glory in Arabia: The British Retreat from Aden*. London: I. B. Tauris, 2006.

Hitchens, Christopher. *Blood, Class and Empire: The Enduring Anglo-American Relationship*. London: Atlantic Books, 2006.

Holmes, Richard. *Dusty Warriors: Modern Soldiers at War*. London: HarperPress, 2006.

Hyam, Ronald. *Britain's Declining Empire: The Road to Decolonisation, 1918–1968*. Cambridge: Cambridge University Press, 2006.

Jeffrey, Keith. *MI6: The History of the Secret Intelligence Service, 1909–1949*. London: Bloomsbury: 2011.

Johnson, Chalmers. *The Sorrows of Empire: Militarism, Secrecy and the End of the Republic*. London: Verso, 2006.

Johnson, Lyndon Baines. *The Vantage Point: Perspectives on the Presidency, 1963–1969*. New York: Holt, Rinehart & Winston, 1971.

Jones, Clive. *Britain and the Yemen Civil War, 1962–65: Ministers, Mercenaries and Mandarins; Foreign Policy and the Limits of Covert Action*. Brighton, UK: Sussex Academic Press, 2004.

Jones, Matthew. *Conflict and Confrontation in South East Asia, 1961–1965: Britain, the United States, Indonesia and the Creation of Malaysia*. Cambridge: Cambridge University Press, 2001.

Kaplan, Fred. *The Insurgents: David Petraeus and the Plot to Change the American Way of War*. New York: Simon & Schuster, 2013.

Karnow, Stanley. *Vietnam: A History*. London: Penguin, 1997.

Keegan, John. *The Iraq War*. London: Hutchinson, 2004.

Kissinger, Henry. *The White House Years*. London: Weidenfeld & Nicholson, 1979.

Kitson, Frank. *Bunch of Five*. London: Faber & Faber, 1977.

Kyle, Keith. *Suez: Britain's End of Empire in the Middle East*. London: I. B. Tauris, 2003.

Ledwidge, Frank. *Investment in Blood: The True Cost of Britain's Afghan War*. New Haven, CT: Yale University Press, 2013.

———. *Losing Small Wars: British Military Failure in Iraq and Afghanistan*. New Haven, CT: Yale University Press, 2012.

Leffler, Melvyn P., and Odd Arne Westad, eds. *The Cambridge History of the Cold War: Volume 1; Origins*. Cambridge: Cambridge University Press, 2010.

Louis, William Roger, and Hedley Bull, eds. *The Special Relationship: Anglo-American Relations since 1945*. Oxford: Clarendon Press, 1986.

Louis, William Roger, and Robert W. Stookey, eds. *The End of the Palestine Mandate*. London: I. B. Tauris, 1986.

MacLeod, Alan. *International Politics and the Northern Ireland Conflict: The USA, Diplomacy and the Troubles*. London: I. B. Tauris, 2016.

Malkesian, Carter. *War Comes to Garmser: Thirty Years of Conflict on the Afghan Frontier*. London: Hurst, 2013.

Mann, Michael. *Incoherent Empire*. London: Verso, 2005.

Mansoor, Peter R. *Surge: My Journey with General David Petraeus and the Remaking of the Iraq War*. New Haven, CT: Yale University Press, 2013.

Martin, Mike. *An Intimate War: An Oral History of the Helmand Conflict, 1978–2012*. London: Hurst, 2014.

Macmillan, Harold. *At the End of the Day, 1961–63*. London: Macmillan, 1973.

McClintock, Michael. *Instruments of Statecraft: US Guerrilla Warfare, Counterinsurgency and Counterterrorism, 1940–1990*. New York: Pantheon Books, 1992.

McCullough, David. *Truman*. New York: Simon & Schuster, 1992.

McNay, John T. *Acheson and Empire: The British Accent in American Foreign Policy*. Columbia: University of Missouri Press, 2001.

Mead, Walter Russell. *God and Gold: Britain, America and the Making of the Modern World*. London: Atlantic Books, 2007.

Mockaitis, Thomas. *British Counter-Insurgency in the Post-Imperial Era*. Manchester: Manchester University Press, 1995.

Mumford, Andrew. *The Counter-Insurgency Myth: The British Experience of Irregular War*. Abingdon, UK: Routledge, 2011.

Nagl, John. *Knife Fights: A Memoir of Modern War in Theory and Practice.* New York: Penguin, 2014.

———. *Learning to Eat Soup with a Knife: Counter-Insurgency Lessons from Malaya to Vietnam.* Chicago: University of Chicago Press, 2005.

Neustadt, Richard. *Alliance Politics.* New York: Columbia University Press, 1970.

Newsinger, John. *British Counterinsurgency: From Palestine to Northern Ireland.* Basingstoke, UK: Macmillan, 2002.

Nixon, Richard. *The Memoirs of Richard Nixon.* London: Book Club Associates, 1978.

Nolan, Victoria. *Military Leadership and Counterinsurgency: The British Army and Small War Strategy since World War Two.* London: I. B. Tauris, 2012.

O'Ballance, Edgar. *The War in the Yemen.* Hamden, CT: Archon Books, 1971.

Ovendale, Ritchie. *Britain, the United States and the End of the Palestine Mandate, 1942–1948.* Woodbridge: Boydell Press, 1989.

Packer, George. *Assassins' Gate: America in Iraq.* London: Faber & Faber, 2007.

Pieragostini, Karl. *Britain, Aden and South Arabia: Abandoning Empire.* Basingstoke, UK: Macmillan, 1991.

Porch, Douglas. *Counterinsurgency: Exposing the Myths of the New Way of War.* Cambridge: Cambridge University Press, 2013.

Reddaway, John. *Burdened with Cyprus: The British Connection.* London: Weidenfeld & Nicholson, 1986.

Renwick, Robin. *Fighting with Allies: America and Britain in Peace and War.* Basingstoke, UK: Macmillan, 1996.

Reynolds, David. *America, Empire of Liberty: A New History.* London: Allen Lane, 2009.

Ricks, Thomas. *Fiasco: The American Military Adventure in Iraq.* London: Penguin, 2006.

———. *The Gamble: General David Petraeus and the American Military Adventure in Iraq.* New York: Allen Lane, 2009.

Rose, Norman. *A Senseless, Squalid War: Voices from Palestine, 1945–1948.* London: Bodley Head, 2009.

Ryan, David, and Victor Pungong, eds. *The United States and Decolonization: Power and Freedom.* Basingstoke, UK: Macmillan Press, 2000.

Sanders, Andrew. *Inside the IRA: Republicans and the War for Legitimacy.* Edinburgh: Edinburgh University Press, 2011.

Sarkesian, Sam C. *Unconventional Conflicts in a New Security Era: Lessons from Malaya and Vietnam.* Westport, CT: Greenwood, 1993.

Segev, Tom. *One Palestine, Complete: Jews and Arabs under the British Mandate.* London: Abacus, 2001.

Shafer, D. Michael. *Deadly Paradigms: The Failure of US Counterinsurgency Policy.* Princeton, NJ: Princeton University Press, 1989.

Shawcross, William. *Allies: The United States, Britain, Europe and the War in Iraq.* London: Atlantic Books, 2003.

Shepherd, Naomi. *Ploughing Sand: British Rule in Palestine, 1917–1948.* London: John Murray, 1999.

Short, Anthony. *The Communist Insurrection in Malaya, 1948–1960.* London: Frederick Muller, 1975.

Smiley, David (with Peter Kemp). *Arabian Assignment.* London: Leo Cooper, 1975.

Stubbs, Richard. *Hearts and Minds in Guerrilla Warfare: The Malayan Emergency, 1948–1960.* Singapore: Eastern Universities Press, 2004.

Taylor, Peter. *Provos: The IRA and Sinn Fein.* London: Bloomsbury, 1997.

Thompson, Robert. *Make for the Hills: Memories of Far Eastern Wars.* London: Leo Cooper, 1989.

Tonge, Jonathon. *Northern Ireland: Conflict and Change.* London: Prentice Hall, 1998.

Truman, Harry S. *Years of Trial and Hope, 1946–1953.* London: Hodder & Stoughton, 1956.

Ucko, David H., and Robert Egnell. *Counterinsurgency in Crisis: Britain and the Challenges of Modern Warfare.* New York: Columbia University Press, 2013.

Urban, Mark. *Big Boys' Rules: The SAS and the Secret Struggle against the IRA.* London: Faber & Faber, 1992.

———. *Task Force Black: The Explosive True Story of the SAS and the Secret War in Iraq.* London: Abacus, 2011.

Walker, Jonathan. *Aden Insurgency: The Savage War in South Arabia, 1962–67.* Staplehurst, UK: Spellmount, 2005.

Walton, Calder. *Empire of Secrets: British Intelligence, the Cold War and the Twilight of Empire.* London: Harper, 2013.

Waltz, Kenneth N. *Man, the State and War: A Theoretical Analysis.* New York: Columbia University Press, 2001. First published 1959.

Watt, Donald Cameron. *Succeeding John Bull: America in Britain's Place, 1900–1975.* Cambridge: Cambridge University Press, 1984.

Williams, William Appleman. *The Tragedy of American Diplomacy.* Rev. ed. New York: Norton, 1972. First published in 1959 by World Publishing.

Wilson, Andrew J. *Irish America and the Ulster Conflict, 1968–1995.* Belfast: Blackstaff Press, 1995.

Wilson, Harold. *Final Term: The Labour Government, 1974–1976.* London: Weidenfeld & Nicholson, 1979.

———. *The Labour Government, 1964–1970: A Personal Record.* London: Weidenfeld & Nicholson, 1971.

Windrow, Martin. *The Last Valley: Dien Bien Phu and the French Defeat in Vietnam.* London: Cassell, 2005.

Woodward, Bob. *State of Denial.* London: Simon & Schuster, 2006.

Journal Articles

Adamthwaite, Anthony. "Suez Revisited." *International Affairs* 64, no. 3 (1988): 449–64.

Alderson, Alexander. "Learning, Adapting, Applying: US Counter-Insurgency Doctrine and Practice." *RUSI Journal* 152, no. 6 (2007): 12–19.

Aylwin-Foster, Nigel. "Changing the Army for Counterinsurgency Operations." *Military Review* (November/December 2005): 2–15.

Ball, S. J. "Military Nuclear Relations between the United States and Great Britain under the Terms of the McMahon Act, 1946–1958." *Historical Journal* 38, no. 2 (1995): 439–54

Barber, Benjamin. "Imperialism or Interdependence?" *Security Dialogue* 35, no. 2 (2004): 237–42.

Baylis, John. "Exchanging Nuclear Secrets: Laying the Foundation of the Anglo-American Nuclear Relationship." *Diplomatic History* 25, no. 1 (2001): 33–61.

Bearden, Milton. "Afghanistan, Graveyard of Empires." *Foreign Affairs* 80, no. 6 (November/December 2001). http://www.foreignaffairs.com/articles/57411/milton-bearden/afghanistan-graveyard-of-empires.

Biddle, Stephen. "Afghanistan's Legacy: Emerging Lessons of an Ongoing War." *Washington Quarterly* 37, no. 2 (2014): 73–86.

Cavanagh, Matt. "Ministerial Decision-Making in the Run-Up to the Helmand Deployment." *RUSI Journal* 157, no. 2 (2012): 48–54.

Chang, King-yuh. "The United Nations and Decolonisation: The Case of Southern Yemen." *International Organisation* 26, no. 1 (1972): 37–61.

Charters, David A. "Jewish Terrorism and the Modern Middle East." *Journal of Conflict Studies* 27, no. 2 (2007): 80–89.

Chin, Warren. "British Counter-Insurgency in Afghanistan." *Defense and Security Analysis* 23, no. 2 (2007): 201–25.

Cox, Michael. "The Empire's Back in Town: Or, America's Imperial Temptation—Again." *Millennium* 32, no. 1 (2003): 1–27.

Cunningham, Sir Alan. "Palestine: The Last Days of the Mandate." *International Affairs* 24, no. 4 (1948): 481–90.

Danchev, Alex. "The Cold War 'Special Relationship' Revisited." *Diplomacy and Statecraft* 17, no. 3 (2006): 579–95.

———. "Tony Blair's Vietnam: The Iraq War and the 'Special Relationship' in Historical Perspective." *Review of International Studies* 33, no. 2 (2007): 189–203.

Deery, Phillip. "Malaya 1948: Britain's Asian Cold War?" *Journal of Cold War Studies* 9, no. 1 (2007): 29–54.

DeVore, Marc R. "A More Complex and Conventional Victory: Revisiting the Dhofar Counterinsurgency, 1963–1975." *Small Wars and Insurgencies* 23, no. 1 (2012): 144–73.

Dimitrakis, Panagiotis. "British Intelligence and the Cyprus Insurgency, 1955–59." *International Journal of Intelligence and Counter-Intelligence* 21, no. 2 (2008): 375–94.

Dinnerstein, Leonard. "America, Britain and Palestine: The Anglo-American Committee of Inquiry and the Displaced Persons, 1945–46." *Diplomatic History* 4, no. 3 (1980): 283–301.

Dockrill, M. L. "The Foreign Office, Anglo-American Relations and the Korean War, June 1950–June 1951." *International Affairs* 62, no. 3 (1986): 459–76.

Dockrill, Saki. "Forging the Anglo-American Global Defence Partnership: Harold Wilson, Lyndon Johnson and the Washington Summit, 1964." *Journal of Strategic Studies* 23, no. 4 (2000): 107–29.

Donnelly, Thomas. "The Cousins' Counter-Insurgency Wars." *RUSI Journal* 154, no. 3 (2009): 4–9.

Dumbrell, John, and Sylvia Ellis. "British Involvement in Vietnam Peace Initiatives, 1966–1967: Marigold, Sunflowers and 'Kosygin Week.'" *Diplomatic History* 27, no. 1 (2003): 113–49.

Egnell, Robert. "Lessons from Helmand, Afghanistan: What Now for British Counter-Insurgency?" *International Affairs* 87, no. 2 (2011): 297–315.

Evensen, Bruce J. "A Story of 'Ineptness': The Truman Administration's Struggle to Shape Conventional Wisdom on Palestine at the Beginning of the Cold War." *Diplomatic History* 15, no. 3 (1991): 339–59.

Fain, W. Taylor. "Unfortunate Arabia: The United States, Great Britain and Yemen, 1955–63." *Diplomacy and Statecraft* 12, no. 2 (2001): 125–52.

Farrell, Theo. "The Dynamics of British Military Transformation." *International Affairs* 84, no. 4 (2008): 777–807.

———. "Improving in War: Military Adaptation and the British in Helmand Province, Afghanistan, 2006–2009." *Journal of Strategic Studies* 33, no. 4 (2010): 567–94.

Farrell, Theo, and Stuart Gordon. "COIN Machine: The British Military in Afghanistan." *RUSI Journal* 154, no. 3 (2009): 18–25.

Ferris, Jesse. "Soviet Support for Egypt's Intervention in Yemen, 1962–1963." *Journal of Cold War Studies* 10, no. 4 (2008): 5–36.

Fitzgerald, David. "Sir Robert Thompson, Strategic Patience and Nixon's War in Vietnam." *Journal of Strategic Studies* 37, nos. 6–7 (2014). doi: 10.1080/01402390.2014.898582.

Foot, Rosemary. "Anglo-American Relations in the Korean Crisis: The British Effort to Avert an Expanded War, December 1950–January 1951." *Diplomatic History* 10, no. 1 (1986): 43–58.

Fry, Robert, and Desmond Bowen. "UK National Security Strategy and Helmand." *Whitehall Papers* 77, no. 1 (2011): 68–72.

Garden, Timothy. "Iraq: The Military Campaign." *International Affairs* 79, no. 4 (2003): 701–18.

Gentile, Gian: "Freeing the Army from the Counterinsurgency Strait-Jacket." *Joint Forces Quarterly* 58, no. 3 (2010): 121–22.

Goulding, Cathal. "The New Strategy of the IRA." *New Left Review*, no. 65 (November/December 1970): 50–61.

Greenwood, Sean. "'A War We Don't Want': Another Look at the British Labour Government's Commitment in Korea, 1950–51." *Contemporary British History* 17, no. 4 (2003): 1–24.

Hack, Karl. "Detention, Deportation and Resettlement: British Counterinsurgency and Malaya's Rural Chinese, 1948–60." *Journal of Imperial and Commonwealth History* 43, no. 4 (2015): 611–40.

———. "The Malayan Emergency as a Counter-Insurgency Paradigm." *Journal of Strategic Studies* 32, no. 2 (2009): 383–414.

———. "The Origins of the Asian Cold War: Malaya 1948." *Journal of Southeast Asian Studies* 40, no. 3 (2009): 471–96.

Hammes, T. X. "The Future of Counterinsurgency." *Orbis* 56, no. 4 (2012): 565–87.

Hanning, Hugh. "Britain East of Suez: Facts and Figures." *International Affairs* 42, no. 2 (1966): 253–60.

Harding of Petherton, Field Marshal the Lord. "The Cyprus Problem in Relation to the Middle East." *International Affairs* 34, no. 3 (1958): 291–96.

Hatzivassiliou, Evanthis. "Blocking Enosis: Britain and the Cyprus Question, March–December 1956." *Journal of Imperial and Commonwealth History* 19, no. 2 (1991): 247–63.

Hoffman, Frank G. "Neo-Classical Counterinsurgency?" *Parameters* 37, no. 2 (2007): 71–87.

Iron, Richard. "The Charge of the Knights." *RUSI Journal* 158, no. 1 (2013): 54–62.

Jeffreys-Jones, Rhodri. "The End of an Exclusive Special Intelligence Relationship: British-American Intelligence Co-operation before, during and after the 1960s." *Intelligence and National Security* 27, no. 5 (2012): 707–21.

Johnson, Edward. "Britain and the Cyprus Problem at the United Nations, 1954–1958." *Journal of Imperial and Commonwealth History* 28, no. 3 (2000): 113–30.

Jones, Clive. "'Where the State Feared to Tread': Britain, Britons, Covert Action and the Yemen Civil War." *Intelligence and National Security* 21, no. 5 (2006): 717–37.

Kennedy, Edward. "Ulster Is an International Issue." *Foreign Policy*, no. 11 (Summer 1973): 57–71.

Kennedy-Pipe, Caroline, and Rhiannon Vickers. "'Blowback' for Britain? Blair, Bush and the War in Iraq." *Review of International Studies* 33, no. 2 (2007): 205–21.

King, Anthony. "Understanding the Helmand Campaign: British Military Operations in Afghanistan." *International Affairs* 86, no. 2 (2010): 311–32.

King, Desmond. "When an Empire Is Not an Empire: The US Case." *Government and Opposition* 41, no. 2 (2006): 163–96.

Ladwig, Walter C., III. "Supporting Allies in Counter-Insurgency: Britain and the Dhofar Rebellion." *Small Wars and Insurgencies* 19, no. 1 (2008): 62–88.

Lake, David A. "The New American Empire?" *International Studies Perspectives* 9, no. 3 (2008): 281–89.

Louis, William Roger. "American Anti-Colonialism and the Dissolution of the British Empire." *International Affairs* 61, no. 3 (1985): 395–420.

———. "The British Withdrawal from the Gulf, 1967–71." *Journal of Imperial and Commonwealth History* 31, no. 1 (2003): 83–108.

Lowe, Peter. "Change and Stability in Eastern Asia: Nationalism, Communism and British Policy, 1948–1955." *Diplomacy and Statecraft* 15, no. 1 (2004): 137–47.

Lundestad, Geir. "'Empire by Invitation' in the American Century." *Diplomatic History* 23, no. 2 (1999): 189–217.

Markides, Diana Weston, "Britain's "New Look" Policy for Cyprus and the Makarios-Harding Talks, January 1955–March 1956." *Journal of Imperial and Commonwealth History* 23, no. 3 (1995): 479–502.

Mawby, Spencer. "The Clandestine Defence of Empire: British Special Operations in Yemen, 1951–64." *Intelligence and National Security* 17, no. 3 (2002): 105–30.

McAllister, James, and Ian Schulte. "The Limits of Influence in Vietnam: Britain, the United States and the Diem Regime, 1959–63." *Small Wars and Insurgencies* 17, no. 1 (2006): 22–43.

McLean, David. "American Nationalism, the China Myth and the Truman Doctrine: The Question of Accommodation with Peking, 1949–50." *Diplomatic History* 10, no. 1 (1986): 25–42.

Melvin, Mungo. "Learning the Strategic Lessons from Afghanistan." *RUSI Journal* 157, no. 2 (2012): 56–61.

Mockaitis, Thomas R. "The Phoenix of Counterinsurgency." *Journal of Conflict Studies* 27, no. 1 (2007): 9–21.

Mumford, Andrew. "Sir Robert Thompson's Lessons for Iraq: Bringing the 'Five Basic Principles' of Counter-Insurgency into the Twenty-First Century." *Defence Studies* 10, no. 1/2 (2010): 177–94.

O'Grady, Joseph. "An Irish Policy Born in the USA." *Foreign Affairs* 75, no. 3 (1996): 2–7.

Ovendale, Ritchie. "Britain, the United States and the Recognition of Communist China." *Historical Journal* 26, no. 1 (1983): 139–58.

———. "The Palestine Policy of the British Labour Government, 1945–1946." *International Affairs* 55, no. 3 (1979): 409–31.

Petraeus, David. "Reflections on the Counter-Insurgency Era." *RUSI Journal* 158, no. 4 (2013): 82–87.

Porter, Patrick. "Last Charge of the Knights? Iraq, Afghanistan and the Special Relationship." *International Affairs* 86, no. 2 (2010): 355–75.

Pritchard, James, and M. L. R. Smith. "Thompson in Helmand: Comparing Theory to Practice in British Counter-Insurgency Operations in Afghanistan." *Civil Wars* 12, nos. 1–2 (2010): 65–90.

Putnam, Robert D. "Diplomacy and Domestic Politics: The Logic of Two-Level Games." *International Organization* 42, no. 3 (1988): 427–60.

Robb, Thomas. "The 'Limit of What Is Tolerable': British Defence Cuts and the 'Special Relationship,' 1974–1976." *Diplomacy and Statecraft* 22, no. 2 (2011): 321–37.

Robbins, Simon. "The British Counter-Insurgency in Cyprus." *Small Wars and Insurgencies* 23, nos. 4–5 (2012): 720–43.

Ramakrishna, Kumar. "'Transmogrifying' Malaya: The Impact of Sir Gerald Templer (1952–54)." *Journal of Southeast Asian Studies* 32, no. 1 (2001): 79–92.

Shaw, Geoffrey D. T. "Policemen versus Soldiers, the Debate Leading to MAAG Objections and Washington Rejections of the Core of the British Counter-Insurgency Advice." *Small Wars and Insurgencies* 12, no. 2 (2001): 51–78.

Simes, Dimitri K. "America's Imperial Dilemma." *Foreign Affairs* 82, no. 6 (2003): 91–102.

Slonim, Shlomo. "The 1948 American Embargo on Arms to Palestine." *Political Science Quarterly* 94, no. 3 (1979): 495–514.

Smith, Simon C. "Revolution and Reaction: South Arabia in the Aftermath of the Yemeni Revolution." *Journal of Imperial and Commonwealth History* 28, no. 3 (2000): 193–208.

Spelling, Alex. "Edward Heath and Anglo-American Relations, 1970–1974." *Diplomacy and Statecraft* 20, no. 4 (2009): 638–58.

Steininger, Rolf. " 'The Americans Are in Hopeless Position': Great Britain and the War in Vietnam, 1964–65." *Diplomacy and Statecraft* 8, no. 3 (1997): 237–85.

Strachan, Hew. "British Counter-Insurgency from Malaya to Iraq." *RUSI Journal* 152, no. 6 (2007): 8–11.

Stueck, William. "The Limits of Influence: British Policy and American Expansion of the War in Korea." *Pacific Historical Review* 55, no. 1 (1986): 65–95.

Synnott, Hilary. "Statebuilding in Southern Iraq." *Survival* 47, no. 2 (2005): 33–56.

Ucko, David. "Critics Gone Wild: Counterinsurgency as the Root of All Evil." *Small Wars and Insurgencies* 25, no. 1 (2014): 161–79.

———. "Lessons from Basra: The Future of British Counter-Insurgency." *Survival* 52, no. 4 (2010): 131–58.

Varsori, Antonio. "Britain and US Involvement in the Vietnam War during the Kennedy Administration, 1961–1963." *Cold War History* 3, no. 2 (2003): 83–112.

Vickers, Rhiannon. "Harold Wilson, the British Labour Party and the War in Vietnam." *Journal of Cold War Studies* 10, no. 2 (2008): 41–70.

Wagner, Steven. "British Intelligence and the Jewish Resistance Movement in the Palestine Mandate, 1945–46." *Intelligence and National Security* 23, no. 5 (2008): 629–57.

Walton, Calder. "British Intelligence and the Mandate of Palestine: Threats to British National Security Immediately after the Second World War." *Intelligence and National Security* 23, no. 4 (2008): 435–62.

Williamson, Daniel C. "Taking the Troubles across the Atlantic: Ireland's UN Initiatives and Irish-US Relations in the Early Years of the Conflict in Northern Ireland, 1969–72." *Irish Studies in International Relations* 18 (2007): 175–89.

Wither, James K. "Basra's Not Belfast: The British Army, 'Small Wars' and Iraq." *Small Wars and Insurgencies* 20, nos. 3–4 (2009): 611–35.

———. "British Bulldog or Bush's Poodle? Anglo-American Relations and the Iraq War." *Parameters* (Winter 2003–4): 67–82.

Witty, David M. "A Regular Army in Counter-Insurgency Operations: Egypt in North Yemen, 1966–67." *Journal of Military History* 65, no. 2 (2001): 401–39.

Young, John W. "Britain and 'LBJ's War,' 1964–1968." *Cold War History* 2, no. 3 (2002): 63–92.

———. "The Wilson Government and the Davies Peace Mission to North Vietnam, July 1965." *Review of International Studies* 24, no. 4 (1998): 545–62.

Think Tank Reports

Campbell, Alastair. "Assessing Britain's Legacy: The UK Withdrawal from Iraq." *RUSI Commentary*. https://rusi.org/commentary/assessing-britain%E2%80%99s-legacy-uk-withdrawal-iraq.

Garfield, Andrew. *Succeeding in Phase IV: British Perspectives on the US Effort to Stabilize and Reconstruct Iraq*. Foreign Policy Research Institute report, September 2006. http://www.fpri.org/docs/Garfield.SucceedinginPhaseIV.pdf.

Farrell, Theo. "Appraising Moshtarak: The Campaign in Nad-e-Ali District, Helmand." RUSI Briefing Note, June 2010. https://rusi.org/system/files/Appraising_Moshtarak.pdf.

Index

About the Author

Andrew Mumford is associate professor of politics and international relations at the University of Nottingham in the United Kingdom, where he is also the codirector of the Centre for Conflict, Security and Terrorism. He is the author of *The Counter-Insurgency Myth* (Routledge, 2011) and *Proxy Warfare* (Polity, 2013).

CPSIA information can be obtained
at www.ICGtesting.com
Printed in the USA
BVOW03*0940280917
495676BV00011BB/30/P